THE
LOTUS
SUTRA

TRANSLATIONS
FROM THE
ASIAN CLASSICS

THE LOTUS SUTRA

TRANSLATED BY
BURTON WATSON

COLUMBIA UNIVERSITY PRESS

NEW YORK

Columbia University Press
New York   Chichester, West Sussex
Copyright © 1993 Soka Gakkai
All rights reserved

Library of Congress Cataloging-in-Publication Data

Tripiṭaka. Sūtrapiṭaka. Saddharmapuṇḍarīkasūtra. English
The Lotus Sutra / translated by Burton Watson.
p.   cm. — (Translations from the Asian classics)
Translated from: Miao-fa Lion-hua ching.
Includes index.
ISBN 978-0-231-08160-3 (cloth : alk. paper)
ISBN 978-0-231-08161-0 (pbk. : alk. paper)
I. Watson, Burton, 1925–   . II. Title.   III. Series.
BQ2052.E5W38 1993   294.3'82 — dc20   92-38410
CIP

Casebound editions of Columbia University Press books
are printed on permanent and durable
acid-free paper.

Designed by Audrey Smith
Printed in the United States of America

c 10 9 8 7 6 5 4 3

p 20 19 18 17

CONTENTS

CONTENTS

viii

TRANSLATOR'S INTRODUCTION

The Lotus Sutra is one of the most important and influential of all the sutras or sacred scriptures of Mahayana Buddhism, revered by almost all branches of the Mahayana teachings, and over many centuries the object of intense veneration among Buddhist believers throughout China, Korea, Japan, and other regions of eastern Asia.

We do not know where or when the Lotus Sutra was composed, or in what language. Probably it was initially formulated in some local dialect of India or Central Asia and then later put into Sanskrit to lend it greater respectability. All we can say for certain about the date of its composition is that it was already in existence by 255 CE, when the first Chinese translation of it was made. It was translated into Chinese several times subsequently, but it is through the version done in 406 by the Central Asian scholar-monk Kumarajiva that it has become widely known and read in China and the other countries within the

Chinese cultural sphere of influence. This version has been universally acknowledged as the most authoritative and felicitous in language, and it is from this version that the present English translation has been made.

In recent years several Sanskrit texts of the Lotus Sutra, titled in Sanskrit *Saddharma-pundarika Sutra* or "The Sutra of the Lotus of the Wonderful Law," have been discovered in Nepal, Central Asia, and Kashmir. Some appear to have been copied in the eleventh century or later, though some may have been copied as early as the fifth or sixth century. These Sanskrit versions of the work differ considerably in places from the Kumarajiva translation, being often more verbose in expression, which suggests that the text Kumarajiva followed was earlier in date, and may in fact have been quite close to the original version.

The Lotus Sutra, as just mentioned, was at an early date translated into Chinese, as well as into Tibetan, and in later centuries into Hsi-hsia, Mongol, Manchu, Korean, and Japanese. In recent years several translations into English and other European languages have appeared; now it is established as an important text of world literature.

EARLY BUDDHISM

Gautama, or Shakyamuni Buddha, the founder of Buddhism, appears to have lived in India sometime around the sixth or fifth century BCE. Though it is difficult to describe his doctrines in detail, Buddhologists customarily accept several formulas as representative of his teachings. Most famous of these are the so-called four noble truths, which are referred to several times in the Lotus Sutra. These teach that (1) all existence in the *saha* world, the world in which we live at present, is marked by suffering; (2) that suffering is caused by craving; (3) that by doing away with craving one can gain release from suffering and reach a state of peace and enlightenment, often called nirvana; (4) that there is a method for achieving this goal, namely, the discipline known as the eightfold path. This is a set of moral principles enjoining one to cultivate right views, right thinking, right speech, right action, right way of life, right endeavor, right mindfulness, and right meditation.

Another doctrine, also touched on in the Lotus Sutra, is that of the twelve-linked chain of causation or dependent origination, which illustrates step by step the causal relationship between ignorance and suffering. The purpose of the doctrine, like that of the four noble truths, is to wake one to the true nature of reality and help one to achieve emancipation from ignorance and suffering.

In order to pursue the kind of strenuous discipline needed to gain such release, it was thought all but imperative that one leave secular life and become a member of the Buddhist Order, which consisted of both monks and nuns. There, free from family entanglements and worldly concerns, one could devote oneself to a life of poverty, celibacy, and religious study and discipline, supported by the alms of the lay community. Lay believers could acquire religious merit by assisting the Order, observing the appropriate rules of moral conduct, and carrying out devotional practices such as paying obeisance at the stupas or memorial towers that housed the relics of the Buddha. But it was thought that they would have to wait until future existences before they could hope to gain full release from suffering.

Buddhism, it should be noted, took over from earlier Indian thought the belief in karma. According to this belief, all a person's moral actions, whether good or bad, produce definite effects in the person's life, though such effects may take some time before manifesting themselves. According to the Indian view, living beings pass through an endless cycle of death and rebirth, and the ill effects of an evil action in one life may not become evident until some future existence; but that they will appear eventually is inescapable. Hence only by striving to do good in one's present existence can one hope to escape even greater suffering in a future life.

Buddhism vehemently denied that there is any individual soul or personal identity that passes over from one existence to the next—to suppose there is is simply to open the way for further craving—but it did accept the idea of rebirth or transmigration, and taught that the circumstances or realm into which a being is reborn are determined by the good or bad acts done by that being in previous existences. This meant, among other things, that one did not necessarily have to struggle for release from suffering within a single lifetime, but could work at the goal of salvation step by step, performing good moral and devotional acts that would insure one of rebirth in more favorable circumstances in the future, and in this way gradually raising one's level of spiritual attainment.

The tenets and practices of the religion I have described above are often referred to as Hinayana Buddhism. But Hinayana, which means "Lesser Vehicle," is a derogatory term, applied to early Buddhism by a group within the religion that called itself Mahayana or the "Great Vehicle" and represented its doctrines as superior to and superseding those of earlier Buddhism. In keeping with the spirit of religious tolerance and mutual understanding that prevails in most quarters today, writers usually try to avoid use of the term "Hinayana," instead referring to the earlier form of Buddhism as "Theravada" or "The Teachings of the Elders," which is the name used by the branch of it that continues in existence today. This is the form of Buddhism that prevails at present in Sri Lanka, Burma, Thailand, Cambodia, and Laos.

The Mahayana movement appears to have begun in India around the first or second century of the Common Era. In part it was probably a reaction against the great emphasis upon monastic life that marked earlier Buddhism and against the arid psychological and metaphysical speculations that characterize much of early Buddhist philosophy. It aimed to open up the religious life to a wider proportion of the population, to accord a more important role to lay believers, to give more appealing expression to the teachings and make them more readily accessible.

In earlier Buddhism the goal of religious striving had been to achieve the state of arhat or "worthy," one who has "nothing more to learn" and has escaped rebirth in the lower realms of existence. Even to reach this state, however, it was believed, required many lifetimes of strenuous exertion. But Mahayana urged men and women to aim for nothing less than the achievement of the highest level of enlightenment, that of Buddhahood. Enormous help in reaching this exalted goal, it was stressed, would come to them through figures known as bodhisattvas, beings who are dedicated not only to attaining enlightenment for themselves but, out of their immense compassion, to helping others to do likewise. Earlier Buddhism often described Shakyamuni Buddha as a bodhisattva in his previous existences, when he was still advancing toward enlightenment. But in Mahayana texts such as the Lotus Sutra the bodhisattvas are pictured as unlimited in number, all- seeing and all-caring, capable of extending boundless aid and succor to those who call upon them in sincere faith. Indeed, this great

emphasis upon the role of the bodhisattva is one of the main characteristics that distinguish Mahayana thought from that of earlier Buddhism.

At first the proponents of these new Mahayana beliefs seem in
many cases to have lived side by side in the same monasteries as the
adherents of the earlier teachings, their religious practice centering
around the worship of the Buddha's relics housed in the stupas or
memorial towers. But doctrinal clashes arose from time to time and
the two groups eventually drew apart. The Mahayana doctrines appear
to have dominated in northwestern India, where they spread into the
lands of Central Asia and thence into China. As a result, Chinese
Buddhism was from the first overwhelmingly Mahayana in character,
and it was this Mahayana version of the faith that in time was intro-
duced to Korea, Japan, and Vietnam, where it continues in existence
today.

THE WORLD OF THE LOTUS SUTRA

The Lotus Sutra depicts events that take place in a cosmic world of
vast dimensions, a world in many ways reflecting traditional Indian
views of the structure of the universe. For those who are not familiar
with such views, it may be well to describe them here in brief. The
world in which we live at present, it was believed, is made up of four
continents ranged around a great central mountain, Mount Sumeru.
We live in the continent located to the south, known as Jambudvipa or
the "continent of the *jambu* trees." Outside of our present world
there exist countless others spread out in all directions, some similarly
made up of four continents, others realms presided over by various
Buddhas. All these worlds, like our own, are caught up in a never-
ending cycle of formation, continuance, decline, and disintegration, a
process that takes place over vast kalpas or eons of time.

The ordinary beings living in our present world fall into six categories or occupy six realms of existence, arranged in hierarchical order
in terms of their desirability. Lowest are the hell dwellers, beings who
because of their evil actions in the past are compelled, for a time at
least, to suffer in the various hells that exist beneath the earth, the
most terrible of which is the Avichi hell or the hell of incessant
suffering. On a slightly higher level are the hungry ghosts or spirits,

beings who are tormented by endless hunger and craving. Above this is the level of beasts or beings of animal nature, and above that the realm of the *asuras*, demons who are pictured in Indian mythology as constantly engaged in angry warfare. These first three or four realms represent the "evil paths," the lowest, most painful and undesirable states of existence.

Above these is the fifth level, the realm of human beings, and the sixth, that of the heavenly beings or gods. The gods, though they lead far happier lives than the beings in the other realms, are doomed in time to die. Whatever the realm, all the beings in these six realms repeat the never-ending cycle of death and rebirth, moving up or down from one level to another depending upon the good or evil deeds they have committed, but never gaining release from the cycle.

To these six lower worlds or levels Mahayana Buddhism adds four more, the "holy states," representative of the life of enlightenment. On the seventh level are the *shravakas* or voice-hearers. This term, by which they are known in the Lotus Sutra, originally referred to the Buddha's disciples, those who had entered the Buddhist Order and learned the doctrines and practices directly from him, though later it came to refer to those monks and nuns who followed the teachings of early Buddhism such as the four noble truths and strove to attain the state of arhat. Once they attained that state they ceased their endeavors, convinced that they had gained the highest goal possible for them.

Above these, on the eighth level, are the *pratyekabuddhas* or "self-enlightened ones," beings who have won an understanding of the truth through their own efforts but who make no effort to teach others or assist them to enlightenment. On the ninth level are the bodhisattvas, already described above, who out of compassion postpone their entry into Buddhahood and remain in the *saha* world to alleviate the sufferings of others. On the tenth and highest level are the Buddhas or the state of Buddhahood. It is this level, according to Mahayana doctrine, that all living beings should seek to attain, and which, it insists, they can in time attain if they will not content themselves with lesser goals but have faith in the Buddha and his teachings as these are embodied in the sacred scriptures.

Before passing on to a discussion of the particular doctrines set forth in the Lotus Sutra, there is one more aspect of the Mahayana worldview that must be touched upon, difficult though it is to treat in the limited space that can be allotted here. This is the concept of Emptiness or Void (*shunyata*) which is so central to the whole Mahayana system of belief.

The concept, often described in English as "nondualism," is extremely hard for the mind to grasp or visualize, since the mind engages constantly in the making of distinctions and nondualism represents the rejection or transcendence of all distinctions. The world perceived through the senses, the phenomenal world as we know it, was described in early Buddhism as "empty" because it was taught that all such phenomena arise from causes and conditions, are in a constant state of flux, and are destined to change and pass away in time. They are also held to be "empty" in the sense that they have no inherent or permanent characteristics by which they can be described, changing as they do from instant to instant. But in Mahayana thought it became customary to emphasize not the negative but rather the positive aspects or import of the doctrine of Emptiness. If all phenomena are characterized by the quality of Emptiness, then Emptiness must constitute the unchanging and abiding nature of existence, and therefore the absolute or unchanging world must be synonymous with the phenomenal one. Hence all mental and physical distinctions that we perceive or conceive of with our minds must be part of a single underlying unity. It is this concept of Emptiness or nonduality that leads the Mahayana texts to assert that *samsara*, the ordinary world of suffering and cyclical birth and death, is in the end identical with the world of nirvana, and that earthly desires are enlightenment.

THE PRINCIPAL DOCTRINES OF
THE LOTUS SUTRA

The Kumarajiva translation of the Lotus Sutra as it exists at present is made up of twenty-eight chapters. Nearly all the chapters consist of a combination of prose and verse passages. Verse form was used to make it easier for the followers of the religion to memorize the teachings and retain them in mind, and the *gathas* or verse passages were probably composed first. Later, as the sutra moved toward its final form, prose passages were added that incorporated the verse sections into a continuous narrative. In the present arrangement of the text, the verse sections usually repeat what has already been stated in a preceding prose passage.

Like nearly all sutras, the Lotus begins with the Buddha's close disciple Ananda speaking the words, "This is what I heard." Ananda, who was present at all the Buddha's expositions of the Dharma or doctrine, then proceeds to describe the occasion when, at Mount Gridhrakuta or Eagle Peak near the city of Rajagriha, the Buddha preached the Lotus Sutra.

In these opening sentences we are still in the world of historical reality or possibility, in a setting in the outskirts of the city of Rajagriha in northern India in which Gautama or Shakyamuni very probably did in fact propound his doctrines in the sixth or fifth century BCE.

But as Ananda proceeds to describe the staggering number and variety of human, nonhuman, and heavenly beings who have gathered to listen to the Buddha's discourse, we realize that we have left the world of factual reality far behind. This is the first point to keep in mind in reading the Lotus Sutra. Its setting, its vast assembly of listeners, its dramatic occurrences in the end belong to a realm that totally transcends our ordinary concepts of time, space, and possibility. Again and again we are told of events that took place countless, indescribable numbers of kalpas or eons in the past, or of beings or worlds that are as numerous as the sands of millions and billions of Ganges rivers. Such "numbers" are in fact no more than pseudo-numbers or non-numbers, intended to impress on us the impossibility of measuring the immeasurable. They are not meant to convey any statistical data but simply to boggle the mind and jar it loose from its conventional concepts of time and space. For in the realm of Emptiness, time and space as we conceive them are meaningless; anywhere is the same as everywhere, and now, then, never, forever are all one.

After several astounding events that impress upon us the truly cosmic scale of the drama that is unfolding, the Buddha begins to preach. The first important point he wishes to convey is that there is only one vehicle or one path to salvation, that which leads to the goal of Buddhahood. Earlier in his preaching career, he had described three paths for the believer, what he calls the three vehicles. One was that of the *shravaka* or voice-hearer, which leads to the realm of the arhat. Second was that of the *pratyekabuddha*, the being who gains enlightenment by himself and for himself alone, and the third was that of the bodhisattva. But now, the Buddha tells us, these lesser paths or goals are to be set aside and all beings are to aim for the single goal of Buddhahood, the one and only vehicle to true enlightenment or perfect understanding, a state designated in the Lotus Sutra by the rather daunting Sanskrit term *anuttara-samyak-sambodhi*.

When asked why, if there is only the single vehicle or truth, the Buddha has earlier taught his followers the doctrine of the three vehicles, he replies that at that time they were not yet ready to comprehend or accept the highest truth. Therefore he had to employ what he terms an expedient means in order to lead them gradually along the road to greater understanding. He then illustrates his point through the famous parable of the burning house.

The first lesson the sutra wishes to teach, then, is that its doctrines, delivered by the Buddha some forty or more years after the start of his preaching career, which is how the Lotus Sutra depicts them, represent the highest level of truth, the summation of the Buddha's message, superseding his earlier pronouncements, which had only provisional validity.

In some Mahayana texts Shariputra and the other close disciples of the Buddha, who represent the Lesser Vehicle outlook and path of endeavor, are held up to ridicule or portrayed as figures of fun. But the prevailing mood of the Lotus Sutra is one of compassion, and in it the voice-hearers are shown responding to the Buddha's words with understanding and gratitude. In return, the Buddha bestows on each of them a prophecy of the attainment of Buddhahood in a future existence, and in many cases reveals the type of Buddha land each will preside over.

The mood of revelation and rejoicing continues in the chapters that follow as the Buddha names more persons who are assured of attaining Buddhahood. The company of nuns who are attending the assembly, headed by the Buddha's aunt, Mahaprajapati, and his wife in his younger years, Yashodhara, at one point grow apprehensive because their names have not been mentioned, but the Buddha assures them that they too are included in his predictions of Buddhahood.

All these monks and nuns have been personal followers of Shakyamuni Buddha, diligent in religious practice and faultless in their observance of the rules of conduct, and it is hardly surprising to learn that

their efforts are to be crowned with success. Truly surprising, however, is the prophecy set forth in chapter twelve concerning Devadatta,
who gives his name to the chapter.

Devadatta is described in accounts of the life of Shakyamuni Buddha as a disciple and cousin of the Buddha who, though full of zeal at
first, later grew envious of Shakyamuni, made several attempts on his
life, and schemed to foment division in the Order. For these crimes,
among the most heinous in the eyes of Buddhism, he was said to have
fallen into hell alive. Yet in chapter twelve of the Lotus Sutra the
Buddha reveals that in a past existence this epitome of evil was in fact
a good friend and teacher of the Buddha, preaching the way of enlightenment for him, and that in an era to come, Devadatta will without
fail become a Buddha himself. From this we learn that even the most
depraved of persons can hope for salvation, and that in the realm of
nondualism good and evil are not the eternal and mutually exclusive
opposites we had supposed them to be.

Chapter twelve relates another affair of equally astounding import.
In it, the bodhisattva Manjushri describes how he has been preaching
the Lotus Sutra at the palace of the dragon king at the bottom of the
sea. The *nagas* or dragons, it should be noted, are one of eight kinds
of nonhuman beings who are believed to protect Buddhism. They
were revered in early Indian folk religion and were taken over by
Buddhism, whose scriptures often portray them as paying homage to
the Buddha and seeking knowledge of his teachings.

Asked if there were any among his listeners who succeeded in
gaining enlightenment, Manjushri mentions the daughter of the dragon
king Sagara, a girl just turned eight, who was able to master all the
teachings. The questioner expresses understandable skepticism, point-
ing out that even Shakyamuni himself required many eons of religious
practice before he could achieve enlightenment.

The girl herself then appears and before the astonished assembly
performs various acts that demonstrate she has in fact achieved the
highest level of understanding and can "in an instant" attain Buddhahood. Earlier Buddhism had asserted that women are gravely ham-
pered in their religious endeavors by "five obstacles," one of which is
the fact that they can never hope to attain Buddhahood. But all such
assertions are here in the Lotus Sutra unequivocally thrust aside. The
child is a dragon, a nonhuman being, she is of the female sex, and she

has barely turned eight, yet she reaches the highest goal in the space
of a moment. Once again the Lotus Sutra reveals that its revolutionary
doctrines operate in a realm transcending all petty distinctions of sex
or species, instant or eon.

These joyous revelations concerning the universal accessibility of
Buddhahood, which occupy the middle chapters of the sutra, constitute
the second important message of the work. The third is set forth in
chapter sixteen. In chapter fifteen we are told how a vast multitude of
bodhisattvas spring up from the earth in a miraculous manner in order
that they may undertake the task of transmitting and protecting the
teachings of the Buddha. When the Buddha is asked who these bodhisattvas are, he replies that they are persons whom he has taught and
guided to enlightenment. His questioner quite naturally asks how
Shakyamuni could possibly have taught and converted such immeasurable multitudes in the course of only forty years of preaching.

In chapter sixteen Shakyamuni reveals the answer to this riddle.
The Buddha, he says, is an eternal being, ever present in the world,
ever concerned for the salvation of all beings. He attained Buddhahood
an incalculably distant time in the past, and has never ceased to abide
in the world since then. He seems at times to pass away into nirvana,
and at other times to make a new appearance in the world. But he does
this only so that living beings will not take his presence for granted
and be slack in their quest for enlightenment. His seeming disappear-
ance is no more than an expedient means which he employs to encour-
age them in their efforts, one of many such expedients that he adopts
in order to fit his teachings to the different natures and capacities of
individual beings and insure that they will have relevance for all. From
this we see that in the Lotus Sutra the Buddha, who had earlier been
viewed as a historical personality, is now conceived as a being who
transcends all boundaries of time and space, an ever-abiding principle
of truth and compassion that exists everywhere and within all beings.

These then are the principal teachings of the Lotus Sutra, concepts
that are basic to all Mahayana thought. In the sutra they are often
very beautifully and persuasively expounded, especially in the various
parables for which the Lotus is famous. But one should not approach
the Lotus expecting to find in it a methodical exposition of a system of
philosophy. Some of the most important principles of Buddhism are
only touched upon in passing, as though the reader or hearer is

expected to be acquainted with them already, while many of the more revolutionary doctrines are not presented in any orderly fashion or supported by careful or detailed arguments but rather thrust upon him with the suddenness of divine revelation.

The text, with its long lists of personages, its astronomical numbers, its formulaic language and frequent repetitions, its vivid parables, is incantatory in effect, appealing not so much to the intellect as to the emotions. It may be noted that in the early centuries of Buddhism it was customary not to put the teachings into written form but to transmit them orally, the works being committed to memory as had been the practice in earlier Indian religion. This was thought to be the proper way, the respectful way to transmit them and insure that they were not revealed to persons who were unqualified or unworthy to receive them. The formulaic language, the recapitulations in verse, the repetitions were all designed to assist the memory of the reciter, and these stylistic features were retained even after the scriptures had been put into written form.

Very early in the sutra the Buddha warns us that the wisdom of the Buddhas is extremely profound and difficult to comprehend, and this warning is repeated frequently in later chapters. The Lotus Sutra tells us at times that the Lotus Sutra is about to be preached, at other times it says that the Lotus Sutra has already been preached with such-and-such results, and at still other times it gives instructions on just how the Lotus Sutra is to be preached or enumerates in detail the merits that accrue to one who pays due honor to the text. But the reader may be forgiven if he comes away from the work wondering just which of the chapters that make it up was meant to be the Lotus Sutra itself. One writer has in fact been led to describe the sutra as a text "about a discourse that is never delivered, . . . a lengthy preface without a book."[1] This is no doubt because Mahayana Buddhism has always insisted that its highest truth can never in the end be expressed in words, since words immediately create the kind of distinctions that violate the unity of Emptiness. All the sutra can do, therefore, is to talk around it, leaving a hole in the middle where truth can reside.

[1] George J. Tanabe, Jr. and Wilma Jane Tanabe, eds., *The Lotus Sutra in Japanese Culture* (Honolulu: University of Hawaii Press, 1989), p. 2 in the introductory chapter by Professor George Tanabe.

But of course in the view of religion there are other approaches to truth than merely through words and intellectual discourse. The sutra therefore exhorts the individual to approach the wisdom of the Buddhas through the avenue of faith and religious practice. The profound influence which the Lotus Sutra has exerted upon the cultural and religious life of the countries of eastern Asia is due as much to its function as a guide to devotional practice as to the actual ideas that it expounds. It calls upon us to act out the sutra with our bodies and minds rather than merely reading it, and in that way to enter into its meaning.

Much of the Lotus Sutra is taken up with injunctions to the believer to "accept and uphold, read, recite, copy and teach" it to others, and with descriptions of the bountiful merits to be gained by such action, as well as warnings of the evil effects of speaking ill of the sutra and its practices. In addition, one is encouraged to make offerings to the Buddhas and bodhisattvas, to the stupas or memorial towers, and to the monastic Order. Flowers, incense, music, and chants of praise are the customary offerings cited in the sutra, along with food, clothing, bedding, and other daily necessities in the case of members of the Order. Gold, silver, gems and other valuables are also listed among the offerings, but lest this would seem to put the rich at an advantage, the sutra early on emphasizes that it is the spirit in which the offering is made rather than the article itself that is important. Even a tower of sand fashioned by children in play, if offered in the proper spirit, will be acceptable in the sight of the Buddha and bring reward, we are told. It may be noted that the animal sacrifices so central to the earlier Vedic religion were rejected by Buddhism as abhorrent. One chapter of the Lotus does in fact describe a bodhisattva who burned his own body as a form of sacrifice, but the passage is clearly meant to be taken metaphorically. Despite this fact, some believers of later times, in their eagerness to emulate the bodhisattva's example, have interpreted it with tragic literalness.

Most famous and influential of the devotional chapters of the Lotus Sutra are those with which the work closes and which portray various bodhisattvas who can render particular aid and protection to the believer. Noteworthy among these is chapter twenty-five, which centers on a bodhisattva named Avalokiteshvara or Perceiver of the World's

Sounds, known in China as Kuan-yin and in Japan as Kannon. The chapter relates in very concrete terms the wonderful types of assistance that the bodhisattva can render to persons of all different social levels and walks of life, ranging from kings and high ministers to traveling merchants or criminals in chains. In order to make his teaching and aid most readily acceptable to all kinds of beings, the bodhisattva is prepared to take on thirty-three different forms, matching his form to that of the being who calls upon him, whether that being be man or woman, exalted or humble, human or nonhuman in nature. Through chapters such as these, which have been recited with fervor by countless devotees over the centuries, the sutra has brought comfort and hope to all levels of society.

Because of its importance as an expression of basic Mahayana thought, its appeal as a devotional work, its dramatic scenes and memorable parables, the Lotus, as already emphasized, has exerted an incalculable influence upon the culture of East Asia. More commentaries have been written on it than on any other Buddhist scripture. The great works of Chinese and Japanese literature such as *The Dream of the Red Chamber* and *The Tale of Genji* are deeply imbued with its ideas and imagery, and its scenes are among the most frequently depicted in the religious art of the area.

The Lotus is not so much an integral work as a collection of religious texts, an anthology of sermons, stories and devotional manuals, some speaking with particular force to persons of one type or in one set of circumstances, some to those of another type or in other circumstances. This is no doubt one reason why it has had such broad and lasting appeal over the ages and has permeated so deeply into the cultures that have been exposed to it.

The present translation is offered in the hope that through it readers of English may come to appreciate something of the power and appeal of the Lotus Sutra, and that among its wealth of profound religious ideas and striking imagery they may find passages that speak compellingly to them as well.

BURTON WATSON

TRANSLATOR'S
NOTE

Why another English translation of the Lotus Sutra, one may ask, when there are several already in existence? First, I would reply, because language changes and translations grow old. The great works of world literature deserve to be translated again and again so that they will continue to be in language that is appealing to contemporary readers. The earliest English translation of the Lotus Sutra, that done by Kern from a Sanskrit version and published in 1884, assuredly no longer is.

Second, because each translator has a certain kind of reader in mind as the work progresses, and certain aspects of the text he or she is especially concerned to do justice to in the translation, perhaps at the expense of other important aspects of the original. The present translation, as should be apparent from the translator's introduction, is designed for readers who have no special background in Buddhist studies or Asian literature. Thus, for example, Sanskrit names and terms have been romanized in a form that differs slightly from the standard form used in works intended for specialists, a form that it is hoped will help guide them to the correct pronunciation; standard romanization for all such words may be found in the Glossary at the back of the book. The Glossary will also provide background information on personal and place names and technical terms that recur frequently in the text.

The translation, it is hoped, will not only convey the ideas for which the work is so important, but at the same time give some sense of its rich literary appeal. The translation is intended to be in straightforward modern English. No attempt has been made, as in some translations of Buddhist scriptures, to impart a "religious" tone by employing an archaic or biblical-sounding style. Despite the often-noted resemblance between one of its parables and the New Testament story of the prodigal son, the Lotus Sutra, particularly in its thought, is rather far removed from the world of the Bible.

Why, one may also ask, if the Lotus Sutra is a work of Indian Buddhism, has the translation been made from the Kumarajiva Chinese translation of the text rather than from one of the Sanskrit versions? First, as already mentioned in my introduction, though we do not know what language the Lotus Sutra was first composed in, it was very probably not Sanskrit, and therefore the Sanskrit versions of the text are already one step removed from the original. Second, none of the extant Sanskrit versions are as early in date as Kumarajiva's Chinese translation, done in 406, and all differ in some respects from his version. Thus his almost certainly represents an earlier version of the text, one nearer to the original. But most important of all, Kumarajiva's Chinese translation is the version in which the Lotus Sutra has been known and read over the centuries throughout the countries of eastern Asia. Buddhism died out in India long ago and the Sanskrit versions of the text were lost for many hundreds of years, only coming to light again in recent times. Today no one but a handful of scholars read the Lotus Sutra in its Sanskrit versions, whereas Kumarajiva's text is read and recited daily by millions of priests and lay believers of East Asia. It is the language and imagery of the Chinese Lotus Sutra that has molded the religious life and thought of the peoples of that part of the world and made its way into their art and literature. So it seemed wholly justifiable to make the English translation from this still living and vital version of the scripture.

For readers not familiar with the remarkable story of Kumarajiva's life, it may be mentioned here that he lived from 344 to 413 and was a native of the small state of Kucha in Central Asia. His father was an Indian of distinguished family who later in life became a Buddhist monk. His mother was a younger sister of the ruler of Kucha. He entered the Buddhist Order as a boy, and with his mother, who had become a nun, traveled extensively around India, acquiring a profound knowledge of Buddhist texts and teachings. Returning to Kucha, he devoted himself there to the propagation of Mahayana Buddhism.

In time his fame as a Buddhist scholar reached China. The Chinese ruler, eager to have so distinguished a religious figure at his own court, dispatched one of his generals to invade Kucha and bring Kumarajiva to the Chinese capital at Ch'ang-an. Because of a change in the ruling dynasty, Kumarajiva was detained for a number of years in Liang-chou in Kansu, but finally reached Ch'ang-an in 401. There, with the support of the ruler, he immediately embarked on a strenuous translation program, producing in rapid succession a series of authoritative Chinese versions of important Buddhist sutras and treatises, thirty-five works in all, among them the Lotus Sutra. He was greatly aided in his work by a large body of Chinese disciples and scholar-monks who carefully checked his translations against earlier versions, discussed the meaning with him, and helped him to polish the wording of his own versions. This is no doubt one reason why Kumarajiva's translation of the Lotus Sutra is so superior to other Chinese translations and why it has been so widely and enthusiastically read.

The origin of the present translation goes back to a day in Tokyo in December 1973 when I had an opportunity to meet and talk with President Daisaku Ikeda, head of the Soka Gakkai International and a world leader in the Buddhist movement. When President Ikeda learned that most of my translation work was from texts in classical Chinese, he said, "In that case, you must do us a new translation of the Kumarajiva Lotus Sutra!" The project appealed to me immediately, and though it was some years before I could begin actual work, I am extremely grateful for the opportunity it has afforded me to deal with a text of such lasting importance.

The translation was prepared with the assistance of the Nichiren Shoshu International Center in Tokyo, which is connected with Soka Gakkai International. The translation is based on the Chinese text and Japanese *yomikudashi* found in the *Myōhō-renge-kyō narabi ni kaiketsu*, compiled and edited by the Soka Gakkai and published in Tokyo in 1961. The Chinese text of the Kumarajiva translation was fixed long ago and there are no significant textual variations. I would like here to express my deep gratitude to the many persons associated with Soka Gakkai International and the Nichiren Shoshu International Center who lent their assistance to the undertaking. They not only checked over my translation with care and thoroughness, but offered invaluable advice at many points on questions of interpretation and presentation.

A word may be said here as to the sort of problems in interpretation that arose. Classical Chinese, the language of the Kumarajiva Lotus, is highly spare and compressed in style, and hence often ambiguous in meaning or construction and open to varying interpretations. Thus, for example, it is easy to tell where a passage of direct speech begins, but often difficult to determine exactly where it ends. Verbs frequently lack an expressed subject, and a quite legitimate case can be made for several different interpretations of the passage. One must often guess at the tense of a verb, or whether a noun is to be taken as singular or plural. Particularly in the verse sections, where the language has been unusually compressed or distorted in order to fit into lines of uniform length, the meaning can sometimes scarcely be made out at all without consulting the parallel passage in the prose section.

Because of such recurring problems and ambiguities, no two translators of the Chinese will ever come up with exactly identical renderings of the text. This does not mean in most cases that one translator is wrong and the other right, but simply that they have made different choices in their interpretation. In the present translation I have tried to render the text in the way that it has traditionally been understood in China and Japan. That is why I have carefully taken into consideration the Japanese *yomikudashi* reading in the edition cited above, which rearranges the Chinese characters of the text so that they conform to the patterns of Japanese syntax. This reading is based on the interpretation of the text followed by Nichiren (1222–1282), the founder of Nichiren Buddhism in Japan, who throughout his life constantly lectured on the Lotus Sutra to his disciples and lay followers and gave detailed expositions of its teachings. His interpretation is in turn based on the commentaries on the Lotus Sutra by the great scholar of Chinese Buddhism, Chih-i (538–597), the founder of the T'ien-t'ai school.

It may be noted here that Chih-i in his commentaries on the Lotus Sutra developed an extremely complex and sophisticated hermeneutical system by which he attempted to bring out the sutra's deepest meaning and define its position and importance in the body of the Buddhist writings as a whole. This system was further elaborated and refined in subcommentaries on Chih-i's works written by his disciples or later scholars of the T'ien-t'ai school. To fully appreciate the way in which the Lotus Sutra has traditionally been interpreted in East Asian Buddhist circles, one would ideally have to master the ideas and terminology of this system of exegesis. But simply to describe the system adequately would require almost as much space as has been devoted to the translation itself, and would no doubt deter readers from responding to the translation in a direct and personal manner. In the translator's introduction and glossary I have therefore made little reference to this system, but have tried to concentrate on doctrines and motifs that are explicit in the Lotus itself.

But to return to the translation, the single most troublesome problem faced in the translation was how best to handle the Chinese word *fa*, which is used in Buddhist Chinese to render the Sanskrit word *dharma*. Sometimes in the Chinese Lotus the word *fa* seems to refer to the Truth as taught in Buddhism or the doctrine as a whole, in which cases it has been translated "Dharma" or "the Law." But sometimes it is preceded by the pluralizing word *chu*; to translate it in such cases as "the Laws" would give, it was felt, too legalistic a tone, and it has therefore been rendered as "doctrines" or "teachings." The word *dharma* in Sanskrit can also mean a "thing" or a phenomenon, one of the elements that make up existence, and there are places in the Lotus where this meaning is clearly intended. Indeed, one of the most famous phrases in the Chinese version of the sutra is *chu-fa shih-hsiang* (in Japanese *shohō jissō*), which occurs in chapter two and which in the present translation has been rendered as "the true entity of all phenomena." In still other cases *fa* seems to mean merely a rule, a method, or an approach, and has accordingly been rendered by some such equivalent.

One hates to impose distinctions on the translation where they do not exist in the original. But to translate *fa* as "dharma" in all these different cases would not only make for awkward English in places but would fail to convey the real meaning of the passage. I therefore decided to translate the word differently in different contexts. I may not always have made the best choice in deciding what English equivalent to use, but the reader may be assured that I gave careful thought to all such places.

OTHER COMPLETE ENGLISH TRANSLATIONS OF THE LOTUS SUTRA

The Saddharmapundarika; or, The Lotus of the True Law. Tr. by Jan Hendrik Kern. Sacred Books of the East, vol. 21. Oxford: Clarendon Press, 1884.

The first English translation, done from a Sanskrit version of the text that, according to Kern, is dated 1039.

The Sutra of the Lotus Flower of the Wonderful Law. Tr. by Senchu Murano. Tokyo: Nichiren Shu Headquarters, 1974.

Translation of the Kumarajiva version of the Lotus Sutra. Brief introduction, very extensive glossaries, particularly useful to readers with a knowledge of the Japanese readings of Buddhist names and terms.

The Threefold Lotus Sutra: The Sutra of Innumerable Meanings; The Sutra of the Lotus Flower of the Wonderful Law; The Sutra of Meditation on the Bodhisattva Universal Virtue. Tr. by Bunnō Katō, Yoshirō Tamura, and Kojiro Miyasaka. Tokyo: Kosei, 1975.

Translation of the Kumarajiva version of the Lotus, plus two other short sutras that, from the time of Chih-i, have been regarded as an introduction and postscript respectively to the Lotus. Brief introduction and extensive glossary.

Scripture of the Lotus Blossom of the Fine Dharma. Tr. by Leon Hurvitz. New York: Columbia University Press, 1976.

Translation of the Kumarajiva version of the Lotus. Contains a preface, glossary, and extensive section of passages translated from a Sanskrit version of the text to show where and how the Sanskrit differs from the Chinese translation of Kumarajiva. An invaluable work of scholarship.

The Lotus Sutra: The White Lotus of the Marvelous Law. Tr. by Tsugunari Kubo and Akira Yuyama. Tokyo and Berkeley: Bukkyo Dendo Kyokai, 1991.

Translation of the Kumarajiva version of the Lotus. Brief translator's introduction, Sanskrit glossary, and selected bibliography.

THE
LOTUS
SUTRA

1

INTRODUCTION

This is what I heard:

At one time the Buddha was in Rajagriha, staying on Mount Gridhrakuta. Accompanying him were a multitude of leading monks numbering twelve thousand persons. All were arhats whose outflows had come to an end, who had no more earthly desires, who had attained what was to their advantage and had put an end to the bonds of existence, and whose minds had achieved a state of freedom.

Their names were Ajnata Kaundinya, Mahakashyapa, Uruvilvakashyapa, Gayakashyapa, Nadikashyapa, Shariputra, Great Maudgalyayana, Mahakatyayana, Aniruddha, Kapphina, Gavampati, Revata, Pilindavatsa, Bakkula, Mahakaushthila, Nanda, Sundarananda, Purna Maitrayaniputra, Subhuti, Ananda, and Rahula. All were like these, great arhats who were well known to others.

There were also two thousand persons, some of whom were still learning and some who had completed their learning.

There was the nun Mahaprajapati with her six thousand followers. And there was Rahula's mother, the nun Yashodhara, with her followers.

There were bodhisattvas and mahasattvas, eighty thousand of them, none of them ever regressing in their search for anuttara-samyak-sambodhi. All had gained dharanis, delighted in preaching, were eloquent, and turned the wheel of the Law that knows no regression. They had made offerings to immeasurable hundreds and thousands of Buddhas, in the presence of various Buddhas had planted numerous roots of virtue, had been constantly praised by the Buddhas, had trained themselves in compassion, were good at entering the Buddha wisdom, and had fully penetrated the great wisdom and reached the farther shore. Their fame had spread throughout immeasurable worlds and they were able to save countless hundreds of thousands of living beings.

Their names were Bodhisattva Manjushri, Bodhisattva Perceiver of the World's Sounds, Bodhisattva Gainer of Great Authority, Bodhisattva Constant Exertion, Bodhisattva Never Resting, Bodhisattva Jeweled Palm, Bodhisattva Medicine King, Bodhisattva Brave Donor, Bodhisattva Jeweled Moon, Bodhisattva Moonlight, Bodhisattva Full Moon, Bodhisattva Great Strength, Bodhisattva Immeasurable Strength, Bodhisattva Transcending the Threefold World, Bodhisattva Bhadrapala, Bodhisattva Maitreya, Bodhisattva Jeweled Accumulation, and Bodhisattva Guiding Leader. Bodhisattvas and mahasattvas such as these numbering eighty thousand were in attendance.

At that time Shakra Devanam Indra with his followers, twenty thousand sons of gods, also attended. There were also the sons of gods Rare Moon, Pervading Fragrance, Jeweled Glow, and the Four Great Heavenly Kings, along with their followers, ten thousand sons of gods.

Present were the sons of gods Freedom and Great Freedom and their followers, thirty thousand sons of gods. Present were King Brahma, lord of the saha world, the great Brahma Shikhin, and the great

Brahma Light Bright, and their followers, twelve thousand sons of gods.

There were eight dragon kings, the dragon king Nanda, the dragon king Upananda, the dragon king Sagara, the dragon king Vasuki, the dragon king Takshaka, the dragon king Anavatapta, the dragon king Manasvin, and the dragon king Utpalaka, each with several hundreds of thousands of followers.

There were four kimnara kings, the kimnara king Law, the kimnara king Wonderful Law, the kimnara king Great Law, and the kimnara king Upholding the Law, each with several hundreds of thousands of followers.

There were four gandharva kings, the gandharva king Pleasant, the gandharva king Pleasant Sound, the gandharva king Beautiful, and the gandharva king Beautiful Sound, each with several hundreds of thousands of followers.

There were four asura kings, the asura king Balin, the asura king Kharaskandha, the asura king Vemachitrin, and the asura king Rahu, each with several hundreds of thousands of followers.

There were four garuda kings, the garuda king Great Majesty, the garuda king Great Body, the garuda king Great Fullness, and the garuda king As One Wishes, each with several hundreds of thousands of followers. And there was King Ajatashatru, the son of Vaidehi, with several hundreds of thousands of followers.

Each of these, after bowing in obeisance before the Buddha's feet, withdrew and took a seat to one side.

At that time the World-Honored One, surrounded by the four kinds of believers, received offerings and tokens of respect and was honored and praised. And for the sake of the bodhisattvas he preached the Great Vehicle sutra entitled Immeasurable Meanings, a Law to instruct the bodhisattvas, one that is guarded and kept in mind by the Buddhas.

When the Buddha had finished preaching this sutra, he sat with his legs crossed in lotus position and entered into the samadhi of the place of immeasurable meanings, his body and mind never moving. At that time heaven rained down mandarava flowers, great mandarava flowers, manjushaka flowers, and great manjushaka flowers, scattering them over the Buddha and over the great assembly, and everywhere the Buddha world quaked and trembled in six different ways.

At that time the monks, nuns, laymen, laywomen, heavenly beings, dragons, yakshas, gandharvas, asuras, garudas, kimnaras, mahoragas, human and nonhuman beings in the assembly, as well as the petty kings and wheel-turning sage kings—all those in the great assembly, having gained what they had never had before, were filled with joy and, pressing their palms together, gazed at the Buddha with a single mind.

At that time the Buddha emitted a ray of light from the tuft of white hair between his eyebrows, one of his characteristic features, lighting up eighteen thousand worlds in the eastern direction. There was no place that the light did not penetrate, reaching downward as far as the Avichi hell and upward to the Akanishtha heaven.

From this world one could see the living beings in the six paths of existence in all of those other lands. One could likewise see the Buddhas present at that time in those other lands and could hear the sutra teachings which those Buddhas were expounding. At the same time one could see the monks, nuns, laymen, and laywomen who had carried out religious practices and attained the way. One could also see the bodhisattvas and mahasattvas who, through various causes and conditions and various types of faith and understanding and in various forms and aspects were carrying out the way of the bodhisattva. And one could also see the Buddhas who had entered parinirvana, and could also see how, after the Buddhas had entered parinirvana, towers adorned with the seven treasures were erected for the Buddha relics.

At that time Bodhisattva Maitreya had this thought: Now the World-Honored One has manifested these miraculous signs. But what is the cause of these auspicious portents? Now the Buddha, the World-Honored One, has entered into samadhi. An unfathomable event such as this is seldom to be met with. Whom shall I question about this? Who can give me an answer?

And again he had this thought: This Manjushri, son of a Dharma King, has already personally attended and given offerings to immeasurable numbers of Buddhas in the past. Surely he must see these rare signs. I will now question him.

At this time the monks, nuns, laymen and laywomen, as well as the heavenly beings, dragons, spirits, and the others all had this thought: This beam of brightness from the Buddha, these signs of transcendental powers—now whom shall we question about them?

At that time Bodhisattva Maitreya wished to settle his doubts concerning the matter. And in addition he could see what was in the minds of the four kinds of believers, the monks, nuns, laymen and laywomen, as well as the heavenly beings, dragons, spirits, and the others who made up the assembly. So he questioned Manjushri, saying, "What is the cause of these auspicious portents, these signs of transcendental powers, this emitting of a great beam of brightness that illumines the eighteen thousand lands in the eastern direction so we can see all the adornments of the Buddha worlds there?"

Then Bodhisattva Maitreya, wishing to state his meaning once more, asked the question in verse form:

> Manjushri,
> why from the white tuft between the eyebrows
> of our leader and teacher
> does this great light shine all around?
> Why do mandarava
> and manjushaka flowers rain down
> and breezes scented with sandalwood
> delight the hearts of the assembly?
> Because of these
> the earth is everywhere adorned and purified
> and this world
> quakes and trembles in six different ways.
> At this time the four kinds of believers
> are all filled with joy and delight,
> they rejoice in body and mind,
> having gained what they never had before.
> The beam of brightness from between the eyebrows
> illumines the eastern direction
> and eighteen thousand lands
> are all the color of gold.
> From the Avichi hell
> upward to the Summit of Being,
> throughout the various worlds
> the living beings in the six paths,
> the realm to which their births and deaths are tending,
> their good and bad deeds,

and the pleasing or ugly recompense they receive—
all these can be seen from here.
We can also see Buddhas,
those sage lords, lions,
expounding and preaching sutras
that are subtle, wonderful and foremost.
Their voices are clear and pure,
issuing in soft and gentle sounds,
as they teach bodhisattvas
in numberless millions.
Their brahma sounds are profound and wonderful,
making people delight in hearing them.
Each in his own world
preaches the correct Law,
following various causes and conditions
and employing immeasurable similes,
illuminating the Law of the Buddha,
guiding living beings to enlightenment.
If a person should encounter troubles,
loathing old age, sickness and death,
the Buddhas preach to him on nirvana,
explaining how he may put an end to all troubles.
If a person should have good fortune,
having in the past made offerings to the Buddhas,
determined to seek a superior Law,
the Buddhas preach the way of the pratyekabuddha.
If there should be Buddha sons
who carry out various religious practices,
seeking to attain the unsurpassed wisdom,
the Buddhas preach the way of purity.
Manjushri,
I have been dwelling here,
seeing and hearing in this manner
many things numbering in the thousands of millions.
Numerous as they are,
I will now speak of them in brief.
I see in these lands
bodhisattvas numerous as Ganges sands,

according with various causes and conditions
and seeking the way of the Buddha.
Some of them give alms,
gold, silver, coral,
pearls, mani jewels,
seashell, agate,
diamonds and other rarities,
men and women servants, carriages,
jeweled hand carriages and palanquins,
gladly presenting these donations.
Such gifts they give to the Buddha way,
desiring to achieve the vehicle
that is foremost in the threefold world
and praised by the Buddhas.
There are some bodhisattvas
who give jeweled carriages drawn by teams of four,
with railings and flowered canopies
adorning their top and sides.
Again I see bodhisattvas
who give their own flesh, hands and feet,
or their wives and children,
seeking the unsurpassed way.
I also see bodhisattvas
who happily give
heads, eyes, bodies and limbs
in their search for the Buddha wisdom.
Manjushri,
I see kings
going to visit the place of the Buddha
to ask him about the unsurpassed way.
They put aside their happy lands,
their palaces, their men and women attendants,
shave their hair and beard
and don the clothes of the Dharma.
Or I see bodhisattvas
who become monks,
living alone in quietude,
delighting in chanting the sutras.

Again I see bodhisattvas
bravely and vigorously exerting themselves,
entering the deep mountains,
their thoughts on the Buddha way.
And I see them removing themselves from desire,
constantly dwelling in emptiness and stillness,
advancing deep into the practice of meditation
till they have gained the five transcendental powers.
And I see bodhisattvas
resting in meditation, palms pressed together,
with a thousand, ten thousand verses
praising the king of the doctrines.
Again I see bodhisattvas,
profound in wisdom, firm in purpose,
who know how to question the Buddhas
and accept and abide by all they hear.
I see Buddha sons
proficient in both meditation and wisdom,
who use immeasurable numbers of similes
to expound the Law to the assembly,
delighting in preaching the Law,
converting the bodhisattvas,
defeating the legions of the devil
and beating the Dharma drum.
And I see bodhisattvas
profoundly still and silent,
honored by heavenly beings and dragons
but not counting that a joy.
And I see bodhisattvas
living in forests, emitting light,
saving those who suffer in hell,
causing them to enter the Buddha way.
And I see Buddha sons
who have never once slept,
who keep circling through the forest
diligently seeking the Buddha way.
And I see those who observe the precepts,
no flaw in their conduct,

pure as jewels and gems,
and in that manner seeking the Buddha way.
And I see Buddha sons
abiding in the strength of fortitude,
taking the abuse and blows
of persons of overbearing arrogance,
willing to suffer all these,
and in that manner seeking the Buddha way.
I see bodhisattvas
removing themselves from frivolity and laughter
and from foolish companions,
befriending persons of wisdom,
unifying their minds, dispelling confusion,
ordering their thoughts in mountain and forest
and for a million, a thousand, ten thousand years
in that manner seeking the Buddha way.
Or I see bodhisattvas
with delicious things to eat and drink
and a hundred kinds of medicinal potions,
offering them to the Buddha and his monks;
fine robes and superior garments
costing in the thousands or ten thousands,
or robes that are beyond cost,
offering them to the Buddha and his monks;
a thousand, ten thousand, a million kinds
of jeweled dwellings made of sandalwood
and numerous wonderful articles of bedding,
offering them to the Buddha and his monks;
immaculate gardens and groves
where flowers and fruit abound,
flowing springs and bathing pools,
offering them to the Buddha and his monks;
offerings of this kind,
of many different wonderful varieties
presented gladly and without regret
as they seek the unsurpassed way.
Or there are bodhisattvas
who expound the Law of tranquil extinction,

giving different types of instruction
to numberless living beings.
Or I see bodhisattvas
viewing the nature of all phenomena
as having no dual characteristics,
as being like empty space.
And I see Buddha sons
whose minds have no attachments,
who use this wonderful wisdom
to seek the unsurpassed way.
Manjushri,
there are also bodhisattvas
who after the Buddha has passed into extinction
make offerings to his relics.
I see Buddha sons
building memorial towers
as numberless as Ganges sands,
ornamenting each land with them,
jeweled towers lofty and wonderful,
five thousand yojanas high,
their width and depth
exactly two thousand yojanas,
each of these memorial towers
with its thousand banners and streamers,
with curtains laced with gems like dewdrops
and jeweled bells chiming harmoniously.
There heavenly beings, dragons, spirits,
human and nonhuman beings,
with incense, flowers and music
constantly make offerings.
Manjushri,
these Buddha sons
in order to make offerings to the relics
adorn the memorial towers
so that each land, just as it is,
is as outstandingly wonderful and lovely
as the heavenly king of trees
when its flowers open and unfold.

When the Buddha emits a beam of light
I and the other members of the assembly
can see these lands
in all their various outstanding wonders.
The supernatural powers of the Buddhas
and their wisdom are rare indeed;
by emitting one pure beam of light,
the Buddhas illuminate countless lands.
I and the others have seen this,
have gained something never known before.
Buddha son, Manjushri,
I beg you to settle the doubts of the assembly.
The four kinds of believers look up in happy anticipation,
gazing at you and me.
Why does the World-Honored One
emit this beam of brightness?
Buddha son, give a timely answer,
settle these doubts and occasion joy!
What rich benefits will come
from the projecting of this beam of brightness?
It must be that the Buddha wishes to expound
the wonderful Law he gained
when he sat in the place of practice.
He must have prophecies to bestow.
He has showed us Buddha lands
with their adornment and purity of manifold treasures,
and we have seen their Buddhas—
this is not done for petty reasons.
Manjushri, you must know.
The four kinds of believers, the dragons and spirits
gaze at you in surmise,
wondering what explanation you will give.

At that time Manjushri said to the bodhisattva and mahasattva
Maitreya and the other great men: "Good men, I suppose that the
Buddha, the World-Honored One, wishes now to expound the great
Law, to rain down the rain of the great Law, to blow the conch of the
great Law, to beat the drum of the great Law, to elucidate the meaning

of the great Law. Good men, in the past I have seen this auspicious portent among the Buddhas. They emitted a beam of light like this, and after that they expounded the great Law. Therefore we should know that now, when the present Buddha manifests this light, he will do likewise. He wishes to cause all living beings to hear and understand the Law, which is difficult for all the world to believe. Therefore he has manifested this auspicious portent.

"Good men, once, at a time that was an immeasurable, boundless, inconceivable number of asamkhya kalpas in the past, there was a Buddha named Sun Moon Bright, Thus Come One, worthy of offerings, of right and universal knowledge, perfect clarity and conduct, well gone, understanding the world, unexcelled worthy, trainer of people, teacher of heavenly and human beings, Buddha, World-Honored One, who expounded the correct Law. His exposition was good at the beginning, good in the middle, good at the end. The meaning was profound and far-reaching, the words were skillful and wondrous. It was pure and without alloy, complete, clean and spotless, and bore the marks of brahma practice.

"For the sake of those seeking to become voice-hearers he responded by expounding the Law of the four noble truths, so that they could transcend birth, old age, sickness and death and attain nirvana. For the sake of those seeking to become pratyekabuddhas he responded by expounding the Law of the twelve-linked chain of causation. For the sake of the bodhisattvas he responded by expounding the six paramitas, causing them to gain anuttara-samyak-sambodhi and to acquire the wisdom that embraces all species.

"Then there was another Buddha who was also named Sun Moon Bright, and then another Buddha also named Sun Moon Bright. There were twenty thousand Buddhas like this, all with the same appellation, all named Sun Moon Bright. And all had the same surname, the surname Bharadvaja. Maitreya, you should understand that from the first Buddha to the last, all had the same appellation, all were named Sun Moon Bright. They were worthy of all the ten epithets and the Law they expounded was good at the beginning, in the middle, and at the end.

"The last Buddha, when he had not yet left family life, had eight princely sons. The first was named Having Intention, the second Good Intention, the third Immeasurable Intention, the fourth Jeweled Intention, the fifth Increased Intention, the sixth Cleansed of Doubt Intention, the seventh Echoing Intention, and the eighth Law Intention. Dignity and virtue came easily to them, and each presided over a four-continent realm.

"When these princes heard that their father had left family life and had gained anuttara-samyak-sambodhi, they all cast aside their princely positions and followed him by leaving family life. Conceiving a desire for the Great Vehicle, they constantly carried out brahma practices, and all became teachers of the Law. They had already planted good roots in the company of a thousand, ten thousand Buddhas.

"At that time the Buddha Sun Moon Bright preached the Great Vehicle sutra entitled Immeasurable Meanings, a Law to instruct the bodhisattvas, one that is guarded and kept in mind by the Buddhas. When he had finished preaching the sutra, he sat cross-legged in the midst of the great assembly and entered into the samadhi of the place of immeasurable meanings, his body and mind never moving. At this time heaven rained down mandarava flowers, great mandarava flowers, manjushaka flowers, and great manjushaka flowers, scattering them over the Buddha and over the great assembly, and everywhere the Buddha world quaked and trembled in six different ways.

"At that time the monks, nuns, laymen, laywomen, heavenly beings, dragons, yakshas, gandharvas, asuras, garudas, kimnaras, and mahoragas, the human and nonhuman beings in the assembly, as well as the petty kings and wheel-turning sage kings—all those in this great assembly gained what they had never had before and, filled with joy, pressed their palms together and gazed at the Buddha with a single mind.

"At that time the Thus Come One emitted a ray of light from the tuft of white hair between his eyebrows, one of his characteristic features, lighting up eighteen thousand Buddha lands in the eastern direction. There was no place that the light did not penetrate, just as you have seen it light up these Buddha lands now.

"Maitreya, you should understand this. At that time in the assembly there were twenty million bodhisattvas who were happy and eager to hear the Law. When these bodhisattvas saw this beam of light that illumined the Buddha lands everywhere, they gained what they had never had before. They wished to know the causes and conditions that had occasioned this light.

"At that time there was a bodhisattva named Wonderfully Bright who had eight hundred disciples. At this time the Buddha Sun Moon Bright arose from his samadhi and, because of the bodhisattva Wonderfully Bright, preached the Great Vehicle sutra called the Lotus of the Wonderful Law, a Law to instruct the bodhisattvas, one that is guarded and kept in mind by the Buddhas. For sixty small kalpas the Buddha remained in his seat without rising, and the listeners in the assembly at that time also remained seated there for sixty small kalpas, their bodies and minds never moving. And yet it seemed to them that they had been listening to the Buddha preach for no more than the space of a meal. At this time in the assembly there was not a single person who in body or mind had the least feeling of weariness.

"When the Buddha Sun Moon Bright had finished preaching this sutra over a period of sixty small kalpas, he spoke these words to the Brahmas, devils, shramanas and Brahmans, as well as to the heavenly and human beings and asuras in the assembly, saying, 'Tonight at midnight the Thus Come One will enter the nirvana of no remainder.'

"At this time there was a bodhisattva named Virtue Storehouse. The Buddha Sun Moon Bright bestowed a prophecy on him, announcing to the monks, 'This bodhisattva Virtue Storehouse will be the next to become a Buddha. He will be called Pure Body, tathagata, arhat, samyak-sambuddha.'

"After the Buddha had finished bestowing this prophecy, at midnight he entered the nirvana of no remainder.

"After the Buddha had passed away, Bodhisattva Wonderfully Bright upheld the Sutra of the Lotus of the Wonderful Law, for a period of fully eighty small kalpas expounding it for others. The eight sons of the Buddha Sun Moon Bright all acknowledged Wonderfully Bright as their teacher. Wonderfully Bright taught and converted them and roused in them a firm determination to gain anuttara-samyak-sambodhi. Those princely sons gave offerings to immeasurable hundreds, thousands, ten thousands, millions of Buddhas, and after that all were able to achieve the Buddha way. The last to become a Buddha was named Burning Torch.

"Among the eight hundred disciples of Wonderfully Bright was one named Seeker of Fame. He was greedy for gain and support, and though he read and recited numerous sutras, he could not understand them, but for the most part forgot them. Hence he was called Seeker of Fame. Because this man had in addition planted various good roots, however, he was able to encounter immeasurable hundreds, thousands, ten thousands, millions of Buddhas, to make offerings to them, revere, honor and praise them.

"Maitreya, you should understand this. Bodhisattva Wonderfully Bright who lived then—could he be unknown to you? He was no other than I myself. And Bodhisattva Seeker of Fame was you.

"Now when I see this auspicious portent, it is no different from what I saw before. Therefore I suppose that now the Thus Come One is about to preach the Great Vehicle sutra called the Lotus of the Wonderful Law, a Law to instruct the bodhisattvas, one that is guarded and kept in mind by the Buddhas."

At that time Manjushri, wishing in the presence of the great assembly to state his meaning once more, spoke in verse form, saying:

> I recall that in a past age
> immeasurable, innumerable kalpas ago
> there was a Buddha, most honored of men,
> named Sun Moon Bright.
> This World-Honored One expounded the Law,
> saving immeasurable living beings
> and numberless millions of bodhisattvas,
> causing them to enter the Buddha wisdom.
> The eight princely sons whom this Buddha sired
> before taking leave of family life,
> when they saw that the great sage had left his family,
> did likewise, carrying out brahma practices.
> At that time the Buddha preached the Great Vehicle,
> a sutra named Immeasurable Meanings,
> and in the midst of a great assembly
> for the sake of the people established broad distinctions.
> When the Buddha had finished preaching this sutra
> he sat in the seat of the Law,
> sitting cross-legged in the samadhi
> called the place of immeasurable meanings.
> The heavens rained mandarava flowers,
> heavenly drums sounded of themselves,
> and the heavenly beings, dragons and spirits

made offerings to the most honored of men.
All the Buddha lands
immediately quaked and trembled greatly.
The Buddha emitted a light from between his eyebrows,
manifesting signs that are rarely seen.
This light illumined the eastern direction,
eighteen thousand Buddha lands,
showing how all the living beings there
were recompensed in birth and death for their past deeds.
That one could see how these Buddha lands,
adorned with numerous jewels,
shone with hues of lapis lazuli and crystal
was due to the illumination of the Buddha's light.
One could also see the heavenly and human beings,
dragons, spirits, many yakshas,
gandharvas and kimnaras,
each making offerings to his respective Buddha.
One could also see Thus Come Ones
naturally attaining the Buddha way,
their bodies the color of golden mountains,
upright, imposing, very subtle and wonderful.
It was as though in the midst of pure lapis lazuli
there should appear statues of real gold.
In the midst of the great assembly the World-Honored Ones
expounded the principles of the profound Law.
In one after another of the Buddha lands
the voice-hearers in countless multitudes
through the illumination of the Buddha's light
all became visible with their great assemblies.
There were also monks
residing in the midst of forests,
exerting themselves and keeping the pure precepts
as though they were guarding a bright jewel.
One could also see bodhisattvas
carrying out almsgiving, forbearance, and so forth,
their number like Ganges sands,
due to the illumination of the Buddha's light.
One could also see bodhisattvas

entering deep into meditation practices,
their bodies and minds still and unmoving,
in that manner seeking the unsurpassed way.
One could also see bodhisattvas
who knew that phenomena are marked by tranquility
    and extinction,
each in his respective land
preaching the Law and seeking the Buddha way.
At that time the four kinds of believers,
seeing the Buddha Sun Moon Bright
manifest his great transcendental powers,
all rejoiced in their hearts,
and each one asked his neighbor
what had caused these events.
The one honored by heavenly and human beings
just then arose from his samadhi
and praised Bodhisattva Wonderfully Bright, saying,
"You are the eyes of the world,
one whom all can take faith in and believe,
able to honor and uphold the storehouse of the Dharma.
The Law that I preach—
you alone know how to testify to it."
The World-Honored One, having bestowed this praise,
causing Wonderfully Bright to rejoice,
preached the Lotus Sutra
for fully sixty small kalpas.
He never rose from this seat,
and the supreme and wonderful Law that he preached
was accepted and upheld in its entirety
by the Dharma teacher Wonderfully Bright.
After the Buddha had preached the Lotus,
causing all the assembly to rejoice,
on that very same day
he announced to the assembly of heavenly and human beings,
"I have already expounded for you
the meaning of the true entity of all phenomena.
Now when midnight comes
I will enter nirvana.

You must strive with all your hearts
and remove yourselves from indulgence and laxity.
It is very difficult to encounter a Buddha—
you meet one once in a million kalpas.''
When the children of the World-Honored One
heard that the Buddha was to enter nirvana,
each one was filled with sorrow and distress,
wondering why the Buddha should so quickly seek extinction.
The sage lord, king of the Law,
comforted and reassured the countless multitude,
saying, ''When I enter extinction
you must not be concerned or fearful!
This bodhisattva Virtue Storehouse
has already fully understood in his mind
the true entity that is without outflows.
He will be next to become a Buddha,
bearing the name Pure Body,
and he too will save immeasurable multitudes.''
That night the Buddha entered extinction,
as a fire dies out when the firewood is exhausted.
They divided and apportioned his relics
and built immeasurable numbers of towers,
and the monks and nuns
whose number was like Ganges sands
redoubled their exertions,
thereby seeking the unsurpassed way.
This Dharma teacher Wonderfully Bright
honored and upheld the Buddha's storehouse of the Dharma
throughout eighty small kalpas,
broadly propagating the Lotus Sutra.
These eight princely sons
whom Wonderfully Bright converted
held firmly to the unsurpassed way
and were thus able to encounter innumerable Buddhas.
And after they had made offerings to these Buddhas
they followed them in practicing the great way
and one after the other succeeded in becoming a Buddha,
each in turn bestowing a prophecy on his successor.

The last to become a heavenly being among heavenly beings
was named the Buddha Burning Torch.
As leader and teacher of seers
he saved immeasurable multitudes.
This Dharma teacher Wonderfully Bright
at that time had a disciple
whose mind was forever occupied with laziness and sloth,
who was greedy for fame and profit.
He sought fame and profit insatiably,
often amusing himself among clansmen and those of
    other surnames.
He threw away what he had studied and memorized,
neglected and forgot it, failed to understand it.
Because of this
he was named Seeker of Fame.
But he had also carried out many good actions
and thus was able to meet with innumerable Buddhas.
He made offerings to the Buddhas
and followed them in practicing the great way,
carrying out all the six paramitas,
and now he has met the lion of the Shakyas.
Hereafter he will become a Buddha
whose name will be Maitreya,
who will save living beings extensively
in numbers beyond calculation.
After that Buddha passed into extinction,
that lazy and slothful one—he was you,
and the Dharma teacher Wonderfully Bright—
that was the person who is now I myself.
I saw how the Buddha Torch Bright (Sun Moon Bright)
earlier manifested an auspicious portent like this.
And so I know that now this present Buddha
is about to preach the Lotus Sutra.
The signs now are like those of the earlier auspicious portent,
this is an expedient means used by the Buddhas.
Now when the Buddha emits this beam of brightness
he is helping to reveal the meaning of the true entity of
    phenomena.

Human beings now will come to know it.
Let us press our palms together and wait with a single mind.
The Buddha will rain down the rain of the Law
to fully satisfy all seekers of the way.
You who seek the three vehicles,
if you have doubts and regrets,
the Buddha will resolve them for you,
bringing them to an end so that nothing remains.

2

EXPEDIENT MEANS

At that time the World-Honored One calmly arose from his samadhi and addressed Shariputra, saying: "The wisdom of the Buddhas is infinitely profound and immeasurable. The door to this wisdom is difficult to understand and difficult to enter. Not one of the voice-hearers or pratyekabuddhas is able to comprehend it.

"What is the reason for this? A Buddha has personally attended a hundred, a thousand, ten thousand, a million, a countless number of Buddhas and has fully carried out an immeasurable number of religious practices. He has exerted himself bravely and vigorously, and his name is universally known. He has realized the Law that is profound and never known before, and preaches it in accordance with what is appropriate, yet his intention is difficult to understand.

"Shariputra, ever since I attained Buddhahood I have through various causes and various similes widely expounded my teachings and have used countless expedient means to guide living beings and cause them to renounce their attachments. Why is this? Because the Thus Come One is fully possessed of both expedient means and the paramita of wisdom.

"Shariputra, the wisdom of the Thus Come One is expansive and profound. He has immeasurable [mercy], unlimited [eloquence], power, fearlessness, concentration, emancipation, and samadhis, and has deeply entered the boundless and awakened to the Law never before attained.

"Shariputra, the Thus Come One knows how to make various kinds of distinctions and to expound the teachings skillfully. His words are soft and gentle and can delight the hearts of the assembly.

"Shariputra, to sum it up: the Buddha has fully realized the Law that is limitless, boundless, never attained before.

"But stop, Shariputra, I will say no more. Why? Because what the Buddha has achieved is the rarest and most difficult-to-understand Law. The true entity of all phenomena can only be understood and shared between Buddhas. This reality consists of the appearance, nature, entity, power, influence, inherent cause, relation, latent effect, manifest effect, and their consistency from beginning to end."

At that time the World-Honored One, wishing to state his meaning once more, spoke in verse form, saying:

> The hero of the world is unfathomable.
> Among heavenly beings or the people of the world,
> among all living beings,
> none can understand the Buddha.
> The Buddha's power, fearlessness,
> emancipation and samadhis
> and the Buddha's other attributes
> no one can reckon or fathom.
> Earlier, under the guidance of countless Buddhas
> he fully acquired and practiced various ways,
> profound, subtle and wonderful doctrines
> that are hard to see and hard to understand.

For immeasurable millions of kalpas
he has been practicing these ways
until in the place of practice he achieved the goal.
I have already come to see and know completely
this great goal and recompense,
the meaning of these various natures and characteristics.
I and the other Buddhas of the ten directions
can now understand these things.
This Law cannot be described,
words fall silent before it.
Among the other kinds of living beings
there are none who can comprehend it,
except the many bodhisattvas
who are firm in the power of faith.
The many disciples of the Buddhas
in the past have given offerings to the Buddhas,
have already cut off all outflows
and now are dwelling in their last incarnation.
But even such persons as they
have not the power needed.
Even if the whole world
were filled with men like Shariputra,
though they exhausted their thoughts and pooled
     their capacities,
they could not fathom the Buddha's knowledge.
Even if ten directions
were all filled with men like Shariputra
or like the other disciples,
though they filled the lands in the ten directions
and exhausted their thoughts and pooled their capacities,
still they could not understand it.
If pratyekabuddhas, acute in understanding,
without outflows, in their last incarnation,
should fill the worlds in the ten directions,
as numerous as bamboos in a grove,
though they should join together with one mind
for a million or for countless kalpas,
hoping to conceive of the Buddha's true wisdom,

they could not understand the smallest part of it.
If bodhisattvas newly embarked on their course
should give offerings to numberless Buddhas,
completely mastering the intent of the various doctrines
and also able to preach the Law effectively,
like so many rice and hemp plants, bamboos or reeds,
filling the lands in the ten directions,
with a single mind, with their wonderful knowledge,
for kalpas numerous as Ganges sands
should all together pool their thoughts and capacities,
they could not understand the Buddha's knowledge.
If bodhisattvas who never regress,
their number like Ganges sands,
with a single mind should join in pondering and seeking,
they could not understand it either.
I also announce to you, Shariputra,
that this profound, subtle and wonderful Law
without outflows, incomprehensible,
I have now attained in full.
Only I understand its characteristics,
and the Buddhas of the ten directions do likewise.
Shariputra, you should know
that the words of the various Buddhas never differ.
Toward the Law preached by the Buddhas
you must cultivate a great power of faith.
The World-Honored One has long expounded his doctrines
and now must reveal the truth.
I announce this to the assembly of voice-hearers
and to those who seek the vehicle of the pratyekabuddha:
I have enabled people to escape the bonds of suffering
and to attain nirvana.
The Buddha, through the power of expedient means,
has shown them the teachings of the three vehicles,
prying living beings loose from this or that attachment
and allowing them to attain release.

At that time among the great assembly there were voice-hearers,
arhats whose outflows had come to an end, Ajnata Kaundinya and the

others, twelve hundred persons. And there were monks, nuns, laymen and laywomen who had conceived a desire to become voice-hearers or pratyekabuddhas. Each of these had this thought: Now for what reason does the World-Honored One so earnestly praise expedient means and state that the Law attained by the Buddha is profound and difficult to understand, that it is very difficult to comprehend the meaning of the words he preaches, that not one of the voice-hearers or pratyekabuddhas can do so? If the Buddha preaches but one doctrine of emancipation, then we too should be able to attain this Law and reach the state of nirvana. We cannot follow the gist of what he is saying now.

At that time Shariputra understood the doubts that were in the minds of the four kinds of believers, and he himself had not fully comprehended. So he addressed the Buddha, saying, "World-Honored One, what causes and conditions lead you to earnestly praise expedient means, the foremost device of the Buddhas, the profound, subtle and wonderful Law that is difficult to understand? From times past I have never heard this kind of preaching from the Buddha. Now the four kinds of believers all have doubts. We beg that the World-Honored One will expound this matter. For what reason does the World-Honored One earnestly praise this Law that is profound, subtle and wonderful, difficult to understand?"

At that time Shariputra, wishing to state his meaning once more, spoke in verse form, saying:

> Sun of wisdom, great sage and venerable one,
> at long last you preach this Law.
> You yourself declare you have attained
> power, fearlessness, samadhis,
> concentration, emancipation, and these other attributes,
> and the Law that is beyond comprehension.
> This Law attained in the place of practice
> no one is capable of questioning you about.
> "My intention is hard to fathom,
> and no one can question me."
> No one questions, yet you yourself preach,
> praising the path you walk on.
> Your wisdom is very subtle and wonderful,
> that which all the Buddhas attain.

The arhats who are without outflows
and those who seek nirvana
now have all fallen into the net of doubt,
wondering for what reason the Buddha preaches this.
Those who seek to become pratyekabuddhas,
monks and nuns,
heavenly beings, dragons and spirits,
along with the gandharvas and others,
look at one another, filled with perplexity,
gazing upward at the most honored of two-legged beings.
What is the meaning of all this?
I beg the Buddha to explain it for us.
Among the assembly of voice-hearers
the Buddha has said I am foremost,
yet now I lack the wisdom
to solve these doubts and perplexities.
Have I in fact grasped the ultimate Law,
or am I still on the path of practice?
The sons born from the Buddha's mouth
press palms together, gaze upward and wait.
We beg you to put forth subtle and wonderful sounds
and at this time explain to us how it really is.
The heavenly beings, dragons, spirits, and the others,
their numbers like Ganges sands,
the bodhisattvas seeking to be Buddhas
in a great force of eighty thousand,
as well as the wheel-turning sage kings
come from ten thousands of millions of lands,
all press their palms and with reverent minds
wish to hear the teaching of perfect endowment.

At that time the Buddha addressed Shariputra, saying, "Stop, stop! There is no need to speak further. If I speak of this matter, then the heavenly and human beings throughout the worlds will all be astonished and doubtful."

Shariputra once more spoke to the Buddha, saying, "World-Honored One, we beg you to preach! We beg you to preach! What is the reason? Because this assembly of countless hundreds, thousands, ten thousands, millions of asamkhyas of living beings in the past have seen the Buddhas; their faculties are vigorous and acute and their wisdom is bright. If they hear the Buddha preach, they will be capable of reverent belief."

At that time Shariputra, wishing to state his meaning once more, spoke in verse form, saying:

> Dharma King, none more highly honored,
> speak, we beg you, without reserve!
> In this assembly of numberless beings
> are those capable of reverent belief.

The Buddha repeated, "Stop, Shariputra! If I speak of this matter, the heavenly and human beings and asuras throughout the worlds will all be astonished and doubtful. The monks who are overbearingly arrogant will fall into a great pit."

At that time the World-Honored One repeated what he had said in verse form:

> Stop, stop, no need to speak!
> My Law is wonderful and difficult to ponder.
> Those who are overbearingly arrogant
> when they hear it will never show reverent belief.

At that time Shariputra once more spoke to the Buddha, saying, "World-Honored One, we beg you to preach! We beg you to preach! In this assembly at present the persons like myself number in the hundreds, thousands, ten thousands, millions. In age after age we have already attended the Buddhas and received instruction. People of this kind are certain to be capable of reverent belief. Throughout the long night they will gain peace and rest and will enjoy many benefits."

At that time Shariputra, wishing to state his meaning once more, spoke in verse form, saying:

> Supremely honored among two-legged beings,
> we beg you to preach this foremost Law.
> I who am regarded as the Buddha's eldest son
> ask you to favor us by preaching distinctions.

The countless members of this assembly
are capable of according reverent belief to this Law.
The Buddhas have already in age after age
taught and converted them in this manner.
All with a single mind and palms pressed together
desire to hear and receive the Buddha's words.
I and the other twelve hundred of our group,
as well as the others who seek to become Buddhas,
beg that for the sake of this assembly
you will favor us by preaching distinctions.
When we hear this Law
we will be filled with great joy.

At that time the World-Honored One said to Shariputra, "Three times you have stated your earnest request. How can I do other than preach? Now you must listen attentively and carefully ponder. For your sake I will now analyze and explain the matter."

When he had spoken these words, there were some five thousand monks, nuns, laymen and laywomen in the assembly who immediately rose from their seats, bowed to the Buddha, and withdrew. What was the reason for this? These persons had roots of guilt that were deep and manifold, and in addition they were overbearingly arrogant. What they had not attained they supposed they had attained, what they had not understood they supposed they had understood. And because they had this failing, they did not remain where they were.

The World-Honored One was silent and did not try to detain them.

At this time the Buddha said to Shariputra, "Now this assembly of mine is free of branches and leaves, made up solely of the steadfast and truthful. Shariputra, it is well that these persons of overbearing arrogance have withdrawn. Now listen carefully and I will preach for you."

Shariputra said, "So be it, World-Honored One. We are eager to listen!"

The Buddha said to Shariputra, "A wonderful Law such as this is preached by the Buddhas, the Thus Come Ones, at certain times. But like the blooming of the udumbara, such times come very seldom. Shariputra, you and the others must believe me. The words that the Buddhas preach are not empty or false.

"Shariputra, the Buddhas preach the Law in accordance with what is appropriate, but the meaning is difficult to understand. Why is this? Because we employ countless expedient means, discussing causes and conditions and using words of simile and parable to expound the teachings. This Law is not something that can be understood through pondering or analysis. Only those who are Buddhas can understand it. Why is this? Because the Buddhas, the World-Honored Ones, appear in the world for one great reason alone. Shariputra, what does it mean to say that the Buddhas, the World-Honored Ones, appear in the world for one great reason alone?

"The Buddhas, the World-Honored Ones, wish to open the door of Buddha wisdom to all living beings, to allow them to attain purity. That is why they appear in the world. They wish to show the Buddha wisdom to living beings, and therefore they appear in the world. They wish to cause living beings to awaken to the Buddha wisdom, and therefore they appear in the world. They wish to induce living beings to enter the path of Buddha wisdom, and therefore they appear in the world. Shariputra, this is the one great reason for which the Buddhas appear in the world."

The Buddha said to Shariputra, "The Buddhas, the Thus Come Ones, simply teach and convert the bodhisattvas. All the things they do are at all times done for this one purpose. They simply wish to show the Buddha wisdom to living beings and enlighten them to it.

"Shariputra, the Thus Come Ones have only a single Buddha vehicle which they employ in order to preach the Law to living beings. They do not have any other vehicle, a second one or a third one.[1] Shariputra, the Law preached by all the Buddhas of the ten directions is the same as this.

"Shariputra, the Buddhas of the past used countless numbers of expedient means, various causes and conditions, and words of simile and parable in order to expound the doctrines for the sake of living beings. These doctrines are all for the sake of the one Buddha vehicle. These living beings, by listening to the doctrines of the Buddhas, are all eventually able to attain wisdom embracing all species.

"Shariputra, when the Buddhas of the future make their appearance

1. Or perhaps the meaning is "They do not have any other vehicle, not two vehicles or three." The Chinese permits either reading, and Chinese Buddhist sects have disagreed as to which interpretation to follow.

in the world, they too will use countless numbers of expedient means, various causes and conditions, and words of simile and parable in order to expound the doctrines for the sake of living beings. These doctrines will all be for the sake of the one Buddha vehicle. And these living beings, by listening to the doctrines of the Buddhas, will all eventually be able to attain wisdom embracing all species.

"Shariputra, the Buddhas, the World-Honored Ones, who exist at present in the countless hundreds, thousands, ten thousands, and millions of Buddha lands in the ten directions, benefit and bring peace and happiness to living beings in large measure. These Buddhas too use countless numbers of expedient means, various causes and conditions, and words of simile and parable in order to expound the doctrines for the sake of living beings. These doctrines are all for the sake of the one Buddha vehicle. And these living beings, by listening to the doctrines of the Buddhas, are all eventually able to attain wisdom embracing all species.

"Shariputra, these Buddhas simply teach and convert the bodhisattvas. They do it because they wish to show the Buddha wisdom to living beings. They do it because they wish to use the Buddha wisdom to enlighten living beings. They do it because they wish to cause living beings to enter the path of Buddha wisdom.

"Shariputra, I too will now do the same. I know that living beings have various desires, attachments that are deeply implanted in their minds. Taking cognizance of this basic nature of theirs, I will therefore use various causes and conditions, words of simile and parable, and the power of expedient means and expound the Law for them. Shariputra, I do this so that all of them may attain the one Buddha vehicle and wisdom embracing all species.

"Shariputra, in the worlds of the ten directions, there are not two vehicles, much less three! Shariputra, the Buddhas appear in evil worlds of five impurities. These are the so-called impurity of the age, impurity of desire, impurity of living beings, impurity of view, and impurity of life span.

"Shariputra, when the age is impure and the times are chaotic, then the defilements of living beings are grave, they are greedy and jealous and put down roots that are not good. Because of this, the Buddhas, utilizing the power of expedient means, apply distinctions to the one Buddha vehicle and preach as though it were three.

"Shariputra, if any of my disciples should claim to be an arhat or a pratyekabuddha and yet does not heed or understand that the Buddhas, the Thus Come Ones, simply teach and convert the bodhisattvas, then he is no disciple of mine, he is no arhat or pratyekabuddha.

"Again, Shariputra, if there should be monks or nuns who claim that they have already attained the status of arhat, that this is their last incarnation, that they have reached the final nirvana, and that therefore they have no further intention of seeking anuttara-samyak-sambodhi, then you should understand that such as these are all persons of overbearing arrogance. Why do I say this? Because if there are monks who have truly attained the status of arhat, then it would be unthinkable that they should fail to believe this Law. The only exception would be in a time after the Buddha had passed away, when there was no Buddha present in the world. Why is this? Because after the Buddha has passed away it will be difficult to find anyone who can embrace, recite, and understand the meaning of sutras such as this. But if persons at that time encounter another Buddha, then they will attain decisive understanding with regard to this Law.

"Shariputra, you and the others should with a single mind believe and accept the words of the Buddha. The words of the Buddhas, the Thus Come Ones, are not empty or false. There is no other vehicle, there is only the one Buddha vehicle."

At that time the World-Honored One, wishing to state his meaning once more, spoke in verse form, saying:

There are monks and nuns
who behave with overbearing arrogance,
laymen full of self-esteem,
laywomen who are lacking in faith.
Among the four kinds of believers, the likes of these
number five thousand.
They fail to see their own errors,
are heedless and remiss with regard to the precepts,
clinging to their shortcomings, unwilling to change.
But these persons of small wisdom have already left;
the chaff among this assembly
has departed in the face of the Buddha's authority.
These persons were of paltry merit and virtue,

incapable of receiving this Law.
This assembly is now free of branches and leaves,
made up only of those steadfast and truthful.
Shariputra, listen carefully,
for the Law which the Buddhas have attained,
through the power of countless expedient means
they preach for the benefit of living beings.
The thoughts that are in the minds of living beings,
the different types of paths they follow,
their various desires and natures,
the good and bad deeds they have done in previous existences—
all these the Buddha takes cognizance of,
and then he employs causes, similes and parables,
words that embody the power of expedient means,
in order to gladden and please them all.
Sometimes he preaches sutras,
verses, stories of the previous lives of disciples,
stories of the previous lives of the Buddha, of
    unheard-of things.
At other times he preaches regarding causes and conditions,
uses similes, parables, passages of poetry
or discourses.
For those of dull capacities who delight in a little Law,
who greedily cling to birth and death,
who, despite the innumerable Buddhas,
fail to practice the profound and wonderful way
but are perplexed and confused by a host of troubles—
for these I preach nirvana.
I devise these expedient means
and so cause them to enter into the Buddha wisdom.
Up to now I have never told you
that you were certain to attain the Buddha way.
The reason I never preached in that manner
was that the time to preach so had not yet come.
But now is the very time
when I must decisively preach the Great Vehicle.
I use these nine devices,
adapting them to the living beings when I preach,

my basic aim being to lead them into the Great Vehicle,
and that is why I preach this sutra.
There are sons of the Buddha whose minds are pure,
who are gentle and of acute capacities,
who under innumerable Buddhas
have practiced the profound and wonderful way.
For these sons of the Buddha
I preach this sutra of the Great Vehicle.
And I predict that these persons
in a future existence will attain the Buddha way.
Because deep in their minds they think of the Buddha
and practice and uphold the pure precepts,
they are assured they will attain Buddhahood,
and hearing this, their whole bodies are filled with great joy.
The Buddha knows their minds and their practices
and therefore preaches for them the Great Vehicle.
When the voice-hearers and bodhisattvas
hear this Law that I preach,
as soon as they have heard one verse
they will all without doubt be certain of attaining Buddhahood.
In the Buddha lands of the ten directions
there is only the Law of the one vehicle,
there are not two, there are not three,
except when the Buddha preaches so as an expedient means,
merely employing provisional names and terms
in order to conduct and guide living beings
and preach to them the Buddha wisdom.
The Buddhas appear in the world
solely for this one reason, which is true;
the other two are not the truth.
Never do they use a lesser vehicle
to save living beings and ferry them across.
The Buddha himself dwells in this Great Vehicle,
and adorned with the power of meditation and wisdom
that go with the Law he has attained,
he uses it to save living beings.
He himself testifies to the unsurpassed way,
the Great Vehicle, the Law in which all things are equal.

If I used a lesser vehicle
to convert even one person,
I would be guilty of stinginess and greed,
but such a thing would be impossible.
If a person will believe and take refuge in the Buddha,
the Thus Come One will never deceive him,
nor will he ever show greed or jealousy,
for he has rooted out evil from among the phenomena.
Therefore throughout the ten directions
the Buddha alone is without fear.
I adorn my body with the special characteristics
and shine my light upon the world.
I am honored by numberless multitudes
and for them I preach the emblem of the reality of things.
Shariputra, you should know
that at the start I took a vow,
hoping to make all persons
equal to me, without any distinction between us,
and what I long ago hoped for
has now been fulfilled.
I have converted all living beings
and caused them all to enter the Buddha way.
If when I encounter living beings
I were in all cases to teach them the Buddha way,
those without wisdom would become confused
and in their bewilderment would fail to accept my teachings.
I know that such living beings
have never in the past cultivated good roots
but have stubbornly clung to the five desires,
and their folly and craving have given rise to affliction. ·
Their desires are the cause
whereby they fall into the three evil paths,
revolving wheel-like through the six realms of existence
and undergoing every sort of suffering and pain.
Having received a tiny form in the womb,
in existence after existence they constantly grow to maturity.
Persons of meager virtue and small merit,
they are troubled and beset by manifold sufferings.

They stray into the dense forest of mistaken views,
debating as to what exists and what does not,
and in the end cling to such views,
embracing all sixty-two of them.[2]
They are profoundly committed to false and empty doctrines,
holding firmly to them, unable to set them aside.
Arrogant and puffed up with self-importance,
fawning and devious, insincere in mind,
for a thousand, ten thousand, a million kalpas
they will not hear the Buddha's name,
nor will they hear the correct Law—
such people are difficult to save.
For these reasons, Shariputra,
I have for their sake established expedient means,
preaching the way that ends all suffering,
and showing them nirvana.
But although I preach nirvana,
this is not a true extinction.
All phenomena from the very first
have of themselves constantly borne the marks of
    tranquil extinction.
Once the sons of the Buddha have carried out this path,
then in a future existence they will be able to become Buddhas.
I have employed the power of expedient means
to unfold and demonstrate this doctrine of three vehicles,
but the World-Honored Ones, every one of them,
all preach the single vehicle way.
Now before this great assembly
I must clear away all doubts and perplexities.
There is no discrepancy in the words of the Buddhas,
there is only the one vehicle, not two.
For numberless kalpas in the past
countless Buddhas who have now entered extinction,
a hundred, thousand, ten thousand, million types
in numbers incapable of calculation—

2. Sixty-two possible views that arise from the two views that there is existence and
that there is no existence. The term is often used to refer to all the non-Buddhist views
that were current in Shakyamuni's time.

such World-Honored Ones,
using different types of causes, similes, and parables,
the power of countless expedient means,
have expounded the characteristics of teachings.
These World-Honored Ones
have all preached the doctrine of the single vehicle,
converting countless living beings
and causing them to enter the Buddha way.
And these great sage lords,
knowing what is desired deep in the minds
of the heavenly and human beings and the other living things
throughout all the worlds,
have employed still other expedient means
to help illuminate the highest truth.
If there are living beings
who have encountered these past Buddhas,
and if they have listened to their Law, presented alms,
or kept the precepts, shown forbearance,
been assiduous, practiced meditation and wisdom, and so forth,
cultivating various kinds of merit and virtue,
then persons such as these
all have attained the Buddha way.
After the Buddhas have passed into extinction,
if persons are of good and gentle mind,
then living beings such as these
have all attained the Buddha way.
After the Buddhas have passed into extinction,
if persons make offerings to the relics,
raising ten thousand or a million kinds of towers,
using gold, silver and crystal,
seashell and agate,
carnelian, lapis lazuli, pearls
to purify and adorn them extensively,
in this way erecting towers;
or if they raise up stone mortuary temples
or those of sandalwood or aloes,
hovenia or other kinds of timber,
or of brick, tile, clay or earth;

if in the midst of the broad fields
they pile up earth to make a mortuary temple for the Buddhas,
or even if little boys at play
should collect sand to make a Buddha tower,
then persons such as these
have all attained the Buddha way.
If there are persons who for the sake of the Buddha
fashion and set up images,
carving them with many distinguishing characteristics,
then all have attained the Buddha way.
Or if they make things out of the seven kinds of gems,
of copper, red or white copper,
pewter, lead, tin,
iron, wood, or clay,
or use cloth soaked in lacquer or resin
to adorn and fashion Buddha images,
then persons such as these
have all attained the Buddha way.
If they employ pigments to paint Buddha images,
endowing them with the characteristics of hundredfold merit,
if they make them themselves or have others make them,
then all have attained the Buddha way.
Even if little boys in play
should use a piece of grass or wood or a brush,
or perhaps a fingernail
to draw an image of the Buddha,
such persons as these
bit by bit will pile up merit
and will become fully endowed with a mind of
    great compassion;
they all have attained the Buddha way.
Merely by converting the bodhisattvas
they bring salvation and release to numberless multitudes.
And if persons, in the presence of such memorial towers,
such jeweled images and painted images,
should with reverent minds make offerings
of flowers, incense, banners or canopies,
or if they should employ persons to make music,

striking drums or blowing horns or conch shells,
playing pipes, flutes, zithers, harps,
balloon guitars, cymbals and gongs,
and if these many kinds of wonderful notes
are intended wholly as an offering;
or if one with a joyful mind
sings a song in praise of the Buddha's virtue,
even if it is just one small note,
then all who do these things have attained the Buddha way.
If someone with a confused and distracted mind
should take even one flower
and offer it to a painted image,
in time he would come to see countless Buddhas.
Or if a person should bow or perform obeisance,
or should merely press his palms together,
or even should raise a single hand,
or give no more than a slight nod of the head,
and if this were done in offering to an image,
then in time he would come to see countless Buddhas.
And if he himself attains the unsurpassed way
and spreads salvation abroad to countless multitudes,
he will enter the nirvana of no remainder
as a fire dies out when the firewood is exhausted.
If persons with confused and distracted minds
should enter a memorial tower
and once exclaim, "Hail to the Buddha!"
then all have attained the Buddha way.
If from past Buddhas
when they were in the world or after their extinction,
there should be those who heard this Law,
then all have attained the Buddha way.
The World-Honored Ones of the future,
whose numbers will be incalculable,
these Thus Come Ones
will also employ expedient means to preach the Law,
and all these Thus Come Ones
through countless expedient means
will save and bring release to living beings

so that they enter the Buddha's wisdom which is free
   of outflows.
If there are those who hear the Law,
then not a one will fail to attain Buddhahood.
The original vow of the Buddhas
was that the Buddha way, which they themselves practice,
should be shared universally among living beings
so that they too may attain this same way.
The Buddhas of future ages,
although they preach hundreds, thousands, millions,
a countless number of doctrines,
in truth do so for the sake of the single vehicle.
The Buddhas, most honored of two-legged beings,
know that phenomena have no constantly fixed nature,
that the seeds of Buddhahood sprout through causation,
and for this reason they preach the single vehicle.
But that these phenomena are part of an abiding Law,
that the characteristics of the world are constantly abiding—
this they have come to know in the place of practice,
and as leaders and teachers they preach expedient means.
The presently existing Buddhas of the ten directions,
whom heavenly and human beings make offerings to,
who in number are like Ganges sands,
they have appeared in the world
in order to bring peace and comfort to living beings,
and they too preach the Law in this way.
They understand the foremost truth of tranquil extinction
and therefore employ the power of expedient means,
and though they point out various different paths,
in truth they do so for the sake of the Buddha vehicle.
They understand the actions of living beings,
the thoughts that lie deep in their minds,
the deeds they have carried out in the past,
their desires, their nature, the power of their exertions,
and whether their capacities are acute or dull,
and so they employ various causes and conditions,
similes, parables, and other words and phrases,
adapting what expedient means are suitable to their preaching.

Now I too am like this;
in order to bring peace and comfort to living beings
I employ various different doctrines
to disseminate the Buddha way.
Through the power of my wisdom
I know the nature and desires of living beings
and through expedient means I preach these doctrines,
causing all living beings to attain joy and gladness.
Shariputra, you should understand
that I view things through the Buddha eye,
I see the living beings in the six paths,
how poor and distressed they are, without merit or wisdom,
how they enter the perilous road of birth and death,
their sufferings continuing with never a break,
how deeply they are attached to the five desires,
like a yak enamored of its tail,
blinding themselves with greed and infatuation,
their vision so impaired they can see nothing.
They do not seek the Buddha, with his great might,
or the Law that can end their sufferings,
but enter deeply into erroneous views,
hoping to shed suffering through greater suffering.
For the sake of these living beings
I summon up a mind of great compassion.
When I first sat in the place of practice
and gazed at the tree and walked around it,
for the space of three times seven days
I pondered the matter in this way.
The wisdom I have attained, I thought,
is subtle, wonderful, the foremost.
But living beings, dull in capacity,
are addicted to pleasure and blinded by stupidity.
With persons such as this,
what can I say, how can I save them?
At that time the Brahma kings,
along with the heavenly king Shakra,
the Four Heavenly Kings who guard the world,
and the heavenly king Great Freedom,

in company with the other heavenly beings
and their hundreds and thousands and ten thousands
    of followers,
reverently pressed their palms together and bowed,
begging me to turn the wheel of the Law.
Immediately I thought to myself
that if I merely praised the Buddha vehicle,
then the living beings, sunk in their suffering,
would be incapable of believing in this Law.
And because they rejected the Law and failed to believe in it,
they would fall into the three evil paths.
It would be better if I did not preach the Law
but quickly entered into nirvana.
Then my thoughts turned to the Buddhas of the past
and the power of expedient means they had employed,
and I thought that the way I had now attained
should likewise be preached as three vehicles.
When I thought in this manner,
the Buddhas of the ten directions all appeared
and with brahma sounds comforted and instructed me.
"Well done, Shakyamuni!" they said.
"Foremost leader and teacher,
you have attained the unsurpassed Law.
But following the example of all other Buddhas,
you will employ the power of expedient means.
We too have all attained
the most wonderful, the foremost Law,
but for the sake of living beings
we make distinctions and preach the three vehicles.
People of small wisdom delight in a small Law,
unable to believe that they themselves could become Buddhas.
Therefore we employ expedient means,
making distinctions and preaching various goals.
But though we preach the three vehicles,
we do it merely in order to teach the bodhisattvas."
Shariputra, you should understand this.
When I heard these saintly lions
and their deep, pure, subtle, wonderful sounds,

I rejoiced, crying "Hail to the Buddhas!"
Then I thought to myself,
I have come into this impure and evil world,
and as these Buddhas have preached,
I too must follow that example in my actions.
After I had thought of the matter in this way,
I set out at once for Varanasi.
The marks of tranquil extinction borne by all phenomena
cannot be explained in words,
and therefore I used the power of expedient means
to preach to the five ascetics.
This I termed turning the wheel of the Law,
and also with regard to "the sound of nirvana,"
and "arhat," "Dharma" and "Samgha,"
I used these terms to indicate distinctions.
"From infinite kalpas in the past
I have extolled and taught the Law of nirvana,
ending the long sufferings of birth and death."
This is how I customarily preached.
Shariputra, you should know this.
When I looked at the Buddha sons,
I saw incalculable thousands, ten thousands, millions
who had determined to seek the way of the Buddha,
every one with a respectful and reverent mind,
all coming to the place of the Buddha,
persons who in the past had listened to other Buddhas
and heard the Law preached through expedient means.
Immediately the thought came to me
that the reason the Thus Come One has appeared
is so he may preach the Buddha wisdom.
Now is precisely the time to do so.
Shariputra, you should understand
that persons of dull capacity and small wisdom,
who are attached to appearances, proud and overbearing,
are incapable of believing in this Law.
Now I, joyful and fearless,
in the midst of the bodhisattvas,
honestly discarding expedient means,

will preach only the unsurpassed way.
When the bodhisattvas hear this Law,
they will be released from all entanglements of doubt.
The twelve hundred arhats,
they too will all attain Buddhahood.
Following the same fashion that the Buddhas of the
    three existences
employ in preaching the Law,
I now will do likewise,
preaching a Law that is without distinctions.
The times when the Buddhas appear in the world
are far apart and difficult to encounter.
And even when they appear in the world
it is difficult for them to preach this Law.
Throughout incalculable, innumerable kalpas
it is rare that one may hear this Law,
and a person capable of listening to this Law,
such a person is likewise rare.
It is like the udumbara flower
which all the world loves and delights in,
which heavenly and human beings look on as something rare,
but which appears only once in many many ages.
If a person hears this Law, delights and praises it,
even if he utters just one word,
then he has made offerings
to all the Buddhas of the three existences.
But a person like this is very rarely found,
rarer than the udumbara flower.
You should have no doubts.
I, being king of the doctrines,
make this announcement to the entire great assembly.
I employ only the single vehicle way
to teach and convert the bodhisattvas,
I have no voice-hearer disciples.
You, Shariputra,
and the voice-hearers and bodhisattvas,
you should understand that this wonderful Law
is the secret crux of the Buddhas.

In this evil world of the five impurities
those who merely delight in and are attached to the desires,
living beings such as this
in the end will never seek the Buddha way.
When evil persons in ages to come
hear the Buddha preach the single vehicle,
they will be confused, will not believe or accept it,
will reject the Law and fall into the evil paths.
But when there are those with a sense of shame, persons
  of purity
who have determined to seek the Buddha way,
then for the sake of such as these
one should widely praise the way of the single vehicle.
Shariputra, you should understand this.
The Law of the Buddhas is like this.
Employing ten thousand, a million expedient means,
they accord with what is appropriate in preaching the Law.
Those who are not versed in the matter
cannot fully comprehend this.
But you and the others already know
how the Buddhas, the teachers of the world,
accord with what is appropriate in employing expedient means.
You will have no more doubts or perplexities
but, your minds filled with great joy,
will know that you yourselves will attain Buddhahood.

3
SIMILE AND PARABLE

At that time Shariputra's mind danced with joy. Then he immediately stood up, pressed his palms together, gazed up in reverence at the face of the Honored One, and said to the Buddha, "Just now, when I heard from the World-Honored One this voice of the Law, my mind seemed to dance and I gained what I had never had before. Why do I say this? Because in the past when I heard a Law of this kind from the Buddha and saw how the bodhisattvas received prophecies that in time they would attain Buddhahood, I and the others felt that we had no part in the affair. We were deeply grieved to think we would never gain the immeasurable insight of the Thus Come One.

"World-Honored One, I have constantly lived in the mountain

forest or alone under the trees, sometimes sitting, sometimes walking around, and always I have thought to myself, Since I and the others all alike have entered into the nature of the Law, why does the Thus Come One use the Law of the Lesser Vehicle to bring us salvation?

"But the fault is ours, not that of the World-Honored One. Why do I say this? If we had been willing to wait until the true means for attaining anuttara-samyak-sambodhi was preached, then we would surely have obtained release through the Great Vehicle. But we failed to understand that the Buddha was employing expedient means and preaching what was appropriate to the circumstances. So when we first heard the Law of the Buddha, we immediately believed and accepted it, supposing that we had gained understanding.

"World-Honored One, for a long time now, all day and throughout the night, I have repeatedly taxed myself with this thought. But now I have heard from the Buddha what I had never heard before, a Law never known in the past, and it has ended all my doubts and regrets. My body and mind are at ease and I have gained a wonderful feeling of peace and security. Today at last I understand that truly I am the Buddha's son, born from the Buddha's mouth, born through conversion to the Law, gaining my share of the Buddha's Law!"

At that time Shariputra, wishing to state his meaning once more, spoke in verse form, saying:

> When I heard the sound of this Law,
> I gained what I had never had before.
> My mind was filled with great joy,
> I was released from all bonds of the net of doubt.
> From past times I have received the Buddha's teachings
> and have not been denied the Great Vehicle.
> The Buddha's sound is very rarely heard,
> but it can free living beings from distress.
> Already I have put an end to outflows,
> and hearing this, am freed from care and distress.
> I lived in the mountain valleys
> or under the forest trees,
> sometimes sitting, sometimes walking around,
> and constantly I thought of this matter—
> how severely I taxed myself!

"Why have I been deceived?" I said.
"I and the others are sons of the Buddha too,
all alike have entered the Law that is without outflows,
yet in times to come we will never be able
to expound the unsurpassed way.
The golden body, the thirty-two features,
the ten powers, the various emancipations—
though all alike share a single Law,
these we will never attain!
The eighty types of wonderful characteristics,
the eighteen unshared properties—
merits such as these
are all lost to us!"
When I was walking around alone,
I saw the Buddha among the great assembly,
his fame filling the ten directions,
bringing benefit far and wide to living beings,
and I thought to myself, I am deprived of such benefits!
How greatly have I been deceived!
Constantly, day and night,
whenever I pondered over this,
I wanted to ask the World-Honored One
whether I had indeed been deprived or not.
Constantly, when I saw the World-Honored One
praising the bodhisattvas,
then day and night
I would mull this matter over.
But now as I listen to the voice of the Buddha,
I see he preaches the Law in accordance with what
    is appropriate,
using this hard-to-conceive doctrine of no outflows
to lead people to the place of practice.
Formerly I was attached to erroneous views,
acting as teacher to the Brahmans.
But the World-Honored One, knowing what was in my mind,
rooted out my errors and preached nirvana.
I was freed of all my errors
and gained understanding of the Law of emptiness.

At that time my mind told me
I had reached the stage of extinction,
but now I realize
that that was not true extinction.
If the time should come when I can become a Buddha,
then I will possess all the thirty-two features
and heavenly and human beings, the many yakshas,
dragons, spirits and others will hold me in reverence.
When that time comes, then I can say
that at last all has been wiped out without residue.
In the midst of the great assembly, the Buddha
declared that I will become a Buddha.
When I heard the sound of this Law
my doubts and regrets were all wiped away.
At first, when I heard the Buddha's preaching,
there was great astonishment and doubt in my mind.
Is this not a devil pretending to be the Buddha,
trying to vex and confuse my mind? I thought.
But the Buddha employed various causes,
similes, and parables, expounding eloquently.
His mind was peaceful as the sea,
and as I listened, I was freed from the net of doubt.
The Buddha said that in past ages
the countless Buddhas who have passed into extinction
rested and abided in the midst of expedient means,
and all likewise preached this Law.
The Buddhas of the present and future,
whose numbers are beyond calculation,
they too will use expedient means
in expounding this same Law.
Thus the present World-Honored One,
being born and later leaving his family,
attaining the way and turning the wheel of the Law,
likewise employs expedient means in preaching.
The World-Honored One preaches the true way.
Papiyas would not do that.
Therefore I know for certain

this is not a devil pretending to be the Buddha.
But because I fell into the net of doubt
I supposed this to be the devil's work.
Now I hear the Buddha's soft and gentle sound,
profound, far-reaching, very subtle and wonderful,
expounding and discoursing on the pure Law,
and my mind is filled with great joy.
My doubts and regrets are forever ended,
I will rest and abide in true wisdom.
I am certain I will become a Buddha,
to be revered by heavenly and human beings,
turning the wheel of the unsurpassed Law
and teaching and converting the bodhisattvas.

At that time the Buddha said to Shariputra, "Now, in the midst of this great assembly of heavenly and human beings, shramanas, Brahmans and so forth, I say this. In the past, under twenty thousand million Buddhas, for the sake of the unsurpassed way I have constantly taught and converted you. And you throughout the long night followed me and accepted my instruction. Because I used expedient means to guide and lead you, you were born in the midst of my Law.

"Shariputra, in the past I taught you to aspire and vow to achieve the Buddha way. But now you have forgotten all that and instead suppose that you have already attained extinction. Now, because I want to make you recall to mind the way that you originally vowed to follow, for the sake of the voice-hearers I am preaching this Great Vehicle sutra called the Lotus of the Wonderful Law, a Law to instruct the bodhisattvas, one that is guarded and kept in mind by the Buddhas.

"Shariputra, in ages to come, after a countless, boundless, inconceivable number of kalpas have passed, you will make offerings to some thousands, ten thousands, millions of Buddhas, and will honor and uphold the correct Law. You will fulfill every aspect of the way of the bodhisattva and will be able to become a Buddha with the name Flower Glow Thus Come One, worthy of offerings, of right and universal knowledge, perfect clarity and conduct, well gone, understanding the world, unexcelled worthy, trainer of people, teacher of heavenly and human beings, Buddha, World-Honored One.

"Your realm will be called Free from Stain, the land will be level and smooth, pure and beautifully adorned, peaceful, bountiful and happy. Heavenly and human beings will flourish there. The ground will be of lapis lazuli, roads will crisscross it in eight directions, and ropes of gold will mark their boundaries. Beside each road will grow rows of seven-jeweled trees which will constantly flower and bear fruit. And this Flower Glow Thus Come One will employ the three vehicles to teach and convert living beings.

"Shariputra, when this Buddha appears, although it will not be an evil age, because of his original vow he will preach the Law through the three vehicles. His kalpa will be called Great Treasure Adornment. Why will it be called Great Treasure Adornment? Because in that land bodhisattvas will be looked on as a great treasure. Those bodhisattvas will be countless, boundless, inconceivable in number, beyond the reach of reckoning or of simile and parable. Without the power of Buddha wisdom, one cannot understand how many. Whenever these bodhisattvas wish to walk anywhere, jeweled flowers will uphold their feet.

"These bodhisattvas will not have just conceived the desire for enlightenment, but all will have spent a long time planting the roots of virtue. Under countless hundreds, thousands, tens of thousands, millions of Buddhas they will have carried out brahma practices in a flawless manner, and will have been perpetually praised by the Buddhas. Constantly they will have cultivated Buddha wisdom, acquiring great transcendental powers and thoroughly understanding the gateways to all the doctrines. They will be upright in character, without duplicity, firm in intent and thought. Bodhisattvas such as this will abound in that land.

"Shariputra, the life span of the Buddha Flower Glow will be twelve small kalpas, not counting the time when he is still a prince and before he becomes a Buddha. The people of his land will have a life span of eight small kalpas. When Flower Glow Thus Come One has lived for twelve small kalpas, he will prophesy that the bodhisattva Firm Full will attain anuttara-samyak-sambodhi. He will announce to the monks, 'This bodhisattva Firm Full will be the next to become a Buddha. He will be named Flower Feet Safely Walking, tathagata, arhat, samyak-sambuddha. His Buddha land will be like mine.'

"Shariputra, after the Buddha Flower Glow has passed into extinction, the era of the Correct Law will last for thirty-two small kalpas, and the era of the Counterfeit Law will last for another thirty-two small kalpas."

At that time the World-Honored One, wishing to state his meaning once more, spoke in verse form, saying:

> Shariputra, in ages to come
> you will become a Buddha, of universal wisdom, venerable,
> bearing the name Flower Glow,
> and you will save countless multitudes.
> You will make offerings to numberless Buddhas,
> be endowed with all the bodhisattva practices,
> the ten powers and other blessings,
> and will realize the unsurpassed way.
> After countless kalpas have passed,
> your kalpa will be named Great Treasure Adornment.
> Your world will be called Free from Stain,
> pure, without flaw or defilement.
> Its land will be made of lapis lazuli,
> its roads bounded by ropes of gold,
> and seven-jeweled trees in a jumble of colors
> will constantly bear blossoms and fruit.
> The bodhisattvas of that realm
> will always be firm in intent and thought.
> Transcendental powers and paramitas—
> each will be endowed with all of these,
> and under numberless Buddhas
> they will diligently study the bodhisattva way.
> Thus these great men
> will be converted by the Buddha Flower Glow.
> When that Buddha was still a prince,
> he gave up his country, abandoned worldly glory,
> and in his final incarnation
> left his family and attained the Buddha way.
> Flower Glow Buddha will continue in the world
> for a life span of twelve small kalpas.

The numerous people of his land
will have a life span of eight small kalpas.
After that Buddha has passed into extinction,
the Correct Law will endure in the world
for thirty-two small kalpas,
saving living beings far and wide.
When the Correct Law has passed away,
the Counterfeit Law will endure for thirty-two kalpas.
The Buddha's relics will circulate widely;
heavenly and human beings everywhere will make offerings
    to them.
The actions of Flower Glow Buddha
will all be as I have said.
This most saintly and venerable of two-legged beings
will be foremost and without peer.
And he will be none other than you—
you should rejoice and count yourself fortunate!

At that time, when the four kinds of believers, namely, monks, nuns, laymen and laywomen, and the heavenly beings, dragons, yakshas, gandharvas, asuras, garudas, kimnaras, mahoragas, and others in the great assembly saw how Shariputra received from the Buddha this prophecy that he would attain anuttara-samyak-sambodhi, their hearts were filled with great joy and danced without end. Each one removed the upper robe that he or she was wearing and presented it as an offering to the Buddha. Shakra Devanam Indra, King Brahma, and the countless sons of gods likewise took their wonderful heavenly robes, heavenly mandarava flowers and great mandarava flowers and offered them to the Buddha. The heavenly robes they had scattered remained suspended in the air and turned round and round of themselves. Heavenly beings made music, a hundred, a thousand, ten thousand varieties, all at the same time in the midst of the air, raining down quantities of heavenly flowers and speaking these words: "In the past at Varanasi the Buddha first turned the wheel of the Law. Now he turns the wheel again, the wheel of the unsurpassed, the greatest Law of all!"

At that time the sons of gods, wishing to state their meaning once more, spoke in verse form, saying:

In the past at Varanasi
you turned the wheel of the Law of the four noble truths,
making distinctions, preaching that all things
are born and become extinct, being made up of the
    five components.
Now you turn the wheel of the most wonderful,
the unsurpassed great Law.
This Law is very profound and abstruse;
there are few who can believe it.
Since times past often we have heard
the World-Honored One's preaching,
but we have never heard
this kind of profound, wonderful and superior Law.
Since the World-Honored One preaches this Law,
we all welcome it with joy.
Shariputra with his great wisdom
has now received this venerable prophecy.
We too in the same way
will surely be able to attain Buddhahood,
throughout all the many worlds
the most venerable, the unsurpassed goal.
The Buddha way is difficult to fathom,
but you will preach with expedient means, according to what is
    appropriate.
The meritorious deeds we have done
in this existence or past existences,
and the blessings gained from seeing the Buddha—
all these we will apply to the Buddha way.

At that time Shariputra said to the Buddha: "World-Honored One,
now I have no more doubts or regrets. In person I have received from
the Buddha this prophecy that I will attain anuttara-samyak-sambodhi. These twelve hundred persons here whose minds are free—in
the past they remained at the level of learning, and the Buddha
constantly taught and converted them, saying, 'My Law can free you
from birth, old age, sickness and death and enable you at last to
achieve nirvana.' These persons, some of whom were still learning and
some who had completed their learning, each believed that, because he

had shed his views of 'self,' and also his views of 'existing' and 'not existing,' he had attained nirvana. But now from the World-Honored One they hear what they had never heard before, and all have fallen into doubt and perplexity.

"Very well, World-Honored One. I beg that for the sake of the four kinds of believers you will explain the causes and conditions and make it possible for them to shed their doubts and regrets."

At that time the Buddha said to Shariputra, "Did I not tell you earlier that when the Buddhas, the World-Honored Ones, cite various causes and conditions and use similes, parables, and other expressions, employing expedient means to preach the Law, it is all for the sake of anuttara-samyak-sambodhi? Whatever is preached is all for the sake of converting the bodhisattvas.

"Moreover, Shariputra, I too will now make use of similes and parables to further clarify this doctrine. For through similes and parables those who are wise can obtain understanding.

"Shariputra, suppose that in a certain town in a certain country there was a very rich man. He was far along in years and his wealth was beyond measure. He had many fields, houses and menservants. His own house was big and rambling, but it had only one gate. A great many people—a hundred, two hundred, perhaps as many as five hundred—lived in the house. The halls and rooms were old and decaying, the walls crumbling, the pillars rotten at their base, and the beams and rafters crooked and aslant.

"At that time a fire suddenly broke out on all sides, spreading through the rooms of the house. The sons of the rich man, ten, twenty, perhaps thirty, were inside the house. When the rich man saw the huge flames leaping up on every side, he was greatly alarmed and fearful and thought to himself, I can escape to safety through the flaming gate, but my sons are inside the burning house enjoying themselves and playing games, unaware, unknowing, without alarm or fear. The fire is closing in on them, suffering and pain threaten them, yet their minds have no sense of loathing or peril and they do not think of trying to escape!

"Shariputra, this rich man thought to himself, I have strength in my body and arms. I can wrap them in a robe or place them on a bench and carry them out of the house. And then again he thought, This house has only one gate, and moreover it is narrow and small.

My sons are very young, they have no understanding, and they love their games, being so engrossed in them that they are likely to be burned in the fire. I must explain to them why I am fearful and alarmed. The house is already in flames and I must get them out quickly and not let them be burned up in the fire!

"Having thought in this way, he followed his plan and called to all his sons, saying, 'You must come out at once!' But though the father was moved by pity and gave good words of instruction, the sons were absorbed in their games and unwilling to heed him. They had no alarm, no fright, and in the end no mind to leave the house. Moreover, they did not understand what the fire was, what the house was, what danger was. They merely raced about this way and that in play and looked at their father without heeding him.

"At that time the rich man had this thought: The house is already in flames from this huge fire. If I and my sons do not get out at once, we are certain to be burned. I must now invent some expedient means that will make it possible for the children to escape harm.

"The father understood his sons and knew what various toys and curious objects each child customarily liked and what would delight them. And so he said to them, 'The kind of playthings you like are rare and hard to find. If you do not take them when you can, you will surely regret it later. For example, things like these goat-carts, deer-carts, and ox-carts. They are outside the gate now where you can play with them. So you must come out of this burning house at once. Then whatever ones you want, I will give them all to you!'

"At that time, when the sons heard their father telling them about these rare playthings, because such things were just what they had wanted, each felt emboldened in heart and, pushing and shoving one another, they all came wildly dashing out of the burning house.

"At this time the rich man, seeing that his sons had gotten out safely and all were seated on the open ground at the crossroads and were no longer in danger, was greatly relieved and his mind danced for joy. At that time each of the sons said to his father, 'The play-things you promised us earlier, the goat-carts and deer-carts and ox-carts—please give them to us now!'

"Shariputra, at that time the rich man gave to each of his sons a large carriage of uniform size and quality. The carriages were tall and spacious and adorned with numerous jewels. A railing ran all around them and bells hung from all four sides. A canopy was stretched over the top, which was also decorated with an assortment of precious jewels. Ropes of jewels twined around, a fringe of flowers hung down, and layers of cushions were spread inside, on which were placed vermilion pillows. Each carriage was drawn by a white ox, pure and clean in hide, handsome in form and of great strength, capable of pulling the carriage smoothly and properly at a pace fast as the wind. In addition, there were many grooms and servants to attend and guard the carriage.

"What was the reason for this? This rich man's wealth was limitless and he had many kinds of storehouses that were all filled and over-flowing. And he thought to himself, There is no end to my posses-sions. It would not be right if I were to give my sons small carriages of inferior make. These little boys are all my sons and I love them without partiality. I have countless numbers of large carriages adorned with seven kinds of gems. I should be fair-minded and give one to each of my sons. I should not show any discrimination. Why? Because even if I distributed these possessions of mine to every person in the whole country I would still not exhaust them, much less could I do so by giving them to my sons!

"At that time each of the sons mounted his large carriage, gaining something he had never had before, something he had originally never expected. Shariputra, what do you think of this? When this rich man impartially handed out to his sons these big carriages adorned with rare jewels, was he guilty of falsehood or not?"

Shariputra said, "No, World-Honored One. This rich man simply made it possible for his sons to escape the peril of fire and preserve their lives. He did not commit a falsehood. Why do I say this? Because if they were able to preserve their lives, then they had already ob-tained a plaything of sorts. And how much more so when, through an expedient means, they are rescued from that burning house! World-Honored One, even if the rich man had not given them the tiniest carriage, he would still not be guilty of falsehood. Why? Because this rich man had earlier made up his mind that he would employ an expedient means to cause his sons to escape. Using a device of this kind was no act of falsehood. How much less so, then, when the rich man knew that his wealth was limitless and he intended to enrich and benefit his sons by giving each of them a large carriage."

The Buddha said to Shariputra, "Very good, very good. It is just as you have said. And Shariputra, the Thus Come One is like this. That is, he is a father to all the world. His fears, cares and anxieties, ignorance and misunderstanding, have long come to an end, leaving no residue. He has fully succeeded in acquiring measureless insight, power and freedom from fear and gaining great supernatural powers and the power of wisdom. He is endowed with expedient means and the paramita of wisdom, his great pity and great compassion are constant and unflagging; at all times he seeks what is good and will bring benefit to all.

"He is born into the threefold world, a burning house, rotten and old, in order to save living beings from the fires of birth, old age, sickness and death, care, suffering, stupidity, misunderstanding, and the three poisons; to teach and convert them and enable them to attain anuttara-samyak-sambodhi.

"He sees living beings seared and consumed by birth, old age, sickness and death, care and suffering, sees them undergo many kinds of pain because of the five desires and the desire for wealth and profit. Again, because of their greed and attachment and striving they undergo numerous pains in their present existence, and later they undergo the pain of being reborn in hell or as beasts or hungry spirits. Even if they are reborn in the heavenly realm or the realm of human beings, they undergo the pain of poverty and want, the pain of parting from loved ones, the pain of encountering those they detest—all these many different kinds of pain.

"Yet living beings, drowned in the midst of all this, delight and amuse themselves, unaware, unknowing, without alarm or fear. They feel no sense of loathing and make no attempt to escape. In this burning house which is the threefold world, they race about to east and west, and though they encounter great pain, they are not distressed by it.

"Shariputra, when the Buddha sees this, then he thinks to himself, I am the father of living beings and I should rescue them from their sufferings and give them the joy of the measureless and boundless Buddha wisdom so that they may find their enjoyment in that.

"Shariputra, the Thus Come One also has this thought: If I should merely employ supernatural powers and the power of wisdom; if I should set aside expedient means and for the sake of living beings should praise the Thus Come One's insight, power and freedom from fear, then living beings would not be able to gain salvation. Why? Because these living beings have not yet escaped from birth, old age, sickness, death, care and suffering, but are consumed by flames in the burning house that is the threefold world. How could they be able to understand the Buddha's wisdom?

"Shariputra, that rich man, though he had strength in his body and arms, did not use it. He merely employed a carefully contrived expedient means and thus was able to rescue his sons from the peril of the burning house, and afterward gave each of them a large carriage adorned with rare jewels. And the Thus Come One does the same. Though he possesses power and freedom from fear, he does not use these. He merely employs wisdom and expedient means to rescue living beings from the burning house of the threefold world, expounding to them the three vehicles, the vehicle of the voice-hearer, that of the pratyekabuddha, and that of the Buddha.

"He says to them, 'You must not be content to stay in this burning house of the threefold world! Do not be greedy for its coarse and shoddy forms, sounds, scents, tastes and sensations! If you become attached to them and learn to love them, you will be burned up! You must come out of this threefold world at once so that you can acquire the three vehicles, the vehicles of the voice-hearer, the pratyekabuddha and the Buddha. I promise you now that you will get them, and that promise will never prove false. You have only to apply yourselves with diligent effort!'

"The Thus Come One employs this expedient means to lure living beings into action. And then he says to them, 'You should understand that these doctrines of the three vehicles are all praised by the sages. They are free, without entanglements, leaving nothing further to depend upon or seek. Mount these three vehicles, gain roots that are without outflows, gain powers, awareness, the way, meditation, emancipation, samadhis, and then enjoy yourselves. You will gain the delight of immeasurable peace and safety.'

"Shariputra, if there are living beings who are inwardly wise in nature, and who attend the Buddha, the World-Honored One, hear the Law, believe and accept it, and put forth diligent effort, desiring to escape quickly from the threefold world and seeking to attain nirvana, they shall be called [those who ride] the vehicle of the voice-hearer.

They are like those sons who left the burning house in the hope of acquiring goat-carts.

"If there are living beings who attend the Buddha, the World-Honored One, hear the Law, believe and accept it, and put forth diligent effort, seeking wisdom that comes of itself, taking solitary delight in goodness and tranquility, and profoundly understanding the causes and conditions of all phenomena, they shall be called [those who ride] the vehicle of the pratyekabuddha. They are like the sons who left the burning house in the hope of acquiring deer-carts.

"If there are living beings who attend the Buddha, the World-Honored One, hear the Law, believe and accept it, and put forth diligent effort, seeking comprehensive wisdom, Buddha wisdom, wisdom that comes of itself, teacherless wisdom, the insight of the Thus Come One, powers and freedom from fear, who pity and comfort countless living beings, bring benefit to heavenly and human beings, and save them all, they shall be called [those who ride] the Great Vehicle. Because the bodhisattvas seek this vehicle, they are called mahasattvas. They are like the sons who left the burning house in the hope of acquiring ox-carts.

"Shariputra, that rich man, seeing that his sons had all gotten out of the burning house safely and were no longer threatened, recalled that his wealth was immeasurable and presented each of his sons with a large carriage. And the Thus Come One does likewise. He is the father of all living beings. When he sees that countless thousands of millions of living beings, through the gateway of the Buddha's teaching, can escape the pains of the threefold world, the fearful and perilous road, and gain the delights of nirvana, the Thus Come One at that time has this thought: I possess measureless, boundless wisdom, power, fearlessness, the storehouse of the Law of the Buddhas. These living beings are all my sons. I will give the Great Vehicle to all of them equally so that there will not be those who gain extinction by themselves, but that all may do so through the extinction of the Thus Come One.

"To all the living beings who have escaped from the threefold world he then gives the delightful gifts of the meditation, emancipation, and so forth, of the Buddhas. All these are uniform in characteristics, uniform in type, praised by the sages, capable of producing pure, wonderful, supreme delight.

"Shariputra, that rich man first used three types of carriages to entice his sons, but later he gave them just the large carriage adorned with jewels, the safest, most comfortable kind of all. Despite this, that rich man was not guilty of falsehood. The Thus Come One does the same, and he is without falsehood. First he preaches the three vehicles to attract and guide living beings, but later he employs just the Great Vehicle to save them. Why? The Thus Come One possesses measureless wisdom, power, freedom from fear, the storehouse of the Law. He is capable of giving to all living beings the Law of the Great Vehicle. But not all of them are capable of receiving it.

"Shariputra, for this reason you should understand that the Buddhas employ the power of expedient means. And because they do so, they make distinctions in the one Buddha vehicle and preach it as three."

The Buddha, wishing to state his meaning once more, spoke in verse form, saying:

> Suppose there was a rich man
> who had a large house.
> This house was very old,
> and decayed and dilapidated as well.
> The halls, though lofty, were in dangerous condition,
> the bases of the pillars had rotted,
> beams and rafters were slanting and askew,
> foundations and steps were crumbling.
> Walls were cracked and gaping
> and the plaster had fallen off of them.
> The roof thatch was in disrepair or missing,
> the tips of the eaves had dropped off.
> The fences surrounding it were crooked or collapsed
> and heaped rubbish was piled all around.
> Some five hundred persons
> lived in the house.
> Kites, owls, hawks, eagles,
> crows, magpies, doves, pigeons,
> lizards, snakes, vipers, scorpions,
> centipedes and millipedes,
> newts and ground beetles,

weasels, raccoon dogs, mice, rats,
hordes of evil creatures
scurried this way and that.
Places that stank of excrement
overflowed in streams of filth
where dung beetles and other creatures gathered.
Foxes, wolves and jackals
gnawed and trampled in the filth
or tore apart dead bodies,
scattering bones and flesh about.
Because of this, packs of dogs
came racing to the spot to snatch and tear,
driven by hunger and fear,
searching everywhere for food,
fighting, struggling, seizing,
baring their teeth, snarling and howling.
That house was fearful, frightening,
so altered was its aspect.
In every part of it
there were goblins and trolls,
yakshas and evil spirits
who feed on human flesh
or on poisonous creatures.
The various evil birds and beasts
bore offspring, hatched and nursed them,
each hiding and protecting its young,
but the yakshas outdid one another
in their haste to seize and eat them.
And when they had eaten their fill,
their evil hearts became fiercer than ever;
the sound of their wrangling and contention
was terrifying indeed.
Kumbhanda demons
crouched on clumps of earth
or leaped one or two feet
off the ground,
idling, wandering here and there,
amusing themselves according to their whim.

Sometimes they seized a dog by two of its legs
and beat it till it had lost its voice,
or planted their feet on the dog's neck,
terrifying it for their own delight.
Again there were demons
with large tall bodies,
naked in form, black and emaciated,
constantly living there,
who would cry out in loud ugly voices,
shouting and demanding food.
There were other demons
whose throats were like needles,
or still other demons
with heads like the head of an ox,
some feeding on human flesh,
others devouring dogs.
Their hair like tangled weeds,
cruel, baleful, ferocious,
driven by hunger and thirst,
they dashed about shrieking and howling.
The yakshas and starving spirits
and the various evil birds and beasts
hungrily pressed forward in all directions,
peering out at the windows.
Such were the perils of this house,
threats and terrors beyond measure.
This house, old and rotting,
belonged to a certain man
and that man had gone nearby
and had not been out for long
when a fire
suddenly broke out in the house.
In one moment from all four sides
the flames rose up in a mass.
Ridgepoles, beams, rafters, pillars
exploded with a roar, quivering, splitting,
broke in two and came tumbling down
as walls and partitions collapsed.

The various demons and spirits
lifted their voices in a great wail,
the hawks, eagles and other birds,
the kumbhanda demons,
were filled with panic and terror,
not knowing how to escape.
The evil beasts and poisonous creatures
hid in their holes and dens,
and the pishacha demons,
who were also living there,
because they had done so little that was good,
were oppressed by the flames
and attacked one another,
drinking blood and gobbling flesh.
The jackals and their like
were already dead by this time
and the larger of the evil beasts
vied in devouring them.
Foul smoke swirled and billowed up,
filling the house on every side.
The centipedes and millipedes,
the poisonous snakes and their kind,
scorched by the flames,
came scurrying out of their lairs,
whereupon the kumbhanda demons
pounced on them and ate them.
In addition, the starving spirits,
the fire raging about their heads,
hungry, thirsty, tormented by the heat,
raced this way and that in terror and confusion.
Such was the state of that house,
truly frightening and fearful;
malicious injury, the havoc of fire—
many ills, not just one, afflicted it.
At this time the owner of the house
was standing outside the gate
when he heard someone say,
"A while ago your various sons,

in order to play their games,
went inside the house.
They are very young and lack understanding
and will be wrapped up in their amusements."
When the rich man heard this,
he rushed in alarm into the burning house,
determined to rescue his sons
and keep them from being burned by the flames.
He urged his sons to heed him,
explaining the many dangers and perils,
the evil spirits and poisonous creatures,
the flames spreading all around,
the multitude of sufferings
that would follow one another without end,
the poisonous snakes, lizards and vipers,
as well as the many yakshas
and kumbhanda demons,
the jackals, foxes and dogs,
hawks, eagles, kites, owls,
ground beetles and similar creatures,
driven and tormented by hunger and thirst,
truly things to be feared.
His sons could not stay in such a perilous place,
much less when it was all on fire!
But the sons had no understanding
and though they heard their father's warnings,
they continued engrossed in their amusements,
never ceasing their games.
At that time the rich man
thought to himself:
My sons behave in this manner,
adding to my grief and anguish.
In this house at present
there is not a single joy,
and yet my sons,
wrapped up in their games,
refuse to heed my instructions
and will be destroyed by the fire!

Then it occurred to him
to devise some expedient means,
and he said to his sons,
"I have many kinds
of rare and marvelous toys,
wonderful jeweled carriages,
goat-carts, deer-carts,
carts drawn by big oxen.
They are outside the gate right now—
you must come out and see them!
I have fashioned these carts
explicitly for you.
You may enjoy whichever you choose,
play with them as you like!"
When the sons heard
this description of the carts,
at once they vied with one another
in dashing out of the house,
till they reached the open ground,
away from all peril and danger.
When the rich man saw that his sons
had escaped from the burning house
and were standing in the crossroads,
he seated himself on a lion seat,
congratulating himself in these words:
"Now I am content and happy.
These sons of mine
have been very difficult to raise.
Ignorant, youthful, without understanding,
they entered that perilous house
with its many poisonous creatures
and its goblins to be feared.
The roaring flames of the great fire
rose up on all four sides,
yet those sons of mine
still clung to their games.
But now I have saved them,
caused them to escape from danger.

That is the reason, good people,
I am content and happy."
At that time the sons,
seeing their father comfortably seated,
all went to where he was
and said to him:
"Please give us
the three kinds of jeweled carriages
you promised us earlier.
You said if we came out of the house
you'd give us three kinds of carts
and we could choose whichever we wished.
Now is the time
to give them to us!"
The rich man was very wealthy
and had many storehouses.
With gold, silver, lapis lazuli,
seashells, agate,
and other such precious things
he fashioned large carriages
beautifully adorned and decorated,
with railings running around them
and bells hanging from all sides.
Ropes of gold twisted and twined,
nets of pearls
stretched over the top,
and fringes of golden flowers
hung down everywhere.
Multicolored decorations
wound around and encircled the carriages,
soft silks and gauzes
served for cushions,
with fine felts of most wonderful make
valued at thousands or millions,
gleaming white and pure,
to spread over them.
There were large white oxen,
sleek, stalwart, of great strength,

handsome in form,
to draw the jeweled carriages,
and numerous grooms and attendants
to accompany and guard them.
These wonderful carriages
the man presented to each of his sons alike.
The sons at that time
danced for joy,
mounting the jeweled carriages,
driving off in all directions,
delighting and amusing themselves
freely and without hindrance.
I say this to you, Shariputra—
I am like this rich man.
I, most venerable of the sages,
am the father of this world
and all living beings
are my children.
But they are deeply attached to worldly pleasures
and lacking in minds of wisdom.
There is no safety in the threefold world;
it is like a burning house,
replete with a multitude of sufferings,
truly to be feared,
constantly beset with the griefs and pains
of birth, old age, sickness and death,
which are like fires
raging fiercely and without cease.
The Thus Come One has already left
the burning house of the threefold world
and dwells in tranquil quietude
in the safety of forest and plain.
But now this threefold world
is all my domain,
and the living beings in it
are all my children.
Now this place
is beset by many pains and trials.

I am the only person
who can rescue and protect others,
but though I teach and instruct them,
they do not believe or accept my teachings,
because, tainted by desires,
they are deeply immersed in greed and attachment.
So I employ an expedient means,
describing to them the three vehicles,
causing all living beings
to understand the pains of the threefold world,
and then I set forth and expound
a way whereby they can escape from the world.
If these children of mine
will only determine in their minds to do so,
they can acquire all the three understandings
and the six transcendental powers,
can become pratyekabuddhas
or bodhisattvas who never regress.
I say to you, Shariputra,
for the sake of living beings
I employ these similes and parables
to preach the single Buddha vehicle.
If you and the others are capable
of believing and accepting my words,
then all of you are certain
to attain the Buddha way.
This vehicle is subtle, wonderful,
foremost in purity;
throughout all worlds
it stands unsurpassed.
The Buddha delights in and approves it,
and all living beings
should praise it,
offer it alms and obeisance.
There are immeasurable thousands of millions
of powers, emancipations,
meditations, wisdoms,
and other attributes of the Buddha.

But if the children can obtain this vehicle,
it will allow them
day and night for unnumbered kalpas
to find constant enjoyment,
to join the bodhisattvas
and the multitude of voice-hearers
in mounting this jeweled vehicle
and proceeding directly to the place of practice.
For these reasons,
though one should seek diligently in the ten directions,
he will find no other vehicles
except when the Buddha preaches them as an expedient means.
I tell you, Shariputra,
you and the others
are all my children,
and I am a father to you.
For repeated kalpas
you have burned in the flames of manifold sufferings,
but I will save you all
and cause you to escape from the threefold world.
Although earlier I told you
that you had attained extinction,
that was only the end of birth and death,
it was not true extinction.
Now what is needed
is simply that you acquire Buddha wisdom.
If there are bodhisattvas
here in this assembly,
let them with a single mind
listen to the true Law of the Buddhas.
Though the Buddhas, the World-Honored Ones,
employ expedient means,
the living beings converted by them
are all bodhisattvas.
If there are persons of little wisdom
who are deeply attached to love and desire,
because they are that way,
the Buddha preaches for them the rule of suffering.

Then the living beings will be glad in mind,
having gained what they never had before.
The rule of suffering which the Buddha preaches
is true and never varies.
If there are living beings
who do not understand the root of suffering,
who are deeply attached to the causes of suffering
and cannot for a moment put them aside,
because they are that way,
the Buddha uses expedient means to preach the way.
As to the cause of all suffering,
it has its root in greed and desire.
If greed and desire are wiped out,
it will have no place to dwell.
To wipe out all suffering—
this is called the third rule.
For the sake of this rule, the rule of extinction,
one practices the way.
And when one escapes from the bonds of suffering,
this is called attaining emancipation.
By what means
can a person attain emancipation?
Separating oneself from falsehood and delusion—
this alone may be called emancipation.
But if a person has not truly
been able to emancipate himself from everything,
then the Buddha will say
he has not achieved true extinction,
because such a person
has not yet gained the unsurpassed way.
My purpose is not to try
to cause them to reach extinction.
I am the Dharma King,
free to do as I will with the Law.
To bring peace and safety to living beings—
that is the reason I appear in the world.
I say to you, Shariputra,
this Dharma seal of mine

I preach because I wish
to bring benefit to the world.
You must not recklessly transmit it
wherever you happen to wander.
If there is someone who hears it,
responds with joy and gratefully accepts it,
you should know that that person
is an avivartika.
If there is someone who believes and accepts
the Law of this sutra,
that person has already seen
the Buddhas of the past,
has respectfully offered alms to them
and listened to this Law.
If there is someone who can
believe what you preach,
then that person has seen me,
and has also seen you
and the other monks
and the bodhisattvas.
This Lotus Sutra
is preached for those with profound wisdom.
If persons of shallow understanding hear it,
they will be perplexed and fail to comprehend.
As for all the voice-hearers
and pratyekabuddhas,
in this sutra there are things
that are beyond their powers.
Even you, Shariputra,
in the case of this sutra
were able to gain entrance through faith alone.
How much more so, then, the other voice-hearers.
Those other voice-hearers—
it is because they have faith in the Buddha's words
that they can comply with this sutra,
not because of any wisdom of their own.
Also, Shariputra,
to persons who are arrogant or lazy

or taken up with views of the self,
do not preach this sutra.
Those with the shallow understanding of ordinary persons,
who are deeply attached to the five desires,
cannot comprehend it when they hear it.
Do not preach it to them.
If a person fails to have faith
but instead slanders this sutra,
immediately he will destroy all the seeds
for becoming a Buddha in this world.
Or perhaps he will scowl with knitted brows
and harbor doubt or perplexity.
Listen and I will tell you
the penalty this person must pay.
Whether the Buddha is in the world
or has already entered extinction,
if this person should slander
a sutra such as this,
or on seeing those who read, recite,
copy and uphold this sutra,
should despise, hate, envy,
or bear grudges against them,
the penalty this person must pay—
listen, I will tell you now:
When his life comes to an end
he will enter the Avichi hell,
be confined there for a whole kalpa,
and when the kalpa ends, be born there again.
He will keep repeating this cycle
for a countless number of kalpas.
Though he may emerge from hell,
he will fall into the realm of beasts,
becoming a dog or jackal,
his form lean and scruffy,
dark, discolored, with scabs and sores,
something for men to make sport of.
Or again he will be
hated and despised by men,

constantly plagued by hunger and thirst,
his bones and flesh dried up,
in life undergoing torment and hardship,
in death buried beneath tiles and stones.
Because he cut off the seeds of Buddhahood
he will suffer this penalty.
If he should become a camel
or be born in the shape of a donkey,
his body will constantly bear heavy burdens
and have the stick or whip laid on it.
He will think only of water and grass
and understand nothing else.
Because he slandered this sutra,
this is the punishment he will incur.
Or he will be born as a jackal
who comes to the village,
body all scabs and sores,
having only one eye,
by the boys
beaten and cuffed,
suffering grief and pain,
sometimes to the point of death.
And after he has died
he will be born again in the body of a serpent,
long and huge in size,
measuring five hundred yojanas,
deaf, witless, without feet,
slithering along on his belly,
with little creatures
biting and feeding on him,
day and night undergoing hardship,
never knowing rest.
Because he slandered this sutra,
this is the punishment he will incur.
If he should become a human being,
his faculties will be blighted and dull,
he will be puny, vile, bent, crippled,
blind, deaf, hunchbacked.

The things he says
people will not believe,
the breath from his mouth will be constantly foul,
he will be possessed by devils,
poor and lowly,
ordered around by others,
plagued by many ailments, thin and gaunt,
having no one to turn to.
Though he attached himself to others,
they would never think of him;
though he might gain something,
he would at once lose or forget it.
Though he might practice the art of medicine
and by its methods cure someone's disease,
the person would grow sicker from some other malady
and perhaps in the end would die.
If he himself had an illness,
no one would aid or nurse him,
and though he took good medicine,
it would only make his condition worse.
If others should turn against him,
he would find himself plundered and robbed.
His sins would be such
that they would bring unexpected disaster on him.
A sinful person of this sort
will never see the Buddha,
the king of the many sages,
preaching the Law, teaching and converting.
A sinful person of this sort
will constantly be born amid difficulties,
crazed, deaf, confused in mind,
and never will hear the Law.
For countless kalpas
numerous as Ganges sands
he will at birth become deaf and dumb,
his faculties impaired,
will constantly dwell in hell,
strolling in it as though it were a garden,

and the other evil paths of existence
he will look on as his own home.
Camel, donkey, pig, dog—
these will be the forms he will take on.
Because he slandered this sutra,
this is the punishment he will incur.
If he should become a human being,
he will be deaf, blind, dumb.
Poverty, want, all kinds of decay
will be his adornment;
water blisters, diabetes,
scabs, sores, ulcers,
maladies such as these
will be his garments.
His body will always smell bad,
filthy and impure.
Deeply attached to views of self,
he will grow in anger and hatred;
aflame with licentious desires,
he will not spurn even birds or beasts.
Because he slandered this sutra,
this is the punishment he will incur.
I tell you, Shariputra,
if I were to describe the punishments that fall
on persons who slander this sutra,
I could exhaust a kalpa and never come to the end.
For this reason
I expressly say to you,
do not preach this sutra
to persons who are without wisdom.
But if there are those of keen capacities,
wise and understanding,
of much learning and strong memory,
who seek the Buddha way,
then to persons such as this
it is permissible to preach it.
If there are persons who have seen
hundreds and thousands and millions of Buddhas,

have planted many good roots
and are firm and deeply committed in mind,
then to persons such as this
it is permissible to preach it.
If there are persons who are diligent,
constantly cultivating a compassionate mind,
not begrudging of life or limb,
then it is permissible to preach it.
If there are persons who are respectful, reverent,
with minds set on nothing else,
who separate themselves from common folly
to live alone among mountains and waters,
then to persons such as this
it is permissible to preach it.
Again, Shariputra,
if you see a person
who thrusts aside evil friends
and associates with good companions,
then to a person such as this
it is permissible to preach it.
If you see a son of the Buddha
observing the precepts, clean and spotless
as a pure bright gem,
seeking the Great Vehicle sutra,
then to a person such as this
it is permissible to preach it.
If a person is without anger,
upright and gentle in nature,
constantly pitying all beings,
respectful and reverent to the Buddhas,
then to a person such as this
it is permissible to preach it.
Again, if a son of the Buddha
in the midst of the great assembly
should with a pure mind
employ various causes and conditions,
similes, parables, and other expressions
to preach the Law in unhindered fashion,

to a person such as this
it is permissible to preach it.
If there are monks who,
for the sake of comprehensive wisdom,
seek the Law in every direction,
pressing palms together, gratefully accepting,
desiring only to accept and embrace
the sutra of the Great Vehicle
and not accepting a single verse
of the other sutras,
to persons such as this
it is permissible to preach it.
If a person, earnest in mind,
seeks this sutra
as though he were seeking the Buddha's relics,
and having gained and gratefully accepted it,
that person shows no intention
of seeking other sutras
and has never once given thought
to the writings of the non-Buddhist doctrines,
to a person such as this
it is permissible to preach it.
I tell you, Shariputra,
if I described all the characteristics
of those who seek the Buddha way,
I could exhaust a kalpa and never be done.
Persons of this type
are capable of believing and understanding.
Therefore for them you should preach
the Lotus Sutra of the Wonderful Law.

4

BELIEF AND
UNDERSTANDING

At that time, when the men of lifelong wisdom Subhuti, Maha-katyayana, Mahakashyapa, and Mahamaudgalyayana heard from the Buddha a Law that they had never known before, and heard the World-Honored One prophesy that Shariputra would attain anuttara-samyak-sambodhi, their minds were moved as seldom before and danced for joy. At once they rose from their seats, arranged their robes, bared their right shoulders and bowed their right knees to the ground. Pressing their palms together with a single mind, they bent their bodies in a gesture of respect and, gazing up in reverence at the face of the Honored One, said to the Buddha: "We stand at the head of the monks and are all of us old and decrepit. We believed that we had already attained nirvana and that we were incapable of doing more, and so we never sought to attain anuttara-samyak-sambodhi.

"It has been a long time since the World-Honored One first began to expound the Law. During that time we have sat in our seats, our bodies weary and inert, meditating solely on the concepts of emptiness, non-form, and non-action. But as to the pleasures and transcendental powers of the Law of the bodhisattva or the purifying of Buddha lands and the salvation of living beings—these our minds took no joy in. Why is this? Because the World-Honored One had made it possible for us to transcend the threefold world and to attain the enlightenment of nirvana.

"Moreover, we are old and decrepit. When we heard of this anuttara-samyak-sambodhi, which the Buddha uses to teach and convert the bodhisattvas, our minds were not filled with any thought of joy or approval. But now in the presence of the Buddha we have heard this voice-hearer receive a prophecy that he will attain anuttara-samyak-sambodhi and our minds are greatly delighted. We have gained what we never had before. Suddenly we have been able to hear a Law that is rarely encountered, something we never expected up to now, and we look upon ourselves as profoundly fortunate. We have gained great goodness and benefit, an immeasurably rare jewel, something unsought that came of itself.

"World-Honored One, we would be pleased now to employ a parable to make clear our meaning. Suppose there was a man, still young in years, who abandoned his father, ran away, and lived for a long time in another land, for perhaps ten, twenty, or even fifty years. As he grew older, he found himself increasingly poor and in want. He hurried about in every direction, seeking for clothing and food, wandering farther and farther afield until by chance he turned his steps in the direction of his homeland.

"The father meanwhile had been searching for his son without success and had taken up residence in a certain city. The father's household was very wealthy, with immeasurable riches and treasures. Gold, silver, lapis lazuli, coral, amber, and crystal beads all filled and overflowed from his storehouses. He had many grooms and menservants, clerks and attendants, and elephants, horses, carriages, oxen, and goats beyond number. He engaged in profitable ventures at home and in all the lands around, and also had dealings with many merchants and traveling vendors.

"At this time the impoverished son wandered from village to village, passing through various lands and towns, till at last he came to the city where his father was residing. The father thought constantly of his son, but though he had been parted from him for over fifty years, he had never told anyone else about the matter. He merely pondered to himself, his heart filled with regret and longing. He thought to himself that he was old and decrepit. He had great wealth and possessions, gold, silver, and rare treasures that filled and overflowed from his storehouses, but he had no son, so that if one day he should die, the wealth and possessions would be scattered and lost, for there was no one to entrust them to.

"This was the reason he constantly thought so earnestly of his son. And he also had this thought: If I could find my son and entrust my wealth and possessions to him, then I could feel contented and easy in mind and would have no more worries.

"World-Honored One, at that time the impoverished son drifted from one kind of employment to another until he came by chance to his father's house. He stood by the side of the gate, gazing far off at his father, who was seated on a lion throne, his legs supported by a jeweled footrest, while Brahmans, noblemen, and householders, uniformly deferential, surrounded him. Festoons of pearls worth thousands or tens of thousands adorned his body, and clerks, grooms, and menservants holding white fly whisks stood in attendance to left and right. A jeweled canopy covered him, with flowered banners hanging from it, perfumed water had been sprinkled over the ground, heaps of rare flowers were scattered about, and precious objects were ranged here and there, brought out, put away, handed over and received. Such were the many different types of adornments, the emblems of prerogative and marks of distinction.

"When the impoverished son saw how great was his father's power and authority, he was filled with fear and awe and regretted he had ever come to such a place. Secretly he thought to himself: This must be some king, or one who is equal to a king. This is not the sort of place where I can hire out my labor and gain a living. It would be better to go to some poor village where, if I work hard, I will find a place and can easily earn food and clothing. If I stay here for long, I may be seized and pressed into service! Having thought in this way, he raced from the spot.

"At that time the rich old man, seated on his lion throne, spied his son and recognized him immediately. His heart was filled with great joy and at once he thought: Now I have someone to entrust my storehouses of wealth and possessions to! My thoughts have constantly been with this son of mine, but I had no way of seeing him. Now suddenly he has appeared of himself, which is exactly what I would have wished. Though I am old and decrepit, I still care what becomes of my belongings.

"Thereupon he dispatched a bystander to go after the son as quickly as possible and bring him back. At that time the messenger raced swiftly after the son and laid hold of him. The impoverished son, alarmed and fearful, cried out in an angry voice, 'I have done nothing wrong! Why am I being seized?' But the messenger held on to him more tightly than ever and forcibly dragged him back.

"At that time the son thought to himself, I have committed no crime and yet I am taken prisoner. Surely I am going to be put to death! He was more terrified than ever and sank to the ground, fainting with despair.

"The father, observing this from a distance, spoke to the messenger, saying, 'I have no need of this man. Don't force him to come here, but sprinkle cold water on his face so he will regain his senses. Then say nothing more to him!'

"Why did he do that? Because the father knew that his son was of humble outlook and ambition, and that his own rich and eminent position would be difficult for the son to accept. He knew very well that this was his son, but as a form of expedient means he refrained from saying to anyone, 'This is my son.'

"The messenger said to the son, 'I am releasing you now. You may go anywhere you wish.' The impoverished son was delighted, having gained what he had not had before, and picked himself up from the ground and went off to the poor village in order to look for food and clothing.

"At that time the rich man, hoping to entice his son back again, decided to employ an expedient means and send two men as secret messengers, men who were lean and haggard and had no imposing appearance. 'Go seek out that poor man and approach him casually. Tell him you know a place where he can earn twice the regular wage. If he agrees to the arrangement, then bring him here and put him to work. If he asks what sort of work he will be put to, say that he will be employed to clear away excrement, and that the two of you will be working with him.'

"The two messengers then set out at once to find the poor man, and when they had done so, spoke to him as they had been instructed. At that time the impoverished son asked for an advance on his wages and then went with the men to help clear away excrement.

"When the father saw his son, he pitied and wondered at him. Another day, when he was gazing out the window, he saw his son in the distance, his body thin and haggard, filthy with excrement, dirt, sweat, and defilement. The father immediately took off his necklaces, his soft fine garments and his other adornments and put on clothes that were ragged and soiled. He smeared dirt on his body, took in his right hand a utensil for removing excrement, and assuming a gruff manner, spoke to the laborers, saying, 'Keep at your work! You mustn't be lazy!' By employing this expedient means, he was able to approach his son.

"Later he spoke to his son again, saying, 'Now then, young man! You must keep on at this work and not leave me anymore. I will increase your wages, and whatever you need in the way of utensils, rice, flour, salt, vinegar, and the like you should be in no worry about. I have an old servant I can lend you when you need him. You may set your mind at ease. I will be like a father to you, so have no more worries. Why do I say this? Because I am well along in years, but you are still young and sturdy. When you are at work, you are never deceitful or lazy or speak angry or resentful words. You don't seem to have any faults of that kind the way my other workers do. From now on, you will be like my own son.' And the rich man proceeded to select a name and assign it to the man as though he were his child.

"At this time the impoverished son, though he was delighted at such treatment, still thought of himself as a person of humble station who was in the employ of another. Therefore the rich man kept him clearing away excrement for the next twenty years. By the end of this time, the son felt that he was understood and trusted, and he could

come and go at ease, but he continued to live in the same place as
before.

"World-Honored One, at that time the rich man fell ill and knew
that he would die before long. He spoke to his impoverished son,
saying, 'I now have great quantities of gold, silver, and rare treasures
that fill and overflow from my storehouses. You are to take complete
charge of the amounts I have and of what is to be handed out and
gathered in. This is what I have in mind, and I want you to carry out
my wishes. Why is this? Because from now on, you and I will not
behave as two different persons. So you must keep your wits about
you and see that there are no mistakes or losses.'

"At that time the impoverished son, having received these instructions, took over the surveillance of all the goods, the gold, silver, and
rare treasures, and the various storehouses, but never thought of
appropriating for himself so much as the cost of a single meal. He
continued to live where he had before, unable to cease thinking of
himself as mean and lowly.

"After some time had passed, the father perceived that his son was
bit by bit becoming more self-assured and magnanimous in outlook,
that he was determined to accomplish great things and despised his
former low opinion of himself. Realizing that his own end was ap-
proaching, he ordered his son to arrange a meeting with his relatives
and the king of the country, the high ministers, and the noblemen and
householders. When they were all gathered together, he proceeded to
make this announcement: 'Gentlemen, you should know that this is
my son, who was born to me. In such-and-such a city he abandoned
me and ran away, and for over fifty years he wandered about suffering
hardship. His original name is such-and-such, and my name is such-
and-such. In the past, when I was still living in my native city, I
worried about him and so I set out in search of him. Sometime after,
I suddenly chanced to meet up with him. This is in truth my son,
and I in truth am his father. Now everything that belongs to me, all
my wealth and possessions, shall belong entirely to this son of mine.
Matters of outlay and income that have occurred in the past this son
of mine is familiar with.'

"World-Honored One, when the impoverished son heard these
words of his father, he was filled with great joy, having gained what

he never had before, and he thought to himself, I originally had no mind to covet or seek such things. Yet now these stores of treasures have come of their own accord!

"World-Honored One, this old man with his great riches is none other than the Thus Come One, and we are all like the Buddha's sons. The Thus Come One constantly tells us that we are his sons. But because of the three sufferings, World-Honored One, in the midst of birth and death we undergo burning anxieties, delusions, and ignorance, delighting in and clinging to lesser doctrines. But today the World-Honored One causes us to ponder carefully, to cast aside such doctrines, the filth of frivolous debate.

"We were diligent and exerted ourselves in this matter until we had attained nirvana, which is like one day's wages. And once we had attained it, our hearts were filled with great joy and we considered that this was enough. At once we said to ourselves, 'Because we have been diligent and exerted ourselves with regard to the Buddhist Law, we have gained this breadth and wealth of understanding.'

"But the World-Honored One, knowing from past times how our minds cling to unworthy desires and delight in lesser doctrines, pardoned us and let us be, not trying to explain to us by saying, 'You will come to possess the insight of the Thus Come One, your portion of the store of treasures!' Instead the World-Honored One employed the power of expedient means, preaching to us the wisdom of the Thus Come One in such a way that we might heed the Buddha and attain nirvana, which is one day's wages. And because we considered this to be a great gain, we had no wish to pursue the Great Vehicle.

"In addition, though we expounded and set forth the Buddha wisdom for the sake of the bodhisattvas, we ourselves did not aspire to attain it. Why do I say this? Because the Buddha, knowing that our minds delight in lesser doctrines, employed the power of expedient means to preach in a way that was appropriate for us. So we did not know that we were in truth the sons of the Buddha. But now at last we know it.

"With regard to the Buddha wisdom, the World-Honored One is never begrudging. Why do I say this? From times past we have in truth been the sons of the Buddha, but we delighted in nothing but lesser doctrines. If we had had the kind of mind that delighted in great ones, then the Buddha would have preached the Law of the Great Vehicle for us.

"Now in this sutra the Buddha expounds only the one vehicle. And in the past, when in the presence of the bodhisattvas he disparaged the voice-hearers as those who delight in a lesser doctrine, the Buddha was in fact employing the Great Vehicle to teach and convert us. Therefore we say that, though originally we had no mind to covet or seek such a thing, now the great treasure of the Dharma King has come to us of its own accord. It is something that the sons of the Buddha have a right to acquire, and now they have acquired all of it."

At that time Mahakashyapa, wishing to state his meaning once more, spoke in verse form, saying:

> We today have heard
> the Buddha's voice teaching
> and we dance for joy,
> having gained what we never had before.
> The Buddha declares that the voice-hearers
> will be able to attain Buddhahood.
> This cluster of unsurpassed jewels
> has come to us unsought.
> It is like the case of a boy who,
> when still young, without understanding,
> abandoned his father and ran away,
> going far off to another land,
> drifting from one country to another
> for over fifty years.
> His father, distressed in thought,
> searched for him in every direction
> till, worn out with searching,
> he halted in a certain city.
> There he built a dwelling
> where he could indulge the five desires.
> His house was large and costly,
> with quantities of gold, silver,
> seashell, agate,
> pearls, lapis lazuli,

elephants, horses, oxen, goats,
palanquins, and carriages,
fields for farming, menservants, grooms,
and other people in great number.
He engaged in profitable ventures
at home and in all the lands around,
and had merchants and traveling vendors
stationed everywhere.
Thousands, ten thousands, millions
surrounded him and paid reverence;
he enjoyed the constant favor
and consideration of the ruler.
The officials and powerful clans
all joined in paying him honor,
and those who for one reason or another
flocked about him were many.
Such was his vast wealth,
the great power and influence he possessed.
But as he grew old and decrepit
he recalled his son with greater distress than ever,
day and night thinking of nothing else:
"Now the time of my death draws near.
Over fifty years have passed
since that foolish boy abandoned me.
My storehouses full of goods—
what will become of them?"
At this time the impoverished son
was searching for food and clothing,
going from village to village,
from country to country,
sometimes finding something,
other times finding nothing,
starving and emaciated,
his body broken out in sores and ring worm.
As he moved from place to place
he arrived in time at the city where his father lived,
shifting from one job to another
until he came to his father's house.

At that time the rich man
had spread a large jeweled canopy
inside his gate
and was seated on a lion throne,
surrounded by his dependents
and various attendants and guards.
Some were counting out
gold, silver, and precious objects,
or recording in ledgers
the outlay and income of wealth.
The impoverished son, observing
how eminent and distinguished his father was,
supposed he must be the king of a country
or the equal of a king.
Alarmed and full of wonder,
he asked himself why he had come here.
Secretly he thought to himself,
If I linger here for long
I will perhaps be seized
and pressed into service!
Once this thought had occurred to him,
he raced from the spot,
and inquiring where there was a poor village,
went there in hopes of gaining employment.
The rich man at the time,
seated on his lion throne,
saw his son in the distance
and silently recognized who he was.
Immediately he instructed a messenger
to hurry after him and bring him back.
The impoverished son, crying out in terror,
sank to the ground in distress.
"This man has seized me
and is surely going to put me to death!
To think that my search for food and clothing
should bring me to this!"
The rich man knew that his son
was ignorant and self-abasing.

"He will never believe my words,
will never believe I am his father."
So he employed an expedient means,
sending some other men to the son,
a one-eyed man, another puny and uncouth,
completely lacking in imposing appearance,
saying, "Speak to him
and tell him I will employ him
to remove excrement and filth,
and will pay him twice the regular wage."
When the impoverished son heard this
he was delighted and came with the messengers
and worked to clear away excrement and filth
and clean the rooms of the house.
From the window the rich man
would constantly observe his son,
thinking how his son was ignorant and self-abasing
and delighted in such menial labor.
At such times the rich man
would put on dirty ragged clothing,
take in hand a utensil for removing excrement
and go to where his son was,
using this expedient means to approach him,
encouraging him to work diligently.
"I have increased your wages
and given you oil to rub on your feet.
I will see that you have plenty to eat and drink,
mats and bedding that are thick and warm."
At times he would speak severely:
"You must work hard!"
Or again he would say in a gentle voice,
"You are like a son to me."
The rich man, being wise,
gradually permitted his son to come and go in the house.
And after twenty years had passed,
he put him in charge of household affairs,
showing him his gold, silver,
pearls, crystal,

and the other things that were handed out or gathered in,
so that he would understand all about them,
though the son continued to live outside the gate,
sleeping in a hut of grass,
for he looked upon himself as poor,
thinking, "None of these things are mine."
The father knew that his son's outlook
was gradually becoming broader and more magnanimous,
and, wishing to hand over his wealth and goods,
he called together his relatives,
the king of the country and the high ministers,
the noblemen and householders.
In the presence of this great assembly
he declared, "This is my son
who abandoned me and wandered abroad
for a period of fifty years.
Since I found him again,
twenty years have gone by.
Long ago, in such-and-such a city,
when I lost my son,
I traveled all around searching for him
until eventually I came here.
All that I possess,
my house and people,
I hand over entirely to him
so he may do with them as he wishes."
The son thought how in the past he had been poor,
humble and self-abasing in outlook,
but now he had received from his father
this huge bequest of rare treasures,
along with the father's house
and all his wealth and goods.
He was filled with great joy,
having gained what he never had before.
The Buddha too is like this.
He knows our fondness for the petty,
and so he never told us,
"You can attain Buddhahood."

Instead he explained to us
how we could become free of outflows,
carry out the Lesser Vehicle
and be voice-hearer disciples.
Then the Buddha commanded us
to preach the supreme way
and explain that those who practice this
will be able to attain Buddhahood.
We received the Buddha's teaching
and for the sake of the great bodhisattvas
made use of causes and conditions,
various similes and parables,
a variety of words and phrases,
to preach the unsurpassed way.
When the sons of the Buddha
heard the Law through us,
day and night they pondered,
diligently and with effort practicing it.
At that time the Buddha
bestowed prophecies on them, saying,
"In a future existence
you will be able to attain Buddhahood."
The various Buddhas
in their Law of the secret storehouse
set forth the true facts
for the sake of bodhisattvas alone;
it is not for our sake
that they expound the true essentials.
The case is like that of the impoverished son
who was able to approach his father.
Though he knew of his father's possessions,
at heart he had no longing to appropriate them.
Thus, although we preached
the treasure storehouse of the Law of the Buddha,
we did not seek to attain it ourselves,
and in this way our case is similar.
We sought to wipe out what was within ourselves,
believing that that was sufficient.

We understood only this one concern
and knew nothing of other matters.
Though we might hear
of purifying the Buddha lands,
of teaching and converting living beings,
we took no delight in such things.
Why is this?
Because all phenomena
are uniformly empty, tranquil,
without birth, without extinction,
without bigness, without smallness,
without outflows, without action.
And when one ponders in this way,
one can feel no delight or joy.
Through the long night,
with regard to the Buddha wisdom
we were without greed, without attachment,
without any desire to possess it.
We believed that with regard to the Law
we possessed the ultimate.
Through the long night
we practiced the Law of emptiness,
gaining release from the threefold world
and its burden of suffering and care.
We dwelt in our final existence,
in the nirvana of remainder.
Through the teaching and conversion of the Buddha
we gained a way that was not vain,
and in doing so we repaid
the debt we owed to the Buddha's kindness.
Although for the sake
of the Buddha's sons
we preached the Law of the bodhisattva,
urging them to seek the Buddha way,
yet we ourselves
never aspired to that Law.
We were thus abandoned by our guide and teacher
because he had observed what was in our minds.

From the first he never encouraged us
or spoke to us of true benefit.
He was like the rich man
who knew that his son's ambitions were lowly
and who used the power of expedient means
to soften and mold his son's mind
so that later he could entrust to him
all his wealth and treasure.
The Buddha is like this,
resorting to a rare course of action.
Knowing that some have a fondness for the petty,
he uses the power of expedient means
to mold and temper their minds,
and only then teaches them the great wisdom.
Today we have gained
what we never had before;
what we previously never hoped for
has now come to us of itself.
We are like the impoverished son
who gained immeasurable treasure.
World-Honored One, now
we have gained the way, gained its fruit;
through the Law of no outflows
we have gained the undefiled eye.
Through the long night
we observed the pure precepts of the Buddha
and today for the first time
we have gained the fruit, the recompense.
In the Law of the Dharma King
we have long carried out brahma practices;
now we obtain the state of no outflows,
the great unsurpassed fruit.
Now we have become
voice-hearers in truth,
for we will take the voice of the Buddha way
and cause it to be heard by all.
Now we have become
true arhats,

for everywhere among
the heavenly and human beings, devils and Brahmas
of the various worlds
we deserve to receive offerings.
The World-Honored One in his great mercy
makes use of a rare thing,
in pity and compassion teaching and converting,
bringing benefit to us.
In numberless millions of kalpas
who could ever repay him?
Though we offer him our hands and feet,
bow our heads in respectful obeisance,
and present all manner of offerings,
none of us could repay him.
Though we lift him on the crown of our heads,
bear him on our two shoulders,
for kalpas numerous as Ganges sands
reverence him with all our hearts;
though we come with delicate foods,
with countless jeweled robes,
with articles of bedding,
various kinds of potions and medicines;
with ox-head sandalwood
and all kinds of rare gems,
construct memorial towers
and spread the ground with jeweled robes;
though we were to do all this
by way of offering
for kalpas numerous as Ganges sands,
still we could not repay him.
The Buddhas possess rarely known,
immeasurable, boundless,
unimaginable great
transcendental powers.
Free of outflows, free of action,
these kings of the doctrines
for the sake of the humble and lowly
exercise patience in these matters;

to common mortals attached to appearances
they preach in accordance with what is appropriate.
With regard to the Law, the Buddhas
are able to exercise complete freedom.
They understand the various desires and joys
of living beings,
as well as their aims and abilities,
and can adjust to what they are capable of,
employing innumerable similes
to expound the Law for them.
Utilizing the good roots
laid down by living beings in previous existences,
distinguishing between those whose roots are mature
and those whose roots are not yet mature,
they exercise various calculations,
discriminations and perceptions,
and then take the one vehicle way and,
in accordance with what is appropriate, preach it as three.

5

THE PARABLE OF
THE MEDICINAL HERBS

At that time the World-Honored One said to Mahakashyapa and the other major disciples: "Excellent, excellent, Kashyapa. You have given an excellent description of the true blessings of the Thus Come One. It is just as you have said. The Thus Come One indeed has immeasurable, boundless, asamkhyas of blessings, and though you and the others were to spend immeasurable millions of kalpas in the effort, you could never finish describing them.

"Kashyapa, you should understand this. The Thus Come One is king of the doctrines. In what he preaches, there is nothing that is vain. With regard to all the various doctrines, he employs wisdom as an expedient means in expounding them. Therefore the doctrines that he expounds all extend to the point where there is comprehensive wisdom. The Thus Come One observes and understands the end to which all doctrines tend. And he also understands the workings of the deepest mind of all living beings, penetrating them completely and without hindrance. And with regard to the doctrines he is thoroughly enlightened, and he reveals to living beings the totality of wisdom.

"Kashyapa, it is like the plants and trees, thickets and groves, and the medicinal herbs, widely ranging in variety, each with its own name and hue, that grow in the hills and streams, the valleys and different soils of the thousand-millionfold world. Dense clouds spread over them, covering the entire thousand-millionfold world and in one moment saturating it all. The moisture penetrates to all the plants and trees, thickets and groves, and medicinal herbs equally, to their little roots, little stems, little limbs, little leaves, their middle-sized roots, middle-sized stems, middle-sized limbs, middle-sized leaves, to their big roots, big stems, big limbs and big leaves. Each of the trees big and small, depending upon whether it is superior, middling or inferior in nature, receives its allotment. The rain falling from one blanket of cloud accords with each particular species and nature, causing it to sprout and mature, to blossom and bear fruit. Though all these plants and trees grow in the same earth and are moistened by the same rain, each has its differences and particulars.

"Kashyapa, you should understand that the Thus Come One is like this. He appears in the world like a great cloud rising up. With a loud voice he penetrates to all the heavenly and human beings and the asuras of the entire world, like a great cloud spreading over the thousand-millionfold lands. And in the midst of the great assembly, he addresses these words, saying: 'I am the Thus Come One, worthy of offerings, of right and universal knowledge, perfect clarity and conduct, well gone, understanding the world, unexcelled worthy, trainer of people, teacher of heavenly and human beings, Buddha, World-Honored One. Those who have not yet crossed over I will cause to cross over, those not yet freed I will free, those not yet at rest I will put at rest, those not yet in nirvana I will cause to attain nirvana. Of this existence and future existences I understand the true circumstances. I am one who knows all things, sees all things, understands the way, opens up the way, preaches the way. You heavenly and human beings, asuras and others, you must all come here so that I may let you hear the Dharma!'

"At that time living beings of countless thousands, ten thousands, millions of species come to the place where the Buddha is, to listen to the Dharma. The Thus Come One then observes whether the capacities of these living beings are keen or dull, whether they are diligent in their efforts or lazy. And in accordance with what each is capable of hearing, he preaches the Law for them in an immeasurable variety of ways so that all of them are delighted and are able to gain excellent benefits therefrom.

"Once these living beings have heard the Law, they will enjoy peace and security in their present existence and good circumstances in future existences, when they will receive joy through the way and again be able to hear the Law. And having heard the Law, they will escape from obstacles and hindrances, and with regard to the various doctrines will be able to exercise their powers to the fullest, so that gradually they can enter into the way. It is like the rain falling from that great cloud upon all the plants and trees, thickets and groves, and medicinal herbs. Each, depending upon its species and nature, receives its full share of moistening and is enabled to sprout and grow.

"The Law preached by the Thus Come One is of one form, one flavor, namely, the form of emancipation, the form of separation, the form of extinction, which in the end comes down to a wisdom embracing all species. When the living beings hear the Law of the Thus Come One, though they may embrace, read and recite it, and practice it as it dictates, they themselves do not realize or understand the blessings they are gaining thereby. Why is this? Because only the Thus Come One understands the species, the form, the substance, the nature of these living beings. He knows what things they dwell on, what things they ponder, what things they practice. He knows how they dwell on them, how they ponder, how they practice. He knows what Law they dwell on, what Law they ponder, what Law they practice, through what Law they attain what Law.

"Living beings exist in a variety of environments, but only the Thus Come One sees the true circumstances and fully understands them without hindrance. It is like those plants and trees, thickets and groves, and medicinal herbs which do not themselves know whether they are superior, middling or inferior in nature. But the Thus Come One knows that this is the Law of one form, one flavor, namely, the form of emancipation, the form of separation, the form of extinction, the form of ultimate nirvana, of constant tranquility and extinction, which in the end finds its destination in emptiness. The Buddha understands all this. But because he can see the desires that are in the minds of living beings, he guides and protects them, and for this reason does not immediately preach to them the wisdom that embraces all species.

"You and the others, Kashyapa, have done a very rare thing, for you can understand how the Thus Come One preaches the Law in accordance with what is appropriate, you can have faith in it, you can accept it. Why do I say this? Because the fact that the Buddhas, the World-Honored Ones, preach the Law in accordance with what is appropriate is hard to comprehend, hard to understand."

At that time the World-Honored One, wishing to state his meaning once more, spoke in verse form, saying:

> The Dharma King, destroyer of being,
> when he appears in the world
> accords with the desires of living beings,
> preaching the Law in a variety of ways.
> The Thus Come One, worthy of honor and reverence,
> is profound and far-reaching in wisdom.
> For long he remained silent regarding the essential,
> in no hurry to speak of it at once.
> If those who are wise hear of it
> they can believe and understand it,
> but those without wisdom will have doubts and regrets
> and for all time will remain in error.
> For this reason, Kashyapa,
> he adjusts to the person's power when preaching,
> taking advantage of various causes
> and enabling the person to gain a correct view.
> Kashyapa, you should understand
> that it is like a great cloud
> that rises up in the world
> and covers it all over.

This beneficent cloud is laden with moisture,
the lightning gleams and flashes,
and the sound of thunder reverberates afar,
causing the multitude to rejoice.
The sun's rays are veiled and hidden,
a clear coolness comes over the land;
masses of darkness descend and spread—
you can almost touch them.
The rain falls everywhere,
coming down on all four sides.
Its flow and saturation are measureless,
reaching to every area of the earth,
to the ravines and valleys of the mountains and streams,
to the remote and secluded places where grow
plants, bushes, medicinal herbs,
trees large and small,
a hundred grains, rice seedlings,
sugar cane, grape vines.
The rain moistens them all,
none fails to receive its full share.
The parched ground is everywhere watered,
herbs and trees alike grow lush.
What falls from the cloud
is water of a single flavor,
but the plants and trees, thickets and groves,
each accept the moisture that is appropriate to its portion.
All the various trees,
whether superior, middling or inferior,
take what is fitting for large or small
and each is enabled to sprout and grow.
Root, stem, limb, leaf,
the glow and hue of flower and fruit—
one rain extends to them
and all are able to become fresh and glossy.
Whether their allotment
of substance, form and nature is large or small,
the moistening they receive is one,
but each grows and flourishes in its own way.

The Buddha is like this
when he appears in the world,
comparable to a great cloud
that covers all things everywhere.
Having appeared in the world,
for the sake of living beings
he makes distinctions in expounding
the truth regarding phenomena.
The great sage, the World-Honored One,
to heavenly and human beings,
in the midst of all beings,
pronounces these words:
I am the Thus Come One,
most honored of two-legged beings.
I appear in the world
like a great cloud
that showers moisture upon
all the dry and withered living beings,
so that all are able to escape suffering,
gain the joy of peace and security,
the joys of this world
and the joy of nirvana.
All you heavenly and human beings of this assembly,
listen carefully and with one mind!
All of you should gather around
and observe the one of unexcelled honor.
I am the World-Honored One,
none can rival me.
In order to bring peace and security to living beings
I have appeared in the world
and for the sake of this great assembly
I preach the sweet dew of the pure Law.
This Law is of a single flavor,
that of emancipation, nirvana.
With a single wonderful sound
I expound and unfold its meaning;
constantly for the sake of the Great Vehicle
I create causes and conditions.

I look upon all things
as being universally equal,
I have no mind to favor this or that,
to love one or hate another.
I am without greed or attachment
and without limitation or hindrance.
At all times, for all things
I preach the Law equally;
as I would for a single person,
that same way I do for numerous persons.
Constantly I expound and preach the Law,
never have I done anything else,
coming, going, sitting, standing,
never to the end growing weary or disheartened.
I bring fullness and satisfaction to the world,
like a rain that spreads its moisture everywhere.
Eminent and lowly, superior and inferior,
observers of precepts, violators of precepts,
those fully endowed with proper demeanor,
those not fully endowed,
those of correct views, of erroneous views,
of keen capacity, of dull capacity—
I cause the Dharma rain to rain on all equally,
never lax or neglectful.
When all the various living beings
hear my Law,
they receive it according to their power,
dwelling in their different environments.
Some inhabit the realm of human and heavenly beings,
of wheel-turning sage kings,
Shakra, Brahma and the other kings—
these are the inferior medicinal herbs.
Some understand the Law of no outflows,
are able to attain nirvana,
to acquire the six transcendental powers
and gain in particular the three understandings,
or live alone in mountain forests,
constantly practicing meditation

and gaining the enlightenment of pratyekabuddhas—
these are the middling medicinal herbs.
Still others seek the place of the World-Honored One,
convinced that they can become Buddhas,
putting forth diligent effort and practicing meditation—
these are the superior medicinal herbs.
Again there are sons of the Buddha
who devote their minds solely to the Buddha way,
constantly practicing mercy and compassion,
knowing that they themselves will attain Buddhahood,
certain of it and never doubting—
these I call the small trees.
Those who abide in peace in their transcendental powers,
turning the wheel of non-regression,
saving innumerable millions
of hundreds of thousands of living beings—
bodhisattvas such as these
I call the large trees.
The equality of the Buddha's preaching
is like a rain of a single flavor,
but depending upon the nature of the living being,
the way in which it is received is not uniform,
just as the various plants and trees
each receive the moisture in a different manner.
The Buddha employs this parable
as an expedient means to open up and reveal the matter,
using various kinds of words and phrases
and expounding the single Law,
but in terms of the Buddha wisdom
this is no more than one drop of the ocean.
I rain down the Dharma rain,
filling the whole world,
and this single-flavored Dharma
is practiced by each according to the individual's power.
It is like those thickets and groves,
medicinal herbs and trees
which, according to whether they are large or small,
bit by bit grow lush and beautiful.

The Law of the Buddhas
is constantly of a single flavor,
causing the many worlds
to attain full satisfaction everywhere;
by practicing gradually and stage by stage,
all beings can gain the fruits of the way.
The voice-hearers and pratyekabuddhas
inhabit the mountain forests,
dwelling in their final existence,
hearing the Law and gaining its fruits—
we may call them medicinal herbs
that grow and mature each in its own way.
If there are bodhisattvas
who are steadfast and firm in wisdom,
who fully comprehend the threefold world
and seek the supreme vehicle,
these we call the small trees
that achieve growth and maturity.
Again there are those who dwell in meditation,
who have gained the strength of transcendental powers,
have heard of the emptiness of all phenomena,
greatly rejoice in it in their minds
and emit countless rays of light
to save living beings—
these we call large trees
that have gained growth and maturity.
In this way, Kashyapa,
the Law preached by the Buddha
is comparable to a great cloud
which, with a single-flavored rain,
moistens human flowers
so that each is able to bear fruit.
Kashyapa, you should understand
that through various causes and conditions,
various kinds of simile and parable,
I open up and reveal the Buddha way.
This is an expedient means I employ
and the same is true of the other Buddhas.

Now for you and the others
I preach the utmost truth:
none in the multitude of voice-hearers
has entered the stage of extinction.
What you are practicing
is the bodhisattva way,
and as you gradually advance in practice and learning
you are all certain to attain Buddhahood.

6
BESTOWAL OF PROPHECY

At that time the World-Honored One, having finished reciting these verses, made an announcement to the great assembly, speaking in these words: "This disciple of mine Mahakashyapa in future existences will be able to enter the presence of three thousand billion Buddhas, World-Honored Ones, to offer alms, pay reverence, honor and praise them, widely proclaiming the innumerable great doctrines of the Buddhas. And in his final incarnation he will be able to become a Buddha named Light Bright Thus Come One, worthy of offerings, of right and universal knowledge, perfect clarity and conduct, well gone, understanding the world, unexcelled worthy, trainer of people, teacher of heavenly and human beings, Buddha, World-Honored One.

His land will be called Light Virtue and his kalpa will be called Great Adornment. The life span of this Buddha will be twelve small kalpas. His Correct Law will endure in the world for twenty small kalpas, and his Counterfeit Law for twenty small kalpas.

"His realm will be majestically adorned, free of defilement or evil, shards or rubble, thorns or briers, or the unclean refuse of latrines. The land will be level and smooth, without high places or sags, pits or knolls. The ground will be of lapis lazuli, with rows of jeweled trees and ropes of gold to mark the boundaries of the roads. Jeweled flowers will be scattered around, and everywhere will be pure and clean. The bodhisattvas of that realm will number countless thousands of millions, and the multitude of voice-hearers will likewise be innumerable. There will be no workings of the devil, and although the devil and the devil's people will be there, they will all protect the Law of the Buddha."

At that time the World-Honored One, wishing to state his meaning once more, spoke in verse form, saying:

> I announce this to the monks:
> when I employ the Buddha eye
> to observe Kashyapa here,
> I see that in a future existence,
> after innumerable kalpas have passed,
> he will be able to attain Buddhahood.
> In future existences
> he will offer alms and enter the presence
> of three thousand billion
> Buddhas, World-Honored Ones.
> For the sake of the Buddha wisdom
> he will carry out brahma practices meticulously
> and will offer alms to the unexcelled ones,
> the most honored of two-legged beings.
> After he has done so, and has practiced
> all the unsurpassed types of wisdom,
> in his final incarnation
> he will be able to become a Buddha.
> His land will be pure and clean,

the ground of lapis lazuli.
Many jeweled trees
will line the roadsides,
with golden ropes to mark the roads,
and those who see it will rejoice.
It will constantly emit a pleasing fragrance,
with heaps of rare flowers scattered around
and many kinds of strange and wonderful things
for its adornment.
The land will be level and smooth,
without hills or depressions.
The multitude of bodhisattvas
will be beyond calculation,
their minds subdued and gentle,
having attained great transcendental powers,
and they will uphold and embrace
the Great Vehicle scriptures of the Buddhas.
The multitude of voice-hearers
will be free of outflows, in their last incarnation,
sons of the Dharma King,
and their number too will be beyond calculation—
even when one looks with the heavenly eye
one cannot determine their number.
This Buddha will have a life span
of twelve small kalpas.
His Correct Law will endure in the world
for twenty small kalpas,
and his Counterfeit Law
for twenty small kalpas.
Light Bright World-Honored One
will be of this description.

At that time the great Maudgalyayana, Subhuti and Mahakatya-yana, all of them trembling with agitation, pressed their palms to-gether with a single mind and gazed up at the World-Honored One, their eyes never leaving him for an instant. Joining their voices in a single sound, they spoke in verse form, saying:

Great hero and stalwart, World-Honored One,
Dharma King of the Shakyas,
because you have pity on us,
favor us with the Buddha voice!
If, because you understand our innermost minds,
you bestow a prophecy of Buddhahood upon us,
it would be like sweet dew bathing us,
washing away fever and imparting coolness.
Suppose that someone coming from a land of famine
should suddenly encounter a great king's feast.
His heart still filled with doubt and fear,
he would not dare to eat the food at once,
but if he were instructed by the king to do so,
then he would venture to eat.
We now are like such a person,
for whenever we recall the errors of the Lesser Vehicle,
we do not know what we should do
to gain the Buddha's unsurpassed wisdom.
Though we hear the Buddha's voice
telling us that we will attain Buddhahood,
in our hearts we still harbor anxiety and fear,
like that person who did not dare to eat.
But now if the Buddha's prophecy is bestowed upon us,
then joy and peace of mind will quickly be ours.
Great hero and stalwart, World-Honored One,
your constant desire is to set the world at ease.
We beg you to bestow such a prophecy on us,
as you would instruct a starving person to eat.

At that time the World-Honored One, understanding the thoughts in the minds of his major disciples, made this announcement to the monks: "Subhuti here in future existences will enter the presence of three hundred ten thousand million nayutas of Buddhas, offering alms, paying reverence, honoring and praising them. He will constantly carry out brahma practices and fulfill the bodhisattva way, and in his final incarnation he will be able to attain Buddhahood. His title will be Rare Form Thus Come One, worthy of offerings, of right and universal knowledge, perfect clarity and conduct, well gone, understanding the world, unexcelled worthy, trainer of people, teacher of heavenly and human beings, Buddha, World-Honored One. His kalpa will be named Possessed of Jewels and his realm will be named Jewel Born. The land will be level and smooth, the ground made of crystal, it will be adorned with jeweled trees and be free of hills and pits, rubble and thorns and the filth from latrines. Jeweled flowers will cover the ground and everywhere will be pure and clean. The people of his realm will all dwell on jeweled terraces, in rare and wonderful towers and pavilions. His voice-hearer disciples will be countless, boundless, beyond the scope of calculation or simile. The multitude of bodhisattvas will number countless thousands, ten thousands, millions of nayutas. The life span of this Buddha will be twelve small kalpas, his Correct Law will endure in the world for twenty small kalpas, and his Counterfeit Law for twenty small kalpas. This Buddha will constantly dwell in midair, preaching the Law for the assembly and saving numberless multitudes of bodhisattvas and voice-hearers."

At that time the World-Honored One, wishing to state his meaning once more, spoke in verse form, saying:

> You multitude of monks,
> I now announce this to you.
> All of you with a single mind
> should hear what I say.
> My major disciple
> Subhuti
> is destined to become a Buddha
> with the title Rare Form.
> He will offer alms to countless
> tens of thousands and millions of Buddhas.
> By following the practices of the Buddhas
> he will gradually fulfill the great way,
> and in his final incarnation
> will acquire the thirty-two features.
> He will be imposing, exceptional, wonderful,
> like a jeweled mountain.
> His Buddha land
> will be foremost in adornment and purity;
> no living being who sees it

will fail to love and delight in it.
There in the midst, that Buddha
will save unreckonable multitudes.
In that Buddha's Law
will be many bodhisattvas,
all of them with keen capacities,
turning the wheel of non-regression.
That land will constantly
be adorned with bodhisattvas.
The multitude of voice-hearers
will be beyond calculation,
all gaining the three understandings
and exercising the six transcendental powers.
They will dwell in the eight emancipations
and possess great authority and virtue.
The Law preached by that Buddha
will manifest immeasurable
transcendental powers and transformations
of a wondrous nature.
Heavenly and human beings
in numbers like Ganges sands
will all press their palms together,
listen to and receive the Buddha's words.
That Buddha will have a life span
of twelve small kalpas,
his Correct Law will endure in the world
for twenty small kalpas
and his Counterfeit Law
for twenty small kalpas.

At that time the World-Honored One once more spoke to the
multitude of monks: "Now I say this to you. Great Katyayana here in
future existences will present various articles as offerings and will
serve eight thousand million Buddhas, paying honor and reverence to
them. After these Buddhas have passed into extinction, he will raise a
memorial tower for each one measuring a thousand yojanas in height
and exactly five hundred yojanas in both width and depth. It will be
made of gold, silver, lapis lazuli, seashell, agate, pearl, and carnelian,

with these seven precious substances joined together. Numerous flowers, necklaces, paste incense, powdered incense, incense for burning, silken canopies, streamers and banners will be presented as offerings to the memorial towers. And after this has been done, he will once more make offerings to twenty thousands of millions of Buddhas, and will repeat the entire process.

"When he has finished offering alms to all the Buddhas, he will fulfill the way of the bodhisattva and will become a Buddha with the title Jambunada Gold Light Thus Come One, worthy of offerings, of right and universal knowledge, perfect clarity and conduct, well gone, understanding the world, unexcelled worthy, trainer of people, teacher of heavenly and human beings, Buddha, World-Honored One.

"His land will be level and smooth, the ground made of crystal, adorned with jeweled trees, with ropes of gold to mark the boundaries of the roads. Wonderful flowers will cover the ground, everywhere will be pure and clean, and all who see it will rejoice. The four evil paths of existence, hell and the realms of hungry spirits, beasts and asuras, will not exist there. There will be many heavenly and human beings, and multitudes of voice-hearers and bodhisattvas in innumerable tens of thousands of millions will adorn the land. That Buddha's life span will be twelve small kalpas, his Correct Law will endure in the world for twenty small kalpas, and his Counterfeit Law for twenty small kalpas."

At that time the World-Honored One, wishing to state his meaning once more, spoke in verse form, saying:

> You multitude of monks,
> listen all of you with a single mind,
> for in what I speak
> there is nothing that departs from the truth.
> Katyayana here
> will give various kinds
> of fine and wonderful articles
> as offerings to the Buddhas.
> And after the Buddhas have entered extinction
> he will raise seven-jeweled towers
> and present flowers and incense
> as offerings to their relics.

And in his final incarnation
he will gain Buddha wisdom
and achieve impartial and correct enlightenment.
His land will be pure and clean
and he will save innumerable
ten thousands of millions of living beings,
and will receive offerings
from all the ten directions.
This Buddha's brilliance
no one will be able to equal.
His Buddha title will be
Jambu Gold Light.
Bodhisattvas and voice-hearers,
cutting off all forms of existence,
countless and immeasurable in number,
will adorn his land.

At that time the World-Honored One spoke again to the great assembly: "Now I say this to you. Great Maudgalyayana here will present various kinds of articles as offerings to eight thousand Buddhas, paying honor and reverence to them. After these Buddhas have passed into extinction, for each of them he will raise a memorial tower measuring a thousand yojanas in height and exactly five hundred yojanas in width and depth. It will be made of gold, silver, lapis lazuli, seashell, agate, pearl, and carnelian, with these seven precious substances joined together. Numerous flowers, necklaces, paste incense, powdered incense, incense for burning, silken canopies, streamers and banners will be presented as offerings. After this has been done, he will also make offerings to two hundred ten thousand million Buddhas, repeating the process.

"Then he will be able to become a Buddha with the title Tamalapatra Sandalwood Fragrance Thus Come One, worthy of offerings, of right and universal knowledge, perfect clarity and conduct, well gone, understanding the world, unexcelled worthy, trainer of people, teacher of heavenly and human beings, Buddha, World-Honored One. His kalpa will be named Joy Replete and his realm Mind Delight. The land will be level and smooth, the ground made of crystal, jeweled trees will adorn it, pearls and flowers will be scattered around, everywhere will be pure and clean, and all who see it will rejoice. There will be many heavenly and human beings, and the bodhisattvas and voice-hearers will be immeasurable in number. That Buddha's life span will be twenty-four small kalpas, his Correct Law will endure in the world for forty small kalpas, and his Counterfeit Law for forty small kalpas."

At that time the World-Honored One, wishing to state his meaning once more, spoke in verse form, saying:

> This disciple of mine,
> the great Maudgalyayana,
> when he has cast off his present body,
> will be able to see eight thousand,
> two hundred ten thousand million
> Buddhas, World-Honored Ones,
> and for the sake of the Buddha way
> will offer alms, honor and reverence them.
> Where these Buddhas are
> he will constantly carry out brahma practices
> and for immeasurable kalpas
> will uphold and embrace the Buddha Law.
> When these Buddhas have passed into extinction
> he will raise seven-jeweled towers,
> with golden implements to mark the spot for all time
> and flowers, incense and music
> presented as offerings
> in the memorial towers of the Buddhas.
> Step by step he will fulfill
> all the duties of the bodhisattva way
> and in the land called Mind Delight
> will be able to become a Buddha
> named Tamalapatra
> Sandalwood Fragrance.
> This Buddha's life span
> will be twenty-four kalpas.
> Constantly for the sake of heavenly and human beings
> he will expound the Buddha way.
> Voice-hearers innumerable
> as Ganges sands,

with the three understandings and six transcendental powers,
will display great authority and virtue.
Countless bodhisattvas
will be of firm will, diligent in effort,
and with regard to the Buddha wisdom
none will ever retrogress.
After this Buddha has passed into extinction,
his Correct Law will endure
for forty small kalpas,
and his Counterfeit Law will do likewise.
My various disciples,
fully endowed with dignity and virtue,
number five hundred,
and every one will receive such a prophecy.
In a future existence
all will be able to attain Buddhahood.
Concerning the causes and conditions of past existences
as they pertain to me and you
I will now preach.
You must listen carefully.

7

THE PARABLE OF
THE PHANTOM CITY

The Buddha made this announcement to the monks: Once in the past, an immeasurable, boundless, inconceivable asamkhya number of kalpas ago, there was at that time a Buddha named Great Universal Wisdom Excellence Thus Come One, worthy of offerings, of right and universal knowledge, perfect clarity and conduct, well gone, understanding the world, unexcelled worthy, trainer of people, teacher of heavenly and human beings, Buddha, World-Honored One. His land was named Well Constituted and his kalpa was named Great Form.

"Now monks, since that Buddha passed into extinction, a very great, a very long time has passed. Suppose, for example, that someone took all the earth particles in the thousand-millionfold world and ground them up to make ink powder, and as he passed through the thousand lands of the east, he dropped one grain of the ink powder no bigger in size than a speck of dust. Again, when he passed through another thousand lands, he dropped another grain of ink. Suppose he went on in this way until he had finished dropping all the grains of ink made from the earth particles. Now what is your opinion? Do you think that, with regard to those lands, the masters of calculation or the disciples of the masters of calculation would be able to determine the number of lands that had been visited in the process, or would they not?"

"That would be impossible, World-Honored One."

"Now monks, suppose that one should take the earth of all the lands this man had passed through, whether he dropped a grain of ink there or not, and should pound it up into dust. And suppose that one particle of dust should represent one kalpa. The kalpas that had elapsed since that Buddha entered extinction would still exceed the number of dust particles by immeasurable, boundless, hundreds, thousands, ten thousands, millions of asamkhya kalpas. But because I employ the Thus Come One's power to know and see, when I look at that far-off time it seems like today."

At that time the World-Honored One, wishing to state his meaning once more, spoke in verse form, saying:

> When I think of it, in the past,
> immeasurable, boundless kalpas ago,
> there was a Buddha, most honored of two-legged beings,
> named Great Universal Wisdom Excellence.
> If a person should use his strength to smash
> the ground of the thousand-millionfold world,
> should completely crush its earth particles
> and reduce them all to powdered ink,
> and if when he passed through a thousand lands
> he should drop one speck of ink,
> and if he continued in this manner
> until he had exhausted all the specks of ink,
> and if one then took the soil of the lands he had passed
>   through,

both those he dropped a speck in and those he did not,
and once more ground their earth into dust,
and then took one grain of dust to represent one kalpa—
the number of tiny grains of dust would be less
than the number of kalpas in the past when that Buddha lived.
Since that Buddha passed into extinction,
an immeasurable number of kalpas such as this have passed.
The Thus Come One, through his unhindered wisdom,
knows the time when that Buddha passed into extinction
and his voice-hearers and bodhisattvas
as though he were witnessing that extinction right now.
You monks should understand
that the Buddha wisdom is pure, subtle, wonderful,
without outflows, without hindrance,
reaching to and penetrating immeasurable kalpas.

The Buddha announced to the monks: "The Buddha Great Universal Wisdom Excellence had a life span of five hundred and forty ten
thousand million nayutas of kalpas. This Buddha at first sat in the
place of practice and, having smashed the armies of the devil, was on
the point of attaining anuttara-samyak-sambodhi, but the doctrines of
the Buddhas did not appear before him. This state continued for one
small kalpa, and so on for ten small kalpas, the Buddha sitting with
legs crossed, body and mind unmoving, but the doctrines of the Buddhas still did not appear before him.

"At that time the heavenly beings of the Trayastrimsha heaven had
earlier spread a lion seat measuring one yojana in height underneath a
bodhi tree for the Buddha, intending that the Buddha should sit on
this when he attained anuttara-samyak-sambodhi. As soon as the
Buddha took his seat there, the Brahma kings caused a multitude of
heavenly flowers to rain down, covering the ground for a hundred
yojanas around. From time to time a fragrant wind would come up
and blow the withered flowers away, whereupon new ones would rain
down. This continued without interruption for the space of ten small
kalpas as an offering to the Buddha. Up until the time he entered
extinction, such flowers constantly rained down. The Four Heavenly
Kings as their offering to the Buddha constantly beat on heavenly

drums, while the other heavenly beings played heavenly musical instruments, all for ten small kalpas. Until the Buddha entered extinction, such was the state of affairs.

"Now, monks, the Buddha Great Universal Wisdom Excellence passed ten small kalpas before the doctrines of the Buddhas finally appeared before him and he was able to attain anuttara-samyak-sambodhi. Before this Buddha left the householder's life, he had sixteen sons, the first of whom was named Wisdom Accumulated. These sons each had various kinds of rare objects and toys of one kind or another, but when they heard that their father had attained anuttara-samyak-sambodhi, they all threw aside their rare objects and went to where the Buddha was. Their mothers, weeping, followed after them.

"Their grandfather, who was a wheel-turning sage king, along with a hundred chief ministers, as well as a hundred, thousand, ten thousand, million of his subjects, all together surrounded the sons and followed them to the place of practice, all wishing to draw close to the Great Universal Wisdom Excellence Thus Come One, to offer alms, pay honor, venerate and praise him. When they arrived, they touched their heads to the ground and bowed before his feet. When they had finished circling the Buddha, they pressed their palms together with a single mind, gazed up in reverence at the World-Honored One, and recited these verses of praise, saying:

> The World-Honored One, of great authority and virtue,
> in order to save living beings
> spent immeasurable millions of years
> and at last succeeded in becoming a Buddha.
> All your vows have now been fulfilled—
> it is well—no fortune could be greater!
> The World-Honored One is very rarely met with;
> having taken his seat, ten small kalpas pass.
> His body and his hands and feet
> rest in stillness, never moving,
> his mind constantly calm and placid,
> never in turmoil or disorder.
> In the end he attains eternal tranquility and extinction,
> resting in the Law of no outflows.
> Now as we observe the World-Honored One

in tranquility, having completed the Buddha way,
we gain excellent benefits
and praise and congratulate him with great joy.
Living beings undergo constant suffering and anguish,
benighted, without teacher or guide,
not realizing there is a way to end suffering,
not knowing how to seek emancipation.
Through the long night increasingly they follow evil paths,
reducing the multitude of heavenly beings;
from darkness they enter into darkness,
to the end never hearing the Buddha's name.
But now the Buddha has attained the unexcelled,
the tranquility of the Law of no outflows.
We and the heavenly and human beings
hereby obtain the greatest benefit.
For this reason all of us bow our heads,
dedicate our lives to the one of unexcelled honor.

At that time the sixteen princes, having praised the Buddha in these verses, urged the World-Honored One to turn the wheel of the Law, speaking all together in these words: "World-Honored One, expound the Law. By doing so, you will bring tranquility to and will comfort and benefit heavenly and human beings in large measure." They repeated this request in verse form, saying:

World hero without peer,
you who adorn yourself with a hundred blessings,
you have attained unsurpassed wisdom—
we beg you to preach for the sake of the world.
Save and free us
and other kinds of living beings.
Draw distinctions, enlighten us
and allow us to attain wisdom.
If we can gain Buddhahood,
then all living beings can do likewise.
World-Honored One, you know the thoughts
that living beings hold deep in their minds.
You know the paths they tread

and you know the strength of their wisdom,
their pleasures, the blessings they have cultivated,
the actions they have carried out in past existences.
World-Honored One, all this you know already—
now you must turn the unsurpassed wheel!

The Buddha announced to the monks: "When the Buddha Great Universal Wisdom Excellence attained anuttara-samyak-sambodhi, five hundred ten thousand million Buddha worlds in each of the ten directions trembled and shook in six different ways. The dark and secluded places within those lands, where the light of the sun and moon is never able to penetrate, were all brightly illuminated and the living beings were all able to see one another, and they all exclaimed, saying, 'How is it that living beings have suddenly come into existence in this place?'

"Also the palaces of the various heavenly beings in those lands and the Brahma palaces trembled and shook in six different ways and a great light shone everywhere, completely filling the worlds and surpassing the light of the heavens. At that time in five hundred ten thousand million lands in the eastern direction the Brahma palaces shone with a brilliant light that was twice its ordinary brightness, and the Brahma kings each thought to himself, Now the brilliance of the palace is greater than ever in the past. What can be the cause of this phenomenon?

"At that time the Brahma kings visited one another to discuss this matter. Among them was a great Brahma king named Save All who, on behalf of the multitude of Brahma kings, spoke these verses, saying:

> Our palaces have a brilliance
> never known in the past.
> What is the cause of this?
> Each of us seeks an answer.
> Is it because of the birth of some heavenly being of great
> virtue,
> or because the Buddha has appeared in the world
> that this great brilliant light
> shines everywhere in the ten directions?

"At that time the Brahma kings of five hundred ten thousand million lands, accompanied by their palaces, each king taking his outer robe and filling it with heavenly flowers, journeyed together to the western region to observe the signs there. They saw the Great Universal Wisdom Excellence Thus Come One in the place of practice, seated on a lion seat underneath a bodhi tree, with heavenly beings, dragon kings, gandharvas, kimnaras, mahoragas, human, and nonhuman beings surrounding him and paying reverence. And they saw the sixteen princes entreating the Buddha to turn the wheel of the Law.

"At once the Brahma kings touched their heads to the ground and bowed before the Buddha, circled around him a hundred thousand times, and then took the heavenly flowers and scattered them over the Buddha. The flowers they scattered piled up like Mount Sumeru. They also offered them as alms to the Buddha's bodhi tree. This bodhi tree was ten yojanas in height. When they had finished offering the flowers, each one took his palace and presented it to the Buddha, speaking these words: 'We hope you will bestow comfort and benefit on us. We beg you to accept and occupy these palaces that we present.'

"At that time the Brahma kings, in the presence of the Buddha, with a single mind and joined voices recited these verses of praise:

> World-Honored One, very rarely met with,
> one whom it is difficult to encounter,
> endowed with immeasurable blessings,
> capable of saving everyone,
> great teacher of heavenly and human beings,
> you bestow pity and comfort on the world.
> Living beings in the ten directions
> all receive benefit everywhere.
> In the five hundred ten thousand million lands
> from which we come,
> we have put aside the joy of deep meditation
> in order to offer alms to the Buddha.
> Because of our good fortune in previous existences
> our palaces are very richly adorned.
> Now we present them to the World-Honored One,
> begging that he be kind enough to accept them.

"At that time, when the Brahma kings had finished praising the Buddha in verse, they each spoke these words: 'We beg the World-Honored One to turn the wheel of the Law, save living beings, and open up the way to nirvana!'

"Then the Brahma kings with a single mind and joined voices spoke in verse form, saying:

> World hero, most honored of two-legged beings,
> we beg you to expound the Law.
> Through the power of your great mercy and compassion,
> save living beings in their suffering and anguish!

"At that time the Great Universal Wisdom Excellence Thus Come One silently agreed to do so. Now, monks, in five hundred ten thousand million lands in the southeast, the Brahma kings each observed that his palace was shining with a brilliant light such as had never been known in the past. Dancing for joy, entering a frame of mind seldom experienced, they went about visiting one another and discussing these things together.

"At that time there was among the assembly a great Brahma king named Great Compassion who, on behalf of the multitude of Brahma kings, spoke in verse form, saying:

> What cause is in operation
> that such a sign should be manifest?
> Our palaces display a brilliance
> never known before.
> Is it because of the birth of some heavenly being of
> great virtue,
> or because the Buddha has appeared in the world?
> We have never seen such a sign
> and with a single mind we seek the reason.
> Though we must travel a thousand, ten thousand, a
> million lands,
> together we will search out the cause of this light.
> Likely it is because the Buddha has appeared in the world
> to save living beings in their suffering.

"At that time the five hundred ten thousand million Brahma kings, accompanied by their palaces, each king taking his outer robe and filling it with heavenly flowers, journeyed together to the northwestern region to observe the signs there. They saw the Great Universal Wisdom Excellence Thus Come One in the place of practice, seated on a lion seat beneath a bodhi tree, with heavenly beings, dragon kings, gandharvas, kimnaras, mahoragas, human and nonhuman beings surrounding him and paying reverence. And they saw the sixteen princes entreating the Buddha to turn the wheel of the Law.

"At once the Brahma kings touched their heads to the ground and bowed before the Buddha, circled around him a hundred thousand times, and then took the heavenly flowers and scattered them over the Buddha. The flowers they scattered piled up like Mount Sumeru. They also offered them as alms to the Buddha's bodhi tree. When they had finished offering the flowers, each one took his palace and presented it to the Buddha, speaking these words: 'We hope you will bestow comfort and benefit on us. We beg you to accept and occupy these palaces that we present.'

"At that time the Brahma kings, in the presence of the Buddha, with a single mind and joined voices recited these verses of praise:

Sage lord, heavenly being among heavenly beings,
voiced like the kalavinka bird,
you who pity and comfort living beings,
we now pay you honor and reverence.
The World-Honored One is very rarely met with,
appearing only once in many long ages.
One hundred and eighty kalpas
have passed in vain without a Buddha,
when the three evil paths were everywhere
and the multitude of heavenly beings was reduced in number.
Now the Buddha has appeared in the world
to be an eye for living beings.
The world will hurry to him
and he will save and guard one and all.
He will be a father to living beings,
comforting and benefiting them.

We, through the good fortune of past existences,
now are able to encounter the World-Honored One.

"At that time, after the Brahma kings had recited these verses in praise of the Buddha, they each spoke these words: 'We beg the World-Honored One to pity and comfort one and all, to turn the wheel of the Law and save living beings.'

"Then the Brahma kings with a single mind and joined voices spoke in verse form, saying:

Great sage, turn the wheel of the Law,
reveal the characteristics of teachings,
save living beings in their suffering and anguish,
allow them to attain great joy.
When living beings hear this Law
they will gain the way or be reborn in heaven;
those in the evil paths will be reduced in number
and those patient in goodness will increase.

"At that time the Great Universal Wisdom Excellence Thus Come One silently agreed to do so. Now, monks, in five hundred ten thousand million lands in the southern region the Brahma kings each observed that his palace was shining with a brilliant light such as had never been known in the past. Dancing with joy, entering a frame of mind seldom experienced, they went about visiting one another and discussing these things together, saying, 'What is the reason our palaces put forth this brilliant light?'

"Among their group there was a great Brahma king named Wonderful Law who, on behalf of the multitude of Brahma kings, spoke in verse form, saying:

Our palaces
shine with exceeding brilliance.
This cannot be without reason—
it is well we should inquire.
In the past hundred thousand kalpas
such a sign has never been seen.

It is because some heavenly being of great virtue has been born, or because the Buddha has appeared in the world.

"At that time the five hundred ten thousand million Brahma kings, accompanied by their palaces, each king taking his outer robe and filling it with heavenly flowers, journeyed together to the northern region to observe the signs there. They saw the Great Universal Wisdom Excellence Thus Come One in the place of practice, seated on a lion seat beneath a bodhi tree, with heavenly beings, dragon kings, gandharvas, kimnaras, mahoragas, human and nonhuman beings surrounding him and paying reverence. And they saw the sixteen princes entreating the Buddha to turn the wheel of the Law.

"At that time the Brahma kings touched their heads to the ground and bowed before the Buddha, circled around him a hundred thousand times, and then took the heavenly flowers and scattered them over the Buddha. The flowers they scattered piled up like Mount Sumeru. They also offered them as alms to the Buddha's bodhi tree. When they had finished offering the flowers, each one took his palace and presented it to the Buddha, speaking these words: 'We hope you will bestow comfort and benefit on us. We beg you to accept and occupy these palaces that we present.'

"At that time the Brahma kings, in the presence of the Buddha, with a single mind and joined voices recited these verses of praise:

World-Honored One, most difficult to encounter,
destroyer of all earthly desires,
one hundred and thirty kalpas have passed
and now at last we can see you.
Living beings in their hunger and thirst
are made full with the rain of the Dharma.
One such as was never seen in the past,
one of immeasurable wisdom,
like the udumbara flower
today at last appears directly before us.
Our palaces because they receive your light
are wonderfully adorned.

World-Honored One, of great mercy and compassion,
we beg you to accept them.

"At that time, after the Brahma kings had recited these verses in
praise of the Buddha, they each spoke these words: 'We beg the
World-Honored One to turn the wheel of the Law and cause the
heavenly beings, devils, Brahma kings, shramanas, and Brahmans
throughout the world all to gain peace and tranquility and to attain
salvation.'

"At that time the Brahma kings with a single mind and joined
voices recited verses in praise, saying:

> We beg the most honored of heavenly and human beings
> to turn the wheel of the unsurpassed Law.
> Strike the great Dharma drum,
> blow the great Dharma conch,
> rain down the great Dharma rain all around
> to save immeasurable living beings!
> We direct all our faith and entreaties to you—
> let your profound and far-reaching voice sound out!

"At that time the Great Universal Wisdom Excellence Thus Come
One silently agreed to do so. In the southwestern region, and so on to
the lower region, a similar succession of events occurred.

"At that time in the upper region, the Brahma kings of five hundred
ten thousand million lands all observed that the palaces where they
were residing shone with a brilliant light such as had never been
known in the past. Dancing with joy, entering a frame of mind seldom
experienced, they went about visiting one another and discussing these
things together, saying, 'What is the reason our palaces put forth this
bright light?'

"Among their group there was a great Brahma king named Shikhin
who, on behalf of the multitude of Brahma kings, spoke in verse form,
saying:

> Now what is the reason
> that our palaces
> glow and shine with such authority and virtue,

adorned as never before?
A wonderful sign of this kind
has never been seen or heard of in the past.
It is because some heavenly being of great virtue has been born,
or because the Buddha has appeared in the world.

"At that time the five hundred ten thousand million Brahma kings, accompanied by their palaces, each king taking his outer robe and filling it with heavenly flowers, journeyed together to the lower region to observe the signs there. They saw the Great Universal Wisdom Excellence Thus Come One in the place of practice, seated on a lion seat beneath a bodhi tree, with heavenly beings, dragon kings, gandharvas, kimnaras, mahoragas, human and nonhuman beings surrounding him and paying reverence. And they saw the sixteen princes entreating the Buddha to turn the wheel of the Law.

"At that time the Brahma kings touched their heads to the ground and bowed before the Buddha, circled around him a hundred thousand times, and then took the heavenly flowers and scattered them over the Buddha. The flowers they scattered piled up like Mount Sumeru. They also offered them as alms to the Buddha's bodhi tree. When they had finished offering the flowers, each one took his palace and presented it to the Buddha, speaking these words: 'We hope you will bestow comfort and benefit on us. We beg you to accept and occupy these palaces that we present.'

"At that time the Brahma kings, in the presence of the Buddha, with a single mind and joined voices recited these verses of praise:

How fine, that we may see the Buddhas,
sage and venerable ones who save the world,
capable of rescuing and releasing living beings
from the hell of the threefold world!
Venerable among heavenly and human beings, of
    universal wisdom,
you pity and have mercy on the mass of burgeoning creatures,
you are capable of opening the gates of sweet dew
and broadly saving one and all.
Formerly, immeasurable kalpas
passed in vain when no Buddha was present.

The time had not yet come for the World-Honored One
    to appear,
and all in the ten directions were in constant darkness.
Those in the three evil paths increased in number
and the realm of the asuras flourished;
the multitude of heavenly beings was reduced,
and many when they died fell into the evil paths.
Since no one could attend the Buddha and hear the Law,
constantly people followed ways that were not good,
and their physical strength and wisdom
all diminished and declined.
Because of the sinful deeds they had done,
they lost all delight or the thought of delight.
They rested in heretical doctrines
and had no knowledge of good customs or rules.
Unable to be converted by the Buddha,
constantly they fell into the evil paths.
But now you, the Buddha, who will be the eye of the world,
after this long time have at last come forth.
In order to bring pity and comfort to living beings
you have appeared in the world.
You have transcended the world to gain correct enlightenment;
we are filled with delight and admiration.
We and all others in the assembly
rejoice, delighting in what we have never known before.
Our palaces because they receive your light
are wonderfully adorned.
Now we present them to the World-Honored One,
hoping he will have pity and accept them.
We beg that the merit gained through these gifts
may be spread far and wide to everyone,
so that we and other living beings
all together may attain the Buddha way.

"At that time, after the five hundred ten thousand million Brahma kings had recited these verses in praise of the Buddha, they each spoke to the Buddha, saying: 'We beg the World-Honored One to turn the wheel of the Law, bringing peace and tranquility to many, bringing salvation to many.' Then the Brahma kings spoke in verse form, saying:

> World-Honored One, turn the wheel of the Law,
> strike the Dharma drum of sweet dew,
> save living beings in their suffering and anguish,
> open up and show us the way to nirvana!
> We beg you to accept our entreaties
> and with a great, subtle and wonderful sound
> to bring pity and comfort by expounding
> the Law you have practiced for immeasurable kalpas.

"At that time the Great Universal Wisdom Excellence Thus Come One, receiving entreaties from the Brahma kings of the ten directions and from the sixteen princes, immediately gave three turnings to the twelve-spoked wheel of the Law. Neither shramana, Brahman, heavenly being, devil, Brahma, nor any other being in the world was capable of such turning. He said, 'Here is suffering, here is the origin of suffering, here is the annihilation of suffering, here is the path to the annihilation of suffering.'

"Then he broadly expounded the Law of the twelve-linked chain of causation: ignorance causes action, action causes consciousness, consciousness causes name and form, name and form cause the six sense organs, the six sense organs cause contact, contact causes sensation, sensation causes desire, desire causes attachment, attachment causes existence, existence causes birth, birth causes old age and death, worry and grief, suffering and anguish. If ignorance is wiped out, then action will be wiped out. If action is wiped out, then consciousness will be wiped out. If consciousness is wiped out, then name and form will be wiped out. If name and form are wiped out, then the six sense organs will be wiped out. If the six sense organs are wiped out, then contact will be wiped out. If contact is wiped out, then sensation will be wiped out. If sensation is wiped out, then desire will be wiped out. If desire is wiped out, then attachment will be wiped out. If attachment is wiped out, then existence will be wiped out. If existence is wiped out, then birth will be wiped out. If birth is wiped out, then old age and death, worry and grief, suffering and anguish will be wiped out.

"When the Buddha in the midst of the great assembly of heavenly and human beings expounded this Law, six hundred ten thousand million nayutas of persons, because they ceased to accept any of the things of the phenomenal world and because their minds were able to attain liberation from the outflows, all achieved profound and wonderful meditation practice, acquired the three understandings and the six transcendental powers, and were endowed with the eight emancipations. And when he expounded the second, third and fourth Laws, living beings equal to a thousand ten thousand millions of Ganges sands of nayutas, because they likewise ceased to accept any of the things of the phenomenal world, were able to liberate their minds from the outflows. From that time on, the multitude of voice-hearers became immeasurable, boundless, incapable of being counted.

"At that time the sixteen princes all left their families while still young boys and became shramaneras. Their faculties were penetrating and sharp, their wisdom was bright and comprehending. Already in the past they had offered alms to a hundred thousand ten thousand million Buddhas, had carried out brahma practices in a flawless manner, and had striven to attain anuttara-samyak-sambodhi. All together they addressed the Buddha, saying: 'World-Honored One, these innumerable thousands, ten thousands, millions of voice-hearers of great virtue have all already achieved success. World-Honored One, now it is fitting that you should preach the Law of anuttara-samyak-sambodhi for our sake so that, once we have heard it, we all may join in practicing and studying it. World-Honored One, we are determined to attain the insight of the Thus Come One. Deep in our minds we have this thought, as the Buddha himself must know.'

"At that time the eighty thousand million persons in the assembly led by the wheel-turning sage king, observing that the sixteen princes had left their families to enter religious life, desired to do likewise. The sage king gave permission for them to do so.

"At that time the Buddha, responding to pleas from the shramaneras, passed a period of twenty thousand kalpas and then at last, in the midst of the four kinds of believers, preached the Great Vehicle sutra entitled the Lotus of the Wonderful Law, a Law to instruct the bodhisattvas, one that is guarded and kept in mind by the Buddhas. After he had preached the sutra, the sixteen shramaneras, for the sake of anuttara-samyak-sambodhi, all together accepted and embraced it, recited and intoned it, penetrated and understood it.

"When the Buddha preached this sutra, the sixteen bodhisattva shramaneras all took faith in it and accepted it, and among the multitude of voice-hearers there were also those who believed in it and understood it. But the other thousand ten thousand million types of living beings all gave way to doubt and perplexity.

"The Buddha preached this sutra for a period of eight thousand kalpas, never once stopping to rest. After he had preached this sutra, he entered a quiet room and dwelled in meditation for a period of eighty-four thousand kalpas.

"At this time the sixteen bodhisattva shramaneras, knowing that the Buddha had entered a room and was in tranquil meditation, each ascended a Dharma seat and likewise for a period of eighty-four thousand kalpas for the sake of the four kinds of believers broadly preached the distinctions put forth in the Lotus Sutra of the Wonderful Law. In this way each of them one by one saved living beings equal in number to six hundred ten thousand million nayutas of Ganges sands, instructing them, bringing them benefit and joy, and causing them to set their minds upon anuttara-samyak-sambodhi.

"The Great Universal Wisdom Excellence Buddha, after passing eighty-four thousand kalpas, arose from his samadhi and approached the Dharma seat. Seating himself calmly, he addressed the whole of the great assembly, saying: 'These sixteen bodhisattva shramaneras are of a kind very rarely to be found, their faculties penetrating and sharp, their wisdom bright and comprehending. Already in the past they have offered alms to immeasurable thousands, ten thousands, millions of Buddhas. In the company of those Buddhas they have constantly carried out brahma practices, received and embraced the Buddha wisdom, and expounded it to living beings, causing them to enter therein. Now all of you should from time to time associate closely with them and offer them alms. Why? Because if any of you, voice-hearers or pratyekabuddhas or bodhisattvas, are able to take faith in the sutra teachings preached by these sixteen bodhisattvas, and will accept and embrace them and never disparage them, then such persons will all be able to attain anuttara-samyak-sambodhi, the wisdom of the Thus Come One.' "

The Buddha, addressing the monks, said: "These sixteen bodhisattvas have constantly desired to expound this Sutra of the Lotus of the Wonderful Law. The living beings converted by each one of these bodhisattvas are equal in number to six hundred ten thousand million nayutas of Ganges sands. Existence after existence these living beings are reborn in company with that bodhisattva, hear the Law from him, and all have faith in and understand it. For this reason they have been able to encounter forty thousand million Buddhas, World-Honored Ones, and have never ceased to do so down to the present.

"You monks, I will now tell you this. These disciples of the Buddha, these sixteen shramaneras, have now all attained anuttara-samyak-sambodhi. In the lands in the ten directions they are at present preaching the Law, with immeasurable hundreds, thousands, ten thousands, millions of bodhisattvas and voice-hearers for their retinue. Two of these shramaneras have become Buddhas in the eastern region. One is named Akshobhya and lives in the Land of Joy. The other is named Sumeru Peak. Two are Buddhas in the southeastern region, one named Lion Voice, the other named Lion Appearance. Two are Buddhas in the southern region, one named Void-Dwelling, the other named Ever Extinguished. Two are Buddhas in the southwestern region, one named Emperor Appearance, the other named Brahma Appearance. Two are Buddhas in the western region, one named Amitayus, the other named Saving All from Worldly Suffering. Two are Buddhas in the northwestern region, one named Tamalapatra Sandalwood Fragrance Transcendental Power, the other named Sumeru Appearance. Two are Buddhas in the northern region, one named Cloud Freedom, the other named Cloud Freedom King. Of the Buddhas of the northeastern region, one is named Destroying All Worldly Fears. The sixteenth is I, Shakyamuni Buddha, who in this saha land have attained anuttara-samyak-sambodhi.

"Monks, when I and these others were shramaneras, each one of us taught and converted living beings equal in number to immeasurable hundreds, thousands, ten thousands, millions of Ganges sands. They heard the Law from us and attained anuttara-samyak-sambodhi. Some of these living beings are now dwelling in the ranks of voice-hearers. But we have constantly instructed them in anuttara-samyak-sambodhi, and these persons should be able, through this Law, to enter into the Buddha way, albeit gradually. Why do I say this? Because the wisdom of the Thus Come One is difficult to believe and difficult to understand. Those living beings equal in number to immeasurable Ganges sands who were converted at that time are you who are now monks, and those who, after I have entered extinction, in ages to come will be voice-hearer disciples.

"After I have entered extinction, there will be other disciples who will not hear this sutra and will not understand or be aware of the practices carried out by the bodhisattvas, but who, through the blessings they have been able to attain, will conceive an idea of extinction and enter into what they believe to be nirvana. At that time I will be a Buddha in another land and will be known by a different name. Those disciples, though they have conceived an idea of extinction and entered into what they take to be nirvana, will in that other land seek the Buddha wisdom and will be able to hear this sutra. For it is only through the Buddha vehicle that one can attain extinction. There is no other vehicle, if one excepts the various doctrines that the Thus Come Ones preach as an expedient means.

"Monks, if a Thus Come One knows that the time has come to enter nirvana, and knows that the members of the assembly are pure and clean, firm in faith and understanding, thorough in their comprehension of the Law of emptiness and deeply entered into meditation practice, then he will call together the assembly of bodhisattvas and voice-hearers and will preach this sutra for them. In the world there are not two vehicles whereby one may attain extinction. There is only the one Buddha vehicle for attaining extinction and one alone.

"Monks, you must understand this. The Thus Come One in his use of expedient means penetrates deeply into the nature of living beings. He knows how their minds delight in petty doctrines and how deeply they are attached to the five desires. And because they are like this, when he expounds nirvana, he does so in such a way that these persons, hearing it, can readily believe and accept it.

"Let us suppose there is a stretch of bad road five hundred yojanas long, steep and difficult, wild and deserted, with no inhabitants around, a truly fearful place. And suppose there are a number of people who want to pass over this road so they can reach a place where there are rare treasures. They have a leader, of comprehensive wisdom and keen understanding, who is thoroughly acquainted with this steep road, knows the layout of its passes and defiles, and is prepared to guide the group of people and go with them over this difficult terrain.

"The group he is leading, after going part way on the road, become disheartened and say to the leader, 'We are utterly exhausted and fearful as well. We cannot go any farther. Since there is still such a long distance ahead, we would like now to turn around and go back.'

"The leader, a man of many expedients, thinks to himself, What a pity that they should abandon the many rare treasures they are seeking and want to turn around and go back! Having had this thought, he resorts to the power of expedient means and, when they have gone three hundred yojanas along the steep road, conjures up a city. He says to the group, 'Don't be afraid! You must not turn back, for now here is a great city where you can stop, rest, and do just as you please. If you enter this city you will be completely at ease and tranquil. Then later, if you feel you can go on to the place where the treasure is, you can leave the city.'

"At that time the members of the group, being utterly exhausted, are overjoyed in mind, exclaiming over such an unprecedented event, 'Now we can escape from this dreadful road and find ease and tranquility!' The people in the group thereupon press forward and enter the city where, feeling that they have been saved from their difficulties, they have a sense of complete ease and tranquility.

"At that time the leader, knowing that the people have become rested and are no longer fearful or weary, wipes out the phantom city and says to the group, 'You must go now. The place where the treasure is is close by. That great city of a while ago was a mere phantom that I conjured up so that you could rest.'

"Monks, the Thus Come One is in a similar position. He is now acting as a great leader for you. He knows that the bad road of birth and death and earthly desires is steep, difficult, long and far-stretching, but that it must be traveled, it must be passed over. If living beings hear only of the one Buddha vehicle, then they will not want to see the Buddha, will not want to draw near him, but will immediately think to themselves, The Buddha road is long and far-stretching and one must labor diligently and undergo difficulties over a long period before he can ever attain success!

"The Buddha knows that the minds of living beings are timid, weak and lowly, and so, using the power of expedient means, he preaches two nirvanas in order to provide a resting place along the road. If living beings choose to remain in these two stages, then the Thus Come One will say to them, 'You have not yet understood what is to be done. This stage where you have chosen to remain is close to the

Buddha wisdom. But you should observe and ponder further. This nirvana that you have attained is not the true one. It is simply that the Thus Come One, using the power of expedient means, has taken the one Buddha vehicle and, making distinctions, has preached it as three.'

"The Buddha is like that leader who, in order to provide a place to rest, conjured up a great city and then, when he knew that the travelers were already rested, said to them, 'The place where the treasure is is nearby. This city is not real. It is merely something I conjured up.' "

At that time the World-Honored One, wishing to state his meaning once more, spoke in verse form, saying:

> The Great Universal Wisdom Excellence Buddha
> sat in the place of practice for ten kalpas,
> but the Law of the Buddha did not appear before him
> and he could not attain the Buddha way.
> The assembly of heavenly gods, dragon kings,
> asuras and others
> constantly rained down heavenly flowers
> as alms offered to that Buddha.
> The heavenly beings beat on heavenly drums
> and made many kinds of music.
> A fragrant wind blew away the withered flowers,
> whereupon fresh and beautiful ones rained down.
> When ten small kalpas had passed,
> then at last he was able to attain the Buddha way.
> The heavenly beings and people of the world
> in their hearts all felt like dancing.
> That Buddha's sixteen sons
> all, in company with their followers,
> a thousand ten thousand million of them gathered around,
> all came to the place of the Buddha,
> touching heads to the ground, bowing at the Buddha's feet
> and entreating him to turn the wheel of the Law, saying,
> "Saintly Lion, let the Dharma rain
> fall in full upon us and all others!"
> The World-Honored One is very difficult to encounter;

only once in a long time does he appear.
In order to bring enlightenment to the many beings
he shakes and moves the regions all around.
In the worlds in the eastern direction
in five hundred ten thousand million lands
the palaces of the Brahma kings glowed with a light
they had never known in the past.
When the Brahma kings saw this sign
they came in search of the Buddha's place,
scattering flowers as a form of offering,
at the same time presenting their palaces,
entreating the Buddha to turn the wheel of the Law
and praising him in verses.
The Buddha knew that the time had not yet come,
and though they entreated, he sat in silence.
In the other three directions and the four directions in between
and in the upper and lower regions, the same occurred,
the Brahma kings scattering flowers, presenting their palaces,
entreating the Buddha to turn the wheel of the Law, saying,
"The World-Honored One is very difficult to encounter.
We beg you in your great mercy and compassion
to open wide the gates of sweet dew
and turn the wheel of the unsurpassed Law."
The World-Honored One, immeasurable in wisdom,
accepted the entreaties of the assembly
and for their sake proclaimed various doctrines,
the four noble truths, the twelve-linked chain of causation,
describing how, from ignorance to old age and death,
all are produced through the cause of birth, saying,
"With regard to these many faults and vexations,
you should understand this about them."
When he expounded this Law,
six hundred ten thousand million trillion beings
were able to reach the end of their sufferings,
all attaining the status of arhat.
The second time he preached the Law
a multitude like a thousand ten thousand Ganges sands
ceased to accept the things of the phenomenal world

and they too were able to become arhats.
Thereafter those who attained the way
were immeasurable in number—
one might calculate for ten thousand million kalpas
and never be able to reckon their extent.
At that time the sixteen princes
left their families and became shramaneras.
All together they entreated that Buddha
to expound the Law of the Great Vehicle, saying,
"We and our attendants
are all certain to attain the Buddha way.
We desire the wisdom eye of foremost purity
such as the World-Honored One possesses."
The Buddha understood their boyish minds
and the actions they had carried out in past existences,
and employing immeasurable causes and conditions
and various similes and parables,
he preached the six paramitas
and matters concerning transcendental powers,
distinguishing the true Law,
the way practiced by bodhisattvas,
preaching this Lotus Sutra
in verses as numerous as Ganges sands.
When the Buddha had finished preaching the sutra
he entered into meditation in a quiet room,
with a single mind sitting in a single place
for eighty-four thousand kalpas.
The shramaneras knew
the Buddha would not yet emerge from meditation
and so for the assembly of immeasurable millions
they preached the unsurpassed wisdom of the Buddha,
each one sitting in a Dharma seat,
preaching this Great Vehicle sutra.
And after the Buddha had entered peaceful tranquility,
they continued to proclaim, helping to convert others to
    the Law.
The living beings saved
by each one of those shramaneras

were equal in number
to six hundred ten thousand million Ganges sands.
After that Buddha had passed into extinction,
those persons who had heard the Law
dwelled here and there in various Buddha lands,
constantly reborn in company with their teachers.
And these sixteen shramaneras,
having fully carried out the Buddha way,
at present are dwelling in the ten directions,
where each has attained correct enlightenment.
The persons who heard the Law at that time
are each in a place where there is one of these Buddhas,
and those who remain at the stage of voice-hearer
are gradually being instructed in the Buddha way.
I myself was numbered among the sixteen
and in the past preached for you.
For this reason I will employ an expedient means
to lead you in the pursuit of Buddha wisdom;
because of these earlier causes and conditions
I now preach the Lotus Sutra.
I will cause you to enter the Buddha way—
be attentive and harbor no fear!
Suppose there was a stretch of steep bad road,
in a remote wasteland with many harmful beasts,
a place moreover without water or grass,
one dreaded by people.
A group of countless thousands and ten thousands
wanted to pass over this steep road,
but the road was very long and far-stretching,
extending five hundred yojanas.
At this time there was a leader,
well informed, possessing wisdom,
of clear understanding and determined mind,
capable of saving endangered persons from manifold difficulties.
The members of the group were all weary and disheartened
and said to their leader,
"We are now exhausted with fatigue
and wish at this point to turn around and go back."

The leader thought to himself,
These people are truly pitiful!
Why do they wish to turn back
and miss the many rare treasures ahead?
At that time he thought of an expedient means,
deciding to exercise his transcendental powers.
He conjured up a great walled city
and adorned its mansions,
surrounding them with gardens and groves,
channels of flowing water, ponds and lakes,
with double gates and tall towers and pavilions,
all filled with men and women.
As soon as he had created this illusion,
he comforted the group, saying, "Have no fear—
you can enter this city
and each amuse himself as he pleases."
When the people had entered the city,
they were all overjoyed in heart.
All had a feeling of ease and tranquility,
telling themselves that they had been saved.
When the leader knew they were rested,
he called them together and announced,
"Now you must push forward—
this is nothing more than a phantom city.
I saw that you were weary and exhausted
and wanted to turn back in mid-journey.
Therefore I used the power of expedient means
to conjure up this city for the moment.
Now you must press forward diligently
so that together you may reach the place where the treasure is."
I too do likewise,
acting as leader to all beings.
I see the seekers of the way
growing disheartened in mid-journey,
unable to pass over the steep road
of birth and death and earthly desires,
and therefore I use the power of expedient means
and preach nirvana to provide them with rest,

saying, "Your sufferings are extinguished,
you have carried out all there is to be done."
When I know they have reached nirvana
and all have attained the stage of arhat,
then I call the great assembly together
and preach the true Law for them.
The Buddhas through the power of expedient means
make distinctions and preach three vehicles,
but there is only the single Buddha vehicle—
the other two nirvanas are preached to provide a resting place.
Now I expound the truth for you—
what you have attained is not extinction.
For the sake of the comprehensive wisdom of the Buddha
you must expend great effort and diligence.
If you gain enlightenment in the Law of the Buddha
with its comprehensive wisdom and ten powers
and are endowed with the thirty-two features,
then this will be true extinction.
The Buddhas in their capacity as leaders
preach nirvana to provide a rest.
But when they know you have become rested,
they lead you onward to the Buddha wisdom.

8

PROPHECY OF ENLIGHTENMENT FOR FIVE HUNDRED DISCIPLES

At that time Purna Maitrayaniputra, hearing from the Buddha this Law as it was expounded through wisdom and expedient means and in accordance with what was appropriate, and also hearing the prophecy that the major disciples would attain anuttara-samyak-sambodhi, hearing matters relating to causes and conditions of previous existences, and hearing how the Buddhas possess great freedom and transcendental powers, obtained what he had never had before, and his mind was purified and felt like dancing. Immediately he rose from his seat, advanced to a position in front of the Buddha, touched his head to the ground and bowed to the Buddha's feet. Then he withdrew to one side, gazed up in reverence at the face of the Honored One, his eyes never leaving it for an instant, and thought to himself: The World-Honored One is very extraordinary, very special, his actions rarely to be encountered! Adapting himself to the various natures of the people of this world and employing expedient means and insight, he preaches the Law for them, drawing living beings away from their greed and attachment to this or that. The Buddha's blessings are such that we cannot set them forth in words. Only the Buddha, the World-Honored One, is capable of knowing the wish that we have had deep in our hearts from the start.

At that time the Buddha said to the monks: "Do you see this Purna Maitrayaniputra? I have always commended him as being foremost among those who preach the Law. And I have always praised his various blessings, his diligence in protecting, upholding, aiding and proclaiming my Law, his ability in teaching, benefiting and delighting the four kinds of believers, the thoroughness with which he understands the correct Law of the Buddha, the great degree to which he enriches those who carry out its brahma practices. If one excepts the Thus Come One, there is no other who can so thoroughly exemplify the eloquence of its theories.

"You should not suppose that Purna is capable of protecting, upholding, aiding and proclaiming my Law only. In the presence of ninety million Buddhas of the past too he protected, upheld, aided and proclaimed the correct Law of the Buddhas. Among all those who at that time preached the Law, he was likewise foremost.

"In addition, concerning the Law of emptiness preached by the Buddhas he has a clear and thorough understanding, he has gained the four unlimited kinds of knowledge, and is at all times capable of preaching the Law in a lucid and pure manner, free of doubts and perplexities. He is fully endowed with the transcendental powers of a bodhisattva. Throughout his allotted life span he constantly carries out brahma practices, so that the other people living in the era of that particular Buddha all think, Here is a true voice-hearer!

"And Purna by employing this expedient means has brought benefit to immeasurable hundreds and thousands of living beings, and has converted immeasurable asamkhyas of persons, causing them to turn toward anuttara-samyak-sambodhi. In order to purify the Buddha lands he constantly devotes himself to the Buddha's work, teaching and converting living beings.

"Monks, Purna was foremost among those who preached the Law in the time of the seven Buddhas. He is also foremost among those who preach the Law in my presence now. And he will likewise be foremost among those who preach the Law in the time of the future Buddhas who appear in the present Wise Kalpa, in all cases protecting, upholding, aiding and proclaiming the Law of the Buddha. In the future too he will protect, uphold, aid and proclaim the Law of immeasurable, boundless Buddhas, teaching, converting and enriching immeasurable living beings and causing them to turn toward anuttara-samyak-sambodhi. In order to purify the Buddha lands he will constantly apply himself with diligence, teaching and converting living beings.

"Little by little he will become fully endowed with the way of the bodhisattva, and when immeasurable asamkhya kalpas have passed, here in the land where he is dwelling he will attain anuttara-samyak-sambodhi. He will be called Law Bright Thus Come One, worthy of offerings, of right and universal knowledge, perfect clarity and conduct, well gone, understanding the world, unexcelled worthy, trainer of people, teacher of heavenly and human beings, Buddha, World-Honored One.

"This Buddha will have thousand-millionfold worlds equal in number to Ganges sands as his Buddha land. The ground will be made of the seven treasures and level as the palm of a hand, without hills or ridges, ravines or gullies. The land will be filled with terraces and towers made of the seven treasures, and the heavenly palaces will be situated close by in the sky, so that human and heavenly beings can communicate and be within sight of each other. There will be no evil paths of existence there, nor will there be any women. All living beings will be born through transformation and will be without lewd desires. They will gain great transcendental powers, their bodies will emit a bright glow, and they will be able to fly at will. They will be firm in intent and thought, diligent and wise, and all alike will be adorned with a golden color and the thirty-two features. All the living beings in that land will regularly take two kinds of food, one being the food of Dharma joy, the other the food of meditation delight. There will be immeasurable asamkhyas, thousands, ten thousands, millions of nayutas of bodhisattvas there, who will gain great transcendental powers and the four unlimited kinds of knowledge, and will be skilled and capable in teaching and converting the different varieties of living beings. The number of voice-hearers will be beyond the power of calculation or reckoning to determine. All will be fully endowed with the six transcendental powers, the three understandings, and the eight emancipations.

"This Buddha land will thus possess measureless blessings of this kind that will adorn and complete it. The kalpa will be named Treasure Bright and the land named Good and Pure. The Buddha's life span will be immeasurable asamkhya kalpas, his Law will endure for a very long time, and after the Buddha has passed into extinction, towers adorned with the seven treasures will be erected to him throughout the entire land."

At that time the World-Honored One, wishing to state his meaning once more, spoke in verse form, saying:

> You monks, listen carefully!
> The way followed by the sons of the Buddha,
> because they are well learned in expedient means,
> is wonderful beyond conception.
> They know how most beings delight in a little Law
> and are fearful of great wisdom.
> Therefore the bodhisattvas
> pose as voice-hearers or pratyekabuddhas,
> employing countless expedient means
> to convert the different kinds of living beings.
> They proclaim themselves to be voice-hearers
> and say they are far removed from the Buddha way,
> and so bring emancipation to immeasurable multitudes,
> allowing them all to achieve success.
> Limited in aspiration, lazy and indolent though the
>   multitudes are,
> bit by bit they are led to the attainment of Buddhahood.
> Inwardly, in secret, the sons act as bodhisattvas,
> but outwardly they show themselves as voice-hearers.
> They seem to be lessening desires out of hatred for birth
>   and death,
> but in truth they are purifying the Buddha lands.
> Before the multitude they seem possessed of the three poisons

or manifest the signs of heretical views.
My disciples in this manner
use expedient means to save living beings.
If I were to describe all the different ways,
the many manifestations they display in converting others,
the living beings who heard me
would be doubtful and perplexed in mind.
Now this Purna in the past
diligently practiced the way
under a thousand million Buddhas,
proclaiming and guarding the Law of those Buddhas.
In order to seek out unsurpassed wisdom
he went to where the Buddhas were,
became a leader among their disciples,
one of wide knowledge and wisdom.
He showed no fear in what he expounded
and was able to delight the assembly.
Never was he weary or disheartened
in assisting the work of the Buddhas.
Already he had passed over into great transcendental powers
and possessed the four unlimited kinds of knowledge.
He knew whether the capacities of the multitude were keen
    or dull
and constantly preached the pure Law.
He expounded such principles as these,
teaching a multitude of thousands of millions,
causing them to reside in the Great Vehicle Law
and himself purifying the Buddha lands.
And in the future too he will offer alms
to immeasurable, countless Buddhas,
protecting, aiding and proclaiming their correct Law
and himself purifying the Buddha lands,
constantly employing various expedient means,
preaching the Law without fear,
saving multitudes beyond calculation,
causing them to realize comprehensive wisdom.
He will offer alms to the Thus Come Ones,
guarding and upholding the treasure storehouse of the Law.

And later he will become a Buddha
known by the name Law Bright.
His land will be called Good and Pure
and will be composed of the seven treasures.
The kalpa will be named Treasure Bright.
The multitude of bodhisattvas will be very numerous,
numbering immeasurable millions,
all having passed over into great transcendental powers,
endowed with dignity, virtue, strength,
filling the entire land.
Voice-hearers too will be numberless,
with the three understandings and eight emancipations,
having attained the four unlimited kinds of knowledge—
such as these will be the monks of the Order.
The living beings of that land
will all be divorced from lewd desires.
They will be born in a pure manner by the process
    of transformation,
with all the features adorning their bodies.
With Dharma joy and meditation delight to feed upon,
they will have no thought of other food.
There will be no women there
and none of the evil paths of existence.
The monk Purna
has won all these blessings to the fullest
and will acquire a pure land such as this,
with its great multitude of worthies and sages.
Of the countless matters pertaining to it
I have now spoken only in brief.

At that time the twelve hundred arhats, being free in mind, thought to themselves, We rejoice at gaining what we have never had before. If the World-Honored One should give each of us a prophecy of enlightenment such as he has given to his other major disciples, would that not be cause for delight?

The Buddha, knowing that this thought was in their minds, said to Mahakashyapa: "On these twelve hundred arhats who are now before me I will one by one bestow a prophecy that they will attain anuttara-samyak-sambodhi. Among this assembly is a major disciple of mine, the monk Kaundinya. He will offer alms to sixty-two thousand million Buddhas, and after that will become a Buddha. He will be designated Universal Brightness Thus Come One, worthy of offerings, of right and universal knowledge, perfect clarity and conduct, well gone, understanding the world, unexcelled worthy, trainer of people, teacher of heavenly and human beings, Buddha, World-Honored One. Five hundred arhats, including Uruvilvakashyapa, Gayakashyapa, Nadikashyapa, Kalodayin, Udayin, Aniruddha, Revata, Kapphina, Bakkula, Chunda, Svagata, and others, will all attain anuttara-samyak-sambodhi. All will have the same designation, being called Universal Brightness."

The World-Honored One, wishing to state his meaning once more, spoke in verse form, saying:

> The monk Kaundinya
> will see immeasurable Buddhas
> and after asamkhya kalpas have passed
> will at last achieve impartial and correct enlightenment.
> Constantly he will emit a great bright light,
> will be endowed with transcendental powers,
> and his name will be known in all ten quarters,
> respected by one and all.
> Constantly he will preach the unsurpassed way;
> therefore he will be named Universal Brightness.
> His realm will be pure and clean,
> his bodhisattvas brave and spirited.
> All will ascend the wonderful towers,
> travel to the lands in ten directions,
> in order to offer unsurpassed articles
> as gifts to the various Buddhas.
> After they have offered these alms
> their minds will be filled with great joy
> and they will speedily return to their native lands—
> such will be their supernatural powers.
> The life span of this Buddha will be sixty thousand kalpas,
> his Correct Law will endure twice that time,
> his Counterfeit Law twice that time again,

and when his Law is extinguished, heavenly and human beings
    will grieve.
The five hundred monks
will one by one become Buddhas,
all with the same name, Universal Brightness.
Each will bestow a prophecy on his successor, saying,
"After I have entered extinction,
you, so-and-so, will become a Buddha.
The world in which you carry out conversions
will be like mine today."
The adornment and purity of their lands,
their various transcendental powers,
their bodhisattvas and voice-hearers,
their Correct Law and Counterfeit Law,
the number of kalpas in their life span—
all will be as I have described above.
Kashyapa, now you know the future
of these five hundred who are free in mind.
The remainder of the multitude of voice-hearers
will also be like this.
As for those not in this gathering,
you must expound and preach to them.

At that time the five hundred arhats in the presence of the Buddha, having received a prophecy of enlightenment, danced for joy. Immediately they rose from their seats, advanced to a position in front of the Buddha, touched their heads to the ground and bowed to the Buddha's feet. They bewailed their error, reproving themselves and saying, "World-Honored One, we always used to think to ourselves, We have already attained the ultimate extinction. But now we know that we were like persons of no wisdom. Why? Because, although we were capable of attaining the wisdom of the Thus Come One, we were willing to content ourselves with petty wisdom.

"World-Honored One, it was like the case of a man who went to the house of a close friend and, having become drunk on wine, lay down to sleep. At that time the friend had to go out on official business. He took a priceless jewel, sewed it in the lining of the man's robe, and left it with him when he went out. The man was asleep drunk and knew nothing about it. When he got up, he set out on a journey to other countries.'In order to provide himself with food and clothing he had to search with all his energy and diligence, encountering very great hardship and making do with what little he could come by.

"Later, the close friend happened to meet him by chance. The friend said, 'How absurd, old fellow! Why should you have to do all this for the sake of food and clothing? In the past I wanted to make certain you would be able to live in ease and satisfy the five desires, and so on such-and-such a day and month and year I took a priceless jewel and sewed it in the lining of your robe. It must still be there now. But you did not know about it, and fretted and wore yourself out trying to provide a living for yourself. What nonsense! Now you must take the jewel and exchange it for goods. Then you can have whatever you wish at all times and never experience poverty or want.'

"The Buddha is like this friend. When he was still a bodhisattva, he taught and converted us, inspiring in us the determination to seek comprehensive wisdom. But in time we forgot all that, became unaware, unknowing. Having attained the way of the arhat, we supposed we had gained extinction. Finding it difficult to provide for our livelihood, as it were, we made do with what little we could come by. However, we have not yet lost the desire for comprehensive wisdom. And now the World-Honored One awakens us and makes us aware, speaking these words: 'Monks, what you have acquired is not the ultimate extinction. For a long time I caused you to cultivate the good roots of Buddhahood, and as an expedient means I showed you the outward signs of nirvana, but you supposed that you had in truth attained nirvana.'

"World-Honored One, now we understand. In fact we are bodhisattvas and have received a prophecy that we will attain anuttara-samyak-sambodhi. For this reason we are filled with great joy, having gained what we never had before."

At that time Ajnata Kaundinya and the others, wishing to state their meaning once more, spoke in verse form, saying:

We have heard the sound of this prophecy
assuring us of unsurpassed ease and tranquility;
we rejoice in gaining what we never had before

and make obeisance to the Buddha of measureless wisdom.
Now in the presence of the World-Honored One
we bewail our faults and errors.
Of the Buddha's immeasurable treasure
we have gained only a small portion of nirvana,
and like ignorant and foolish persons
have taken that to be sufficient.
We are like a poor and impoverished man
who went to the house of a close friend.
The house was a very prosperous one
and he was served many trays of delicacies.
The friend took a priceless jewel,
sewed it in the lining of the poor man's robe,
gave it without a word and then went away,
and the man, being asleep, knew nothing of it.
After the man had gotten up,
he journeyed here and there to other countries,
seeking food and clothing to keep himself alive,
finding it very difficult to provide for his livelihood.
He made do with what little he could get
and never hoped for anything finer,
unaware that in the lining of his robe
he had a priceless jewel.
Later the close friend who had given him the jewel
happened to meet the poor man
and after sharply rebuking him,
showed him the jewel sewed in the robe.
When the poor man saw the jewel
his heart was filled with great joy,
for he was rich, possessed of wealth and goods
sufficient to satisfy the five desires.
We are like that man.
Through the long night the World-Honored One
constantly in his pity teaches and converts us,
causing us to plant the seeds of an unsurpassed aspiration.
But because we are without wisdom,
we are unaware of this, unknowing.
Having gained a small portion of nirvana,

we are satisfied and seek nothing more.
But now the Buddha awakens us,
saying, 'This is not really extinction.
When you have gained the Buddha's unsurpassed wisdom,
then that will be true extinction!'
Now we have heard from the Buddha
these prophecies and descriptions of adornment,
and how each in turn will bestow a prophecy on his successor,
and in body and mind we are filled with joy.

9

PROPHECIES CONFERRED
ON LEARNERS
AND ADEPTS

At that time Ananda and Rahula thought to themselves, Whenever we reflect, we consider how delightful it would be if we should receive a prophecy of enlightenment! Immediately they rose from their seats, advanced to a position in front of the Buddha, touched their heads to the ground and bowed to the Buddha's feet. Together they spoke to the Buddha, saying: "World-Honored One, we too should have a share of this! We have put all our trust in the Thus Come One alone, and we are well known to the heavenly and human beings and asuras of all the world. Ananda constantly attends the Buddha and guards and upholds the Dharma storehouse, and Rahula is the Buddha's son. If the Buddha should bestow on us a prophecy that we will attain anuttara-samyak-sambodhi, then our wishes will be fulfilled and the longings of the multitude will likewise be satisfied."

At that time two thousand of the voice-hearer disciples, both learners and adepts who had nothing more to learn, all rose from their seats, bared their right shoulders, advanced to a position in front of the Buddha, pressed their palms together with a single mind and, gazing up in reverence at the World-Honored One, repeated the wish expressed by Ananda and Rahula and then stood to one side.

At that time the Buddha said to Ananda: "In a future existence you will become a Buddha with the name Mountain Sea Wisdom Unrestricted Power King Thus Come One, worthy of offerings, of right and universal knowledge, perfect clarity and conduct, well gone, understanding the world, unexcelled worthy, and trainer of people, teacher of heavenly and human beings, Buddha, World-Honored One. You will offer alms to sixty-two million Buddhas and will guard and uphold their Dharma storehouses, and after that you will attain anuttara-samyak-sambodhi. You will teach and convert bodhisattvas as numerous as twenty thousand ten thousand million Ganges sands and will cause them to attain anuttara-samyak-sambodhi. Your land will be named Ever Standing Victory Banner, its soil will be clean and pure and made of lapis lazuli. The kalpa will be named Wonderful Sound Filling Everywhere. The life span of that Buddha will be immeasurable thousands, ten thousands, millions of asamkhyas of kalpas—though men should calculate and reckon for thousands, ten thousands, millions of immeasurable asamkhyas of kalpas, they could never ascertain the full number. The Correct Law will endure in the world for twice the life span of the Buddha, and the Counterfeit Law will endure in the world for twice the time of the Correct Law. Ananda, this Mountain Sea Wisdom Unrestricted Power King Buddha will be praised alike by Thus Come Ones of the ten directions who are equal in number to immeasurable thousands, ten thousands, millions of Ganges sands, and they will extol his blessings."

At that time the World-Honored One, wishing to state his meaning once more, spoke in verse form, saying:

> I now say to the monks that
> Ananda, upholder of the Law,
> will give alms to the Buddhas

and after will achieve correct enlightenment.
His name will be Mountain Sea Wisdom
Unrestricted Power King Buddha.
His land will be clean and pure,
named Ever Standing Victory Banner.
He will teach and convert bodhisattvas
in numbers like Ganges sands.
This Buddha will possess great dignity and virtue,
his renown will fill the ten directions.
His life span will be immeasurable
because he takes pity on living beings.
His Correct Law will endure for twice his life span,
his Counterfeit Law, twice that again.
As numerous as Ganges sands
will be the countless living beings
who in the midst of the Buddha's Law
will plant causes and conditions leading to the Buddha way.

At that time in the assembly eight thousand bodhisattvas who had newly conceived the determination to attain enlightenment all thought to themselves, We have never heard of even a great bodhisattva receiving a prophecy such as this. For what reason should these voice-hearers receive such a prediction?

At that time the World-Honored One, knowing the thought that was in the mind of these bodhisattvas, said to them: "Good men, when Ananda and I were at the place of Void King Buddha, we both at the same time conceived the determination to attain anuttara-samyak-sambodhi. Ananda constantly delighted in wide knowledge [of the Law], I constantly put forth diligent effort. Therefore I have already succeeded in attaining anuttara-samyak-sambodhi, while Ananda guards and upholds my Law. And he will likewise guard the Dharma storehouses of the Buddhas of future existences and will teach, convert and bring success to the multitude of bodhisattvas. Such was his original vow, and therefore he has received this prophecy."

When Ananda in the presence of the Buddha heard this prophecy delivered to him and heard of the land and adornments he was to receive, all that he had vowed to achieve was realized and his mind was filled with great joy, for he had gained what he had never had before. Immediately he recalled to mind the Dharma storehouses of immeasurable thousands, ten thousands, millions of Buddhas of the past, and he could fully comprehend them without hindrance, as though he had just now heard them. He also recalled his original vow.

At that time Ananda spoke in verse form, saying:

> The World-Honored One, very rarely met with,
> has caused me to recall the past,
> the Law of immeasurable Buddhas,
> as though I had heard it today.
> Now I have no more doubts
> but dwell securely in the Buddha way.
> As an expedient means I act as attendant,
> guarding and upholding the Law of the Buddhas.

At that time the Buddha said to Rahula: "In a future existence you will become a Buddha with the name Stepping on Seven Treasure Flowers Thus Come One, worthy of offerings, of right and universal knowledge, perfect clarity and conduct, well gone, understanding the world, unexcelled worthy, trainer of people, teacher of heavenly and human beings, Buddha, World-Honored One. You will offer alms to Buddhas and Thus Come Ones as numerous as the dust particles of ten worlds. In all cases you will be the eldest son of those Buddhas, just as you are my son now. The adornments of the land of Stepping on Seven Treasure Flowers Buddha, the number of kalpas in his life span, the disciples he converts, his Correct Law and Counterfeit Law will not differ from those of the Thus Come One Mountain Sea Wisdom Unrestricted Power King. You will be the eldest son of that Buddha, and after that you will attain anuttara-samyak-sambodhi."

At that time the World-Honored One, wishing to state his meaning once more, spoke in verse form, saying:

> When I was crown prince
> Rahula was my eldest son.
> Now that I have gained the Buddha way
> he receives the Dharma and is my Dharma son.
> In existences to come
> he will see immeasurable millions of Buddhas.

As eldest son to all of them,
with a single mind he will seek the Buddha way.
The covert actions of Rahula
I alone am capable of knowing.
He manifests himself as my eldest son,
showing himself to living beings.
With immeasurable millions, thousands, ten thousands
of blessings beyond count,
he dwells securely in the Buddha's Law
and thereby seeks the unsurpassed way.

At that time the World-Honored One observed the two thousand learners and adepts, mild and gentle in will, serenely clean and pure, gazing at the Buddha with a single mind. The Buddha said to Ananda, "Do you see these two thousand learners and adepts?"

"Yes, I see them."

"Ananda, these persons will offer alms to Buddhas and Thus Come Ones equal in number to the dust particles of fifty worlds, paying honor and reverence to them, guarding and upholding their Dharma storehouses. In their final existence they will all at the same time succeed in becoming Buddhas in lands in the ten directions. All will have the identical designation, being called Jewel Sign Thus Come One, worthy of offerings, of right and universal knowledge, perfect clarity and conduct, well gone, understanding the world, unexcelled worthy, trainer of people, teacher of heavenly and human beings, Buddha, World-Honored One. Their life span will be one kalpa, and the adornment of their lands, their voice-hearers and bodhisattvas, Correct Law and Counterfeit Law will in all cases be the same."

At that time the World-Honored One, wishing to state his meaning once more, spoke in verse form, saying:

These two thousand voice-hearers
who now stand in my presence—
on all of them I bestow a prophecy
that in a future existence they will become Buddhas.
The Buddhas to whom they offer alms
will be numerous as the dust particles described above.
They will guard and uphold the Dharma storehouses

and after that will gain correct enlightenment.
Each will have a land in one of the ten directions
and all will share the same name and designation.
All at the same time will sit in the place of practice
and thereby will gain proof of unsurpassed wisdom.
All will be named Jewel Sign
and their lands and disciples,
their Correct Law and Counterfeit Law
will all be identical and without difference.
All will employ transcendental powers
to save living beings in the ten directions.
Their renown will spread everywhere around
and in due time they will enter nirvana.

At that time, when the two thousand learners and adepts heard the Buddha bestow this prophecy, they danced for joy and spoke in verse form, saying:

World-Honored One, bright lamp of wisdom,
we hear your voice bestowing this prophecy
and our hearts are filled with joy
as though we were bathed in sweet dew!

10

THE TEACHER
OF THE LAW

At that time the World-Honored One addressed Bodhisattva Medicine King, and through him the eighty thousand great men, saying: "Medicine King, do you see in this great assembly the immeasurable number of heavenly beings, dragon kings, yakshas, gandharvas, asuras, garudas, kimnaras, mahoragas, human and nonhuman beings, as well as monks, nuns, laymen and laywomen, those who seek to become voice-hearers, who seek to become pratyekabuddhas, or who seek the Buddha way? Upon these various kinds of beings who in the presence of the Buddha listen to one verse or one phrase of the Lotus Sutra of the Wonderful Law and for a moment think of it with joy I will bestow on all of them a prophecy that they will attain anuttara-samyak-sambodhi."

The Buddha said to Medicine King: "In addition, if after the Thus Come One has passed into extinction there should be someone who listens to the Lotus Sutra of the Wonderful Law, even one verse or one phrase, and for a moment thinks of it with joy, I will likewise bestow on him a prophecy that he will attain anuttara-samyak-sambodhi. Again if there are persons who embrace, read, recite, expound and copy the Lotus Sutra of the Wonderful Law, even only one verse, and look upon this sutra with the same reverence as they would the Buddha, presenting various offerings of flowers, incense, necklaces, powdered incense, paste incense, incense for burning, silken canopies, streamers and banners, clothing and music, and pressing their palms together in reverence, then, Medicine King, you should understand that such persons have already offered alms to a hundred thousand million Buddhas and in the place of the Buddhas have fulfilled their great vow, and because they take pity on living beings they have been born in this human world.

"Medicine King, if someone should ask what living beings will be able to attain Buddhahood in a latter-day existence, then you should show him that all these people in a latter-day existence are certain to attain Buddhahood. Why? Because if good men and good women embrace, read, recite, expound and copy the Lotus Sutra, even one phrase of it, offer various kinds of alms to the sutra, flowers, incense, necklaces, powdered incense, paste incense, incense for burning, silken canopies, streamers and banners, clothing and music, and press their palms together in reverence, then these persons will be looked up to and honored by all the world. Alms will be offered to them such as would be offered to the Thus Come One. You should understand that these persons are great bodhisattvas who have succeeded in attaining anuttara-samyak-sambodhi. Pitying living beings, they have vowed to be born among them where they may broadly expound and make distinctions regarding the Lotus Sutra of the Wonderful Law. How much more so is this true, then, of those who can embrace the entire sutra and offer various types of alms to it!

"Medicine King, you should understand that these persons voluntarily relinquish the reward due them for their pure deeds and, in the time after I have passed into extinction, because they pity living beings, they are born in this evil world so they may broadly expound this sutra. If one of these good men or good women in the time after I have passed into extinction is able to secretly expound the Lotus Sutra to one person, even one phrase of it, then you should know that he or she is the envoy of the Thus Come One. He has been dispatched by the Thus Come One and carries out the Thus Come One's work. And how much more so those who in the midst of the great assembly broadly expound the sutra for others!

"Medicine King, if there should be an evil person who, his mind destitute of goodness, should for the space of a kalpa appear in the presence of the Buddha and constantly curse and revile the Buddha, that person's offense would still be rather light. But if there were a person who spoke only one evil word to curse or defame the lay persons or monks or nuns who read and recite the Lotus Sutra, then his offense would be very grave.

"Medicine King, these persons who read and recite the Lotus Sutra—you should understand that these persons adorn themselves with the adornments of the Buddha; they are borne upon the shoulders of the Thus Come One. Wherever they may go, one should greet them with bows, with palms pressed single-mindedly together, with reverence and alms, with respect and praise, flowers, incense, necklaces, powdered incense, paste incense, incense for burning, silken canopies, streamers and banners, clothing, delicacies and the making of music. The finest alms that can be offered to a person should be offered to them. Heavenly treasures should be scattered over them, the treasure hoards of heaven should be given them as gifts. Why do I say this? Because these persons delight in expounding the Law. And if one listens to them for even a moment, he will immediately attain the ultimate anuttara-samyak-sambodhi."

At that time the World-Honored One, wishing to state his meaning once more, spoke in verse form, saying:

> If you wish to abide in the Buddha way
> and successfully gain the wisdom that comes of itself,
> you should be constantly diligent in offering alms
> to those who embrace the Lotus Sutra.
> If you have a wish to quickly obtain

wisdom regarding all species of things,
you should embrace this sutra
and at the same time give alms to those who do so.
If one is capable of embracing
the Lotus Sutra of the Wonderful Law,
know that such a person is an envoy of the Buddha
who thinks with pity of living beings.
Those who are capable of embracing
the Lotus Sutra of the Wonderful Law
relinquish their claim to the pure land
and out of pity for living beings are born here.
Know that persons such as these
freely choose where they will be born,
and choose to be born in this evil world
so they may broadly expound the unsurpassed Law.
You should offer heavenly flowers and incense,
robes decked with heavenly treasures,
the wonderful treasure hoards of heaven
as alms to those who preach the Law.
In the evil world following my extinction
if there are those who can embrace this sutra,
you should press your palms together in reverence
and offer alms to them as you would to the
    World-Honored One.
The choicest delicacies, all that is sweet and tasty,
along with various types of clothing
you should offer as alms to these Buddha sons
in hopes you may hear a moment of their preaching.
If there are those in a later age
who can accept and embrace this sutra,
they are my envoys sent out among the people
to perform the Thus Come One's work.
If for the space of a kalpa
one should constantly harbor a mind destitute of good
and with angry looks should revile the Buddha,
he will be committing an offense of immeasurable gravity.
But if toward those who read, recite and embrace
this Lotus Sutra

one should even for a moment direct evil words,
his offense will be far greater.
If there is someone who seeks the Buddha way
and during a certain kalpa
presses palms together in my presence
and recites numberless verses of praise,
because of these praises of the Buddha
he will gain immeasurable blessings.
And if one lauds and extols those who uphold this sutra,
his good fortune will be even greater.
For the space of eighty million kalpas,
with the most wonderful shapes and sounds,
with that which is pleasing to smell, taste and touch,
offer alms to the upholders of this sutra!
If you have offered alms in this manner
and have heard the teachings for even a moment,
then you will experience joy and good fortune,
saying, "I have gained great benefit!"
Medicine King, now I say to you,
I have preached various sutras,
and among those sutras
the Lotus is the foremost!

At that time the Buddha spoke once more to the bodhisattva and mahasattva Medicine King, saying: "The sutras I have preached number immeasurable thousands, ten thousands, millions. Among the sutras I have preached, now preach, and will preach, this Lotus Sutra is the most difficult to believe and the most difficult to understand. Medicine King, this sutra is the storehouse of the secret crux of the Buddhas. It must not be distributed or recklessly transmitted to others. It has been guarded by the Buddhas, the World-Honored Ones, and from times past until now has never been openly expounded. And since hatred and jealousy toward this sutra abound even when the Thus Come One is in the world, how much more will this be so after his passing?

"Medicine King, you should know that after the Thus Come One has entered extinction, if there are those who can copy, uphold, read and recite this sutra, offer alms to it and expound if for others, then the Thus Come One will cover them with his robe, and they will also be protected and kept in mind by the Buddhas who are now present in other regions. Such persons possess the power of great faith, the power of aspiration, the power of good roots. You should know that such persons lodge in the same place as the Thus Come One, and the Thus Come One pats them on the head with his hand.

"Medicine King, in any place whatsoever where this sutra is preached, where it is read, where it is recited, where it is copied, or where a roll of it exists, in all such places there should be erected towers made of the seven kinds of gems, and they should be made very high and broad and well adorned. There is no need to enshrine the relics of the Buddha there. Why? Because in such towers the entire body of the Thus Come One is already present. All kinds of flowers, incense, necklaces, silken canopies, streamers and banners, music and hymns should be offered as alms to these towers and they should be accorded reverence, honor and praise. If when people see these towers they bow in obeisance and offer alms, then you should know that such persons have all drawn near to anuttara-samyak-sambodhi.

"Medicine King, though there may be many persons, those still living in the household and those who have left it, who practice the way of the bodhisattva, if they are not willing to see, hear, read, recite, copy, embrace and offer alms to this Lotus Sutra, then you should know that such persons are not yet practicing the bodhisattva way in a fitting manner. But if there are those who will listen to this sutra, then they are capable of practicing the bodhisattva way in a fitting manner. If among the living beings who seek the Buddha way there are those who see or hear this Lotus Sutra, and who, having heard it, believe, understand and embrace it, then you should know that these persons can draw near to anuttara-samyak-sambodhi.

"Medicine King, suppose there is a man who is parched with thirst and in need of water. On an upland plateau he begins digging a hole in search of water, but he sees that the soil is dry and knows that water is still far away. He does not cease his efforts, however, and bit by bit he sees the soil becoming damper, until gradually he has worked his way into mud. Now he is determined in his mind to go on, for he knows that he is bound to be nearing water.

"The way of the bodhisattva is the same as this. As long as a person has not yet heard, not yet understood, and not yet been able to practice this Lotus Sutra, then you should know that that person is still far away from anuttara-samyak-sambodhi. But if the person is able to hear, understand, ponder and practice the sutra, then you should know that he can draw near to anuttara-samyak-sambodhi. Why? Because all bodhisattvas who attain anuttara-samyak-sambodhi in all cases do so through this sutra. This sutra opens the gate of expedient means and shows the form of true reality. This storehouse of the Lotus Sutra is hidden deep and far away where no person can reach it. But now the Buddha, teaching, converting and leading to success the bodhisattvas, opens it up for them.

"Medicine King, if there are bodhisattvas who, on hearing this Lotus Sutra, respond with surprise, doubt and fear, then you should know that they are bodhisattvas who have only newly embarked on their course. And if there are voice-hearers who, on hearing this sutra, respond with surprise, doubt, and fear, then you should know that they are persons of overbearing arrogance.

"Medicine King, if there are good men and good women who, after the Thus Come One has entered extinction, wish to expound this Lotus Sutra for the four kinds of believers, how should they expound it? These good men and good women should enter the Thus Come One's room, put on the Thus Come One's robe, sit in the Thus Come One's seat, and then for the sake of the four kinds of believers broadly expound this sutra.

"The 'Thus Come One's room' is the state of mind that shows great pity and compassion toward all living beings. The 'Thus Come One's robe' is the mind that is gentle and forbearing. The 'Thus Come One's seat' is the emptiness of all phenomena. One should seat oneself comfortably therein and after that, with a mind never lazy or remiss, should for the sake of the bodhisattvas and the four kinds of believers broadly expound this Lotus Sutra.

"Medicine King, I will send persons conjured up by magic to other lands to gather together assemblies to listen to the Law. And I will also send monks, nuns, laymen and laywomen conjured up by magic to listen to the preaching of the Law. These persons conjured up by magic will listen to the Law, believe and accept it, and abide by it without violation. If the preachers of the Law are in an empty and silent place, I will at that time send large numbers of heavenly beings, dragons, spirits, gandharvas, asuras, and others to listen to their preaching of the Law. Though I should be in another land, from time to time I will make it possible for the preachers of the Law to see my body. If they should forget a phrase of this sutra, I will appear and prompt them so that they are able to recite the text correctly and in full."

At that time the World-Honored One, wishing to state his meaning once more, spoke in verse form, saying:

> If you wish to put aside all sloth and remissness,
> you must listen to this sutra.
> It is hard to get a chance to hear this sutra,
> and believing and accepting it too is hard.
> If a person is thirsty and wants water
> he may dig a hole in the high plateau,
> but as long as he sees that the soil is dry
> he knows that water is still far away.
> But bit by bit he sees the soil grow damp and muddy
> and then he knows for certain he is nearing water.
> Medicine King, you should understand
> that people are like this—
> if they do not hear the Lotus Sutra,
> they will be far removed from the Buddha's wisdom.
> But if they hear this profound sutra
> which defines the Law of the voice-hearer,
> if they hear this king of the sutras
> and afterward carefully ponder it,
> then you should know that such persons
> are close to the wisdom of the Buddha.
> If a person expounds this sutra,
> he should enter the Thus Come One's room,
> put on the Thus Come One's robe,
> sit in the Thus Come One's seat,
> confront the assembly without fear
> and broadly expound it for them, making distinctions.
> Great pity and compassion are the room,
> gentleness and patience are the robe,
> the emptiness of all phenomena is the seat,
> and from that position one should expound the Law for them.

If when a person expounds this sutra
there is someone who speaks ill and reviles him
or attacks him with swords and staves, tiles and stones,
he should think of the Buddha and for that reason be patient.
In a thousand, ten thousand, a million lands
I will manifest my pure and durable body
and for immeasurable millions of kalpas
will expound the Law for living beings.
If after I have entered extinction
there are those who can expound this sutra,
I will send the four kinds of believers, magically conjured,
monks and nuns
and men and women of pure faith,
to offer alms to the teachers of the Law;
they will lead and guide living beings,
assemble them and cause them to listen to the Law.
If someone thinks to do evil to the preachers
with swords and staves or with tiles and stones,
I will dispatch persons magically conjured
who will act to guard and protect them.
If those who expound the Law
are alone in an empty and silent place,
and in that stillness where no human voice sounds
they read and recite this sutra,
at that time I will manifest
my pure and radiant body for them.
If they forget a passage or a phrase
I will prompt them so they will be thorough and effective.
If persons endowed with these virtues
should expound to the four kinds of believers
and read and recite the sutra in an empty place,
I will enable all of them to see my body.
And if the expounders are in an empty and silent place
I will send heavenly beings, dragon kings,
yakshas, spirits and others
to be an assembly and listen to the Law.
Persons such as this will delight in expounding the Law,
making distinctions and encountering no hindrance.

Because the Buddhas guard and keep them in mind,
they will be able to bring joy to the great assembly.
If one stays close to the teachers of the Law
he will speedily gain the bodhisattva way.
By following and learning from these teachers
he will see Buddhas as numerous as Ganges sands.

11

THE EMERGENCE OF
THE TREASURE TOWER

At that time in the Buddha's presence there was a tower adorned with the seven treasures, five hundred yojanas in height and two hundred and fifty yojanas in width and depth, that rose up out of the earth and stood suspended in the air. Various kinds of precious objects adorned it. It had five thousand railings, a thousand, ten thousand rooms, and numberless streamers and banners decorated it. Festoons of jewels hung down and ten thousand million jeweled bells were suspended from it. All four sides emitted a fragrance of tamalapatra and sandalwood that pervaded the whole world. Its banners and canopies were made of the seven treasures, namely, gold, silver, lapis lazuli, seashell, agate, pearl, and carnelian, and it was so high it reached to the heavenly palaces of the Four Heavenly Kings. The gods of the Trayastrimsha heaven rained down heavenly mandarava flowers as an offering to the treasure tower, and the other heavenly beings and the dragons, yakshas, gandharvas, asuras, garudas, kimnaras, mahoragas, human and nonhuman beings, an assembly of thousands, ten thousands, millions, offered all kinds of flowers, incense, necklaces, streamers, canopies and music as alms to the treasure tower, paying it reverence, honor and praise.

At that time a loud voice issued from the treasure tower, speaking words of praise: "Excellent, excellent! Shakyamuni, World-Honored One, that you can take the great wisdom of equality, a Law to instruct the bodhisattvas, guarded and kept in mind by the Buddhas, the Lotus Sutra of the Wonderful Law, and preach it for the sake of the great assembly! It is as you say, as you say. Shakyamuni, World-Honored One, all that you have expounded is the truth!"

At that time the four kinds of believers saw the great treasure tower suspended in the air, and they heard the voice that issued from the tower. All experienced the joy of the Law, marveling at this thing they had never known before. They rose from their seats, pressed their palms together in reverence, and then retired to one side.

At that time there was a bodhisattva and mahasattva named Great Joy of Preaching, who understood the doubts that were in the minds of the heavenly and human beings, asuras and other beings of all the world. He said to the Buddha: "World-Honored One, for what reason has this treasure tower risen up out of the earth? And why does this voice issue from its midst?"

At that time the Buddha said: "Bodhisattva Great Joy of Preaching, in the treasure tower is the complete body of a Thus Come One. Long ago, an immeasurable thousand, ten thousand, million asamkhyas of worlds to the east, in a land called Treasure Purity, there was a Buddha named Many Treasures. When this Buddha was originally carrying out the bodhisattva way, he made a great vow, saying, 'If, after I have become a Buddha and entered extinction, in the lands in the ten directions there is any place where the Lotus Sutra is preached, then my funerary tower, in order that I may listen to the sutra, will come forth and appear in that spot to testify to the sutra and praise its excellence.'

"When that Buddha had finished carrying out the Buddha way and was on the point of passing into extinction, in the midst of the great assembly of heavenly and human beings he said to the monks, 'After I have passed into extinction, if there are those who wish to offer alms to my complete body, then they should erect a great tower.' That Buddha, through his transcendental powers and the power of his vow, insures that, throughout the worlds in the ten directions, no matter in what place, if there are those who preach the Lotus Sutra, this treasure tower will in all cases come forth and appear in their presence, and his complete body will be in the tower, speaking words of praise and saying, Excellent, excellent!

"Great Joy of Preaching, now this tower of the Thus Come One Many Treasures, because it heard the preaching of the Lotus Sutra, has come forth out of the ground and speaks words of praise, saying, Excellent, excellent!"

At this time Bodhisattva Great Joy of Preaching, knowing the supernatural powers of the Thus Come One, spoke to the Buddha, saying, "World-Honored One, we wish to see the body of this Buddha."

The Buddha said to the bodhisattva and mahasattva Great Joy of Preaching, "This Many Treasures Buddha has taken a profound vow, saying, 'When my treasure tower, in order to listen to the Lotus Sutra, comes forth into the presence of one of the Buddhas, if there should be those who wish me to show my body to the four kinds of believers, then let the various Buddhas who are emanations of that Buddha and who are preaching the Law in the worlds in the ten directions all return and gather around that Buddha in a single spot. Only when that has been done will my body become visible.' Great Joy of Preaching, I will now gather together the various Buddhas that are emanations of my body and that are preaching the Law in the worlds in the ten directions."

Great Joy of Preaching said to the Buddha, "World-Honored One, I and the others also wish to see these Buddhas that are emanations of the World-Honored One, and to make obeisance to them and offer alms."

At that time the Buddha emitted a ray of light from the tuft of white hair [between his eyebrows], immediately making visible the Buddhas in the eastern region in lands as numerous as five hundred ten thousand million nayutas of Ganges sands. The earth in all these lands was made of crystal, and the lands were adorned with jeweled trees and jeweled robes. Countless thousands, ten thousands, millions of bodhisattvas filled them, and everywhere were hung jeweled curtains, with jeweled nets covering them over. The Buddhas in these lands preached the various doctrines of the Law with great and wonderful voices, and one could see immeasurable thousands, ten thousands, millions of bodhisattvas filling all these lands and preaching the Law for the assembly. In the southern, western and northern regions as well, and in the four intermediate quarters and up and down, wherever the beam from the tuft of white hair, a characteristic feature of the Buddha, shone, the same was true.

At that time the Buddhas of the ten directions each spoke to his multitude of bodhisattvas, saying, "Good men, now I must go to the saha world, to the place where Shakyamuni Buddha is, and also offer alms to the treasure tower of Many Treasures Thus Come One."

The saha world thereupon immediately changed into a place of cleanness and purity. The ground was made of lapis lazuli, jeweled trees adorned it, and ropes of gold marked off the eight highways. There were no villages, towns or cities, great seas or rivers, mountains, streams or forests; great jeweled incense was burning there and mandarava flowers covered the ground all over. Jeweled nets and curtains were spread above, hung with jeweled bells, and the members of this assembly alone were gathered there, all other heavenly and human beings having been moved to another region.

At that time the Buddhas, each with a great bodhisattva to act as his attendant, arrived in the saha world and proceeded to a position beneath one of the jeweled trees. Each of these jeweled trees was five hundred yojanas high and adorned with branches, leaves, flowers and fruit in due proportion. Under all the jeweled trees were lion seats five yojanas in height, and these too were decorated with large jewels. At that time each of the Buddhas took one of these seats, seating himself in cross-legged position. In this way the seats were filled throughout the thousand-millionfold world, but still there was no end even to the emanations of Shakyamuni Buddha arriving from merely one direction.

At that time Shakyamuni Buddha, wishing to provide space for all the Buddhas that were emanations of his body, in addition transformed two hundred ten thousand million nayutas of lands in each of the eight directions, making them all clean and pure and without hells, hungry spirits, beasts or asuras. He also moved all their heavenly and human beings to another region. The ground in these lands that he had transformed was also made of lapis lazuli. Jeweled trees adorned them, each tree five hundred yojanas high and adorned with branches, leaves, flowers and fruit in due proportion. There were jeweled lion seats under all the trees, five yojanas in height and ornamented with various kinds of treasures. These lands too were without great seas or rivers, or any kingly ranges of mountains such as the Muchilinda Mountains, Mahamuchilinda Mountains, Iron Encircling Mountains, Great Iron Encircling Mountains, or Mount Sumeru. The whole area comprised a single Buddha land, a jeweled region level and smooth. Curtains crisscrossed with festoons of jewels were spread everywhere, banners and canopies hung down, great jeweled incense burned, and heavenly jeweled flowers covered the ground all around.

Shakyamuni Buddha, in order to provide seats for all the Buddhas that were arriving, once more transformed two hundred ten thousand million nayutas of lands in each of the eight directions, making them all clean and pure and without hells, hungry spirits, beasts or asuras. He also moved all the heavenly and human beings to another region. The ground in these lands that he had transformed was likewise made of lapis lazuli. Jeweled trees adorned the lands, each tree five hundred yojanas in height and adorned with branches, leaves, flowers and fruit in due proportion. There were jeweled lion seats under all the trees, five yojanas in height and ornamented with great jewels. These lands too were without great seas or rivers, or any kingly ranges such as the Muchilinda Mountains, Mahamuchilinda Mountains, Iron Encircling Mountains, Great Iron Encircling Mountains, or Mount Sumeru, the whole area comprising a single Buddha land, a jeweled region level and smooth. Curtains crisscrossed with festoons of jewels were spread everywhere, banners and canopies hung down, great jeweled incense burned, and heavenly jeweled flowers covered the ground all around.

At that time the emanations of Shakyamuni Buddha from the eastern region, Buddhas in lands equal in number to hundreds, thousands, ten thousands, millions of nayutas of Ganges sands, each preaching the Law, had assembled there. And bit by bit the Buddhas from the ten directions all came and assembled in this way and were seated in the eight directions. At this time each of the directions was filled with Buddhas, Thus Come Ones, in four hundred ten thousand million nayutas of lands.

At this time the Buddhas, each seated on a lion seat under one of the jeweled trees, all dispatched their attendants to go and greet Shakyamuni Buddha. Each Buddha presented his attendant with a handful of jeweled flowers and said, "Good man, you must go to Mount Gridhrakuta to the place where Shakyamuni Buddha is and speak to him as I instruct you. Say, 'Are your illnesses few, are your worries few? In spirit and vigor are you well and happy? And are the bodhisattvas and voice-hearers all well and at peace?' Then take these jeweled flowers and scatter them over the Buddha as an offering, and say, 'The Buddha So-and-so would like to participate in the opening of this treasure tower.'

All the Buddhas dispatched their attendants to speak in this manner. At that time Shakyamuni Buddha saw the Buddhas that were his emanations all assembled, each sitting on a lion seat, and heard all these Buddhas say that they wished to participate in the opening of the treasure tower. Immediately he rose from his seat and stationed himself in midair. All the four kinds of believers likewise stood up, pressed their palms together and gazed at the Buddha with a single mind.

Shakyamuni Buddha with the fingers of his right hand then opened the door of the tower of seven treasures. A loud sound issued from it, like the sound of a lock and crossbar being removed from a great city gate, and at once all the members of the assembly caught sight of Many Treasures Thus Come One seated on a lion seat inside the treasure tower, his body whole and unimpaired, sitting as though engaged in meditation. And they heard him say, "Excellent, excellent, Shakyamuni Buddha! You have preached this Lotus Sutra in a spirited manner. I have come here in order that I may hear this sutra."

At that time the four kinds of believers, observing this Buddha who had passed into extinction immeasurable thousands, ten thousands, millions of kalpas in the past speaking in this way, marveled at what they had never known before and took the masses of heavenly jeweled flowers and scattered them over Many Treasures Buddha and Shakyamuni Buddha.

At that time Many Treasures Buddha offered half of his seat in the treasure tower to Shakyamuni Buddha, saying, "Shakyamuni Buddha, sit here!" Shakyamuni Buddha at once entered the tower and took half of the seat, seating himself in cross-legged position.

At that time the members of the great assembly, seeing the two Thus Come Ones seated cross-legged on the lion seat in the tower of seven treasures, all thought to themselves, These Buddhas are seated high up and far away! If only the Thus Come Ones would employ their transcendental powers to enable all of us to join them there in the air!

Immediately Shakyamuni Buddha used his transcendental powers to lift all the members of the great assembly up into the air. And in a loud voice he addressed all the four kinds of believers, saying, "Who is capable of broadly preaching the Lotus Sutra of the Wonderful Law in this saha world? Now is the time to do so, for before long the Thus Come One will enter nirvana. The Buddha wishes to entrust this Lotus Sutra of the Wonderful Law to someone so that it may be preserved."

At that time the World-Honored One, wishing to state his meaning once more, spoke in verse form, saying:

> This holy lord, this World-Honored One,
> though he passed into extinction long ago,
> still seats himself in the treasure tower,
> coming here for the sake of the Law.
> You people, why then do you not also
> strive for the sake of the Law?
> This Buddha passed into extinction
> an endless number of kalpas ago,
> but in many places he comes to listen to the Law
> because such opportunities are hard to encounter.
> This Buddha originally made a vow, saying,
> "After I have passed into extinction,
> wherever I may go, in whatever place,
> my constant aim will be to hear the Law!"
> In addition, these emanations of my body,
> Buddhas in immeasurable numbers
> like Ganges sands,
> have come, desiring to hear the Law,
> and so they may see Many Treasures Thus Come One
> who has passed into extinction.

Each has abandoned his wonderful land,
as well as his host of disciples,
the heavenly and human beings, dragons and spirits,
and all the offerings they give him,
and has come to this place on purpose
to make certain the Law will long endure.
In order to seat these Buddhas
I have employed transcendental powers,
moving immeasurable multitudes,
causing lands to be clean and pure,
leading each of these Buddhas
to the foot of a jeweled tree,
adorned as lotus blossoms
adorn a clear cool pond.
Beneath these jeweled trees
are lion seats,
and the Buddhas seat themselves on them,
adorning them with their brilliance
like a huge torch burning
in the darkness of the night.
A wonderful incense exudes from their bodies,
pervading the lands in the ten directions.
Living beings are wrapped in the aroma,
unable to restrain their joy,
as though a great wind
were tossing the branches of small trees.
Through this expedient means
they make certain that the Law will long endure.
So I say to the great assembly:
After I have passed into extinction,
who can guard and uphold,
read and recite this sutra?
Now in the presence of the Buddha
let him come forward and speak his vow!
This Many Treasures Buddha,
though he passed into extinction long ago,
because of his great vow
roars the lion's roar.

Many Treasures Thus Come One, I myself,
and these emanation Buddhas who have gathered here,
surely know this is our aim.
You sons of the Buddha,
who can guard the Law?
Let him make a great vow
to ensure that it will long endure!
He who is capable of guarding
the Law of this sutra
will thereby have offered alms
to me and to Many Treasures.
This Many Treasures Buddha
dwelling in his treasure tower
journeys constantly throughout the ten directions
for the sake of this sutra.
One who guards this sutra will also have offered alms
to the emanation Buddhas who have come here
adorning and making brilliant
all the various worlds.
If one preaches this sutra,
he will be able to see me
and Many Treasures Thus Come One
and these emanation Buddhas.
All you good men,
each of you must consider carefully!
This is a difficult matter—
it is proper you should make a great vow.
The other sutras
number as many as Ganges sands,
but though you expound those sutras,
that is not worth regarding as difficult.
If you were to seize Mount Sumeru
and fling it far off
to the measureless Buddha lands,
that too would not be difficult.
If you used the toe of your foot
to move the thousand-millionfold world,
booting it far away to other lands,

that too would not be difficult.
If you stood in the Summit of Being heaven
and for the sake of the assembly
preached countless other sutras,
that too would not be difficult.
But if after the Buddha has entered extinction,
in the time of evil,
you can preach this sutra,
that will be difficult indeed!
If there were a person
who took the empty sky in his hand
and walked all around with it,
that would not be difficult.
But if after I have passed into extinction
one can write out and embrace this sutra
and cause others to write it out,
that will be difficult indeed!
If one took the great earth,
placed it on his toenail,
and ascended with it to the Brahma heaven,
that would not be difficult.
But if after the Buddha has passed into extinction,
in the time of evil,
one can even for a little while read this sutra,
that will be difficult indeed!
If, when the fires come at the end of the kalpa,
one can load dry grass on his back
and enter the fire without being burned,
that would not be difficult.
But after I have passed into extinction
if one can embrace this sutra
and expound it to even one person,
that will be difficult indeed!
If one were to embrace this storehouse
of eighty-four thousand doctrines,
the twelve divisions of the sutras,
and expound it to others,
causing listeners

to acquire the six transcendental powers—
though one could do that,
that would not be difficult.
But after I have entered extinction
if one can listen to and accept this sutra
and ask about its meaning,
that will be difficult indeed!
If a person expounds the Law,
allowing thousands, ten thousands, millions,
immeasurable numbers of living beings
equal to Ganges sands
to become arhats
endowed with the six transcendental powers,
though one might confer such benefits,
that would not be difficult.
But after I have entered extinction
if one can honor and embrace
a sutra such as this one,
that will be difficult indeed!
For the sake of the Buddha way
in immeasurable numbers of lands
from the beginning until now
I have widely preached many sutras,
and among them
this sutra is foremost.
If one can uphold this,
he will be upholding the Buddha's body.
All you good men,
after I have entered extinction
who can accept and uphold,
read and recite this sutra?
Now in the presence of the Buddha
let him come forward and speak his vow!
This sutra is hard to uphold;
if one can uphold it even for a short while
I will surely rejoice
and so will the other Buddhas.
A person who can do this

wins the admiration of the Buddhas.
This is what is meant by valor,
this is what is meant by diligence.
This is what is called observing the precepts
and practicing dhuta.
This way one will quickly attain
the unsurpassed Buddha way.
And if in future existences
one can read and uphold this sutra,
he will be a true son of the Buddha,
dwelling in a land spotless and good.
If after the Buddha has passed into extinction
one can understand the meaning of this sutra,
he will be the eyes of the world
for heavenly and human beings.
If in that fearful age
one can preach this sutra for even a moment,
he will deserve to receive alms
from all heavenly and human beings.

12
DEVADATTA

At that time the Buddha addressed the bodhisattvas, the heavenly and human beings, and the four kinds of believers, saying: "Immeasurable kalpas in the past, I sought the Lotus Sutra without ever flagging. During those many kalpas, I constantly appeared as the ruler of a kingdom who made a vow to seek the unsurpassed bodhi. His mind never wavered or turned aside, and in his desire to fulfill the six paramitas he diligently distributed alms, never stinting in heart, whether the gift was elephants or horses, the seven rare articles, countries, cities, wife, children, maidservants, menservants, or his own head, eyes, marrow and brain, his own flesh and limbs. He did not begrudge even his own being and life. At that period the human life span was immeasurably long. But for the sake of the Law this king abandoned his kingdom and throne, delegated the government to the crown prince, sounded drums and sent out proclamations, seeking the Law in four directions and saying, 'Who can expound the Great Vehicle for me? To the end of my life I will be his provider and servant!'

"At that time there was a seer who came to the king and said, 'I have a Great Vehicle text called the Sutra of the Lotus of the Wonderful Law. If you will never disobey me, I will expound it for you.'

"When the king heard these words of the seer, he danced for joy. At once he accompanied the seer, providing him with whatever he needed, picking fruit, drawing water, gathering firewood, setting out meals, even offering his own body as a couch and seat, never stinting in body or mind. He served the seer in this manner for a thousand years, all for the sake of the Law, working diligently, acting as a provider and seeing to it that the seer lacked for nothing."

At that time the World-Honored One, wishing to state his meaning once more, spoke in verse form, saying:

> I recall those departed kalpas of the past
> when in order to seek the great Law,
> though I was the ruler of a worldly kingdom,
> I was not greedy to satisfy the five desires
> but instead struck the bell, crying in four quarters,
> "Who possesses the great Law?
> If he will explain and preach it for me
> I will be his slave and servant!"
> At that time there was a seer named Asita
> who came and announced to this great king,
> "I have a subtle and wonderful Law,
> rarely known in this world.
> If you will undertake religious practice
> I will expound it for you."
> When the king heard the seer's words
> his heart was filled with great joy.
> Immediately he accompanied the seer,
> providing him with whatever he needed,

gathering firewood, fruit and wild rice,
presenting them at appropriate times with respect and
   reverence.
Because the wonderful Law was in his thoughts
he never flagged in body or mind.
For the sake of living beings everywhere
he diligently sought the great Law,
taking no heed for himself
or for the gratification of the five desires.
Therefore the ruler of a great kingdom
through diligent seeking was able to acquire this Law
and eventually to attain Buddhahood,
as I will now explain to you.

The Buddha said to the monks: "The king at that time was I myself, and the seer was the man who is now Devadatta. All because Devadatta was a good friend to me, I was able to become fully endowed with the six paramitas, with pity, compassion, joy, and indifference, with the thirty-two features, the eighty characteristics, the purple-tinged golden color, the ten powers, the four kinds of fearlessness, the four methods of winning people, the eighteen unshared properties, and the transcendental powers and the power of the way. The fact that I have attained impartial and correct enlightenment and can save living beings on a broad scale is all due to Devadatta, who was a good friend."

Then the Buddha said to the four kinds of believers: "Devadatta, after immeasurable kalpas have passed, will attain Buddhahood. He will be called Heavenly King Thus Come One, worthy of offerings, of right and universal knowledge, perfect clarity and conduct, well gone, understanding the world, unexcelled worthy, trainer of people, teacher of heavenly and human beings, Buddha, World-Honored One. His world will be called Heavenly Way, and at that time Heavenly King Buddha will abide in the world for twenty medium kalpas, broadly preaching the wonderful Law for the sake of living beings. Living beings numerous as Ganges sands will attain the fruit of arhatship. Immeasurable numbers of living beings will conceive the desire to become pratyekabuddhas, living beings numerous as Ganges sands will conceive a desire for the unsurpassed way, will gain the truth of birthlessness, and will never regress. After Heavenly King Buddha enters parinirvana, his Correct Law will endure in the world for twenty medium kalpas. The relics from his whole body will be housed in a tower built of the seven treasures, sixty yojanas in height and forty yojanas in width and depth. All the heavenly and human beings will take assorted flowers, powdered incense, incense for burning, paste incense, clothing, necklaces, streamers and banners, jeweled canopies, music and songs of praise and offer them with obeisance to the wonderful seven-jeweled tower. Immeasurable numbers of living beings will attain the fruits of arhatship, numberless living beings will become enlightened as pratyekabuddhas, and unimaginable numbers of living beings will conceive a desire for bodhi and will reach the level of no regression."

The Buddha said to the monks: "In future ages if there are good men or good women who, on hearing the Devadatta chapter of the Lotus Sutra of the Wonderful Law, believe and revere it with pure hearts and harbor no doubts or perplexities, they will never fall into hell or the realm of hungry spirits or of beasts, but will be born in the presence of the Buddhas of the ten directions, and in the place where they are born they will constantly hear this sutra. If they are born among human or heavenly beings, they will enjoy exceedingly wonderful delights, and if they are born in the presence of a Buddha, they will be born by transformation from lotus flowers."

At that time there was a bodhisattva who was among the followers of Many Treasures World-Honored One from the lower region and whose name was Wisdom Accumulated. He said to Many Treasures Buddha, "Shall we return to our homeland?"

Shakyamuni Buddha said to Wisdom Accumulated, "Good man, wait a little while. There is a bodhisattva named Manjushri here whom you should see. Debate and discuss the wonderful Law with him, and then you may return to your homeland."

At that time Manjushri was seated on a thousand-petaled lotus blossom big as a carriage wheel, and the bodhisattvas who had come with him were also seated on jeweled lotus blossoms. Manjushri had emerged in a natural manner from the palace of the dragon king Sagara in the great ocean and was suspended in the air. Proceeding to Holy Eagle Peak, he descended from the lotus blossom and, having entered the presence of the Buddhas, bowed his head and paid obeisance to the feet of the two World-Honored Ones. When he had concluded these gestures of respect, he went to where Wisdom Accumulated was and exchanged greetings with him, and then retired and sat at one side.

Bodhisattva Wisdom Accumulated questioned Manjushri, saying, "When you went to the palace of the dragon king, how many living beings did you convert?"

Manjushri replied, "The number is immeasurable, incapable of calculation. The mouth cannot express it, the mind cannot fathom it. Wait a moment and there will be proof."

Before he had finished speaking, countless bodhisattvas seated on jeweled lotus blossoms emerged from the ocean and proceeded to Holy Eagle Peak, where they remained suspended in the air. These bodhisattvas had all been converted and saved by Manjushri. They had carried out all the bodhisattva practices and all discussed and expounded the six paramitas with one another. Those who had originally been voice-hearers expounded the practices of the voice-hearer when they were in the air, but now all were practicing the Great Vehicle principle of emptiness.

Manjushri said to Wisdom Accumulated, "The work of teaching and converting carried out in the ocean was as you can see."

At that time Bodhisattva Wisdom Accumulated recited these verses of praise:

> Of great wisdom and virtue, brave and stalwart,
> you have converted and saved immeasurable beings.
> Now those in this great assembly,
> as well as I myself, have all seen them.
> You expound the principle of the true entity,
> open up the Law of the single vehicle,
> broadly guiding the many beings,
> causing them quickly to attain bodhi.

Manjushri said, "When I was in the ocean I constantly expounded the Lotus Sutra of the Wonderful Law alone."

Bodhisattva Wisdom Accumulated questioned Manjushri, saying, "This sutra is very profound, subtle and wonderful, a treasure among sutras, a rarity in the world. Are there perhaps any living beings who, by earnestly and diligently practicing this sutra, have been able to attain Buddhahood quickly?"

Manjushri replied, "There is the daughter of the dragon king Sagara, who has just turned eight. Her wisdom has keen roots and she is good at understanding the root activities and deeds of living beings. She has mastered the dharanis, has been able to accept and embrace all the storehouse of profound secrets preached by the Buddhas, has entered deep into meditation, thoroughly grasped the doctrines, and in the space of an instant conceived the desire for bodhi and reached the level of no regression. Her eloquence knows no hindrance, and she thinks of living beings with compassion as though they were her own children. She is fully endowed with blessings, and when it comes to conceiving in mind and expounding by mouth, she is subtle, wonderful, comprehensive and great. Kind, compassionate, benevolent, yielding, she is gentle and refined in will, capable of attaining bodhi."

Bodhisattva Wisdom Accumulated said, "When I observe Shakyamuni Thus Come One, I see that for immeasurable kalpas he carried out harsh and difficult practices, accumulating merit, piling up virtue, seeking the way of the bodhisattva without ever resting. I observe that throughout the thousand-millionfold world, there is not a single spot tiny as a mustard seed where this bodhisattva failed to sacrifice body and life for the sake of living beings. Only after he had done that was he able to complete the bodhi way. I cannot believe that this girl in the space of an instant could actually achieve correct enlightenment."

Before his words had come to an end, the dragon king's daughter suddenly appeared before the Buddha, bowed her head in obeisance, and then retired to one side, reciting these verses of praise:

He profoundly understands the signs of guilt and good fortune
and illuminates the ten directions everywhere.
His subtle, wonderful pure Dharma body
is endowed with the thirty-two features;
the eighty characteristics
adorn his Dharma body.
Heavenly and human beings gaze up in awe,
dragons and spirits all pay honor and respect;
among all living beings,

none who do not hold him in reverence.
And having heard his teachings, I have attained bodhi—
the Buddha alone can bear witness to this.
I unfold the doctrines of the Great Vehicle
to rescue living beings from suffering.

At that time Shariputra said to the dragon girl, "You suppose that in this short time you have been able to attain the unsurpassed way. But this is difficult to believe. Why? Because a woman's body is soiled and defiled, not a vessel for the Law. How could you attain the unsurpassed bodhi? The road to Buddhahood is long and far-stretching. Only after one has spent immeasurable kalpas pursuing austerities, accumulating deeds, practicing all kinds of paramitas, can one finally achieve success. Moreover, a woman is subject to the five obstacles. First, she cannot become a Brahma heavenly king. Second, she cannot become the king Shakra. Third, she cannot become a devil king. Fourth, she cannot become a wheel-turning sage king. Fifth, she cannot become a Buddha. How then could a woman like you be able to attain Buddhahood so quickly?"

At that time the dragon girl had a precious jewel worth as much as the thousand-millionfold world which she presented to the Buddha. The Buddha immediately accepted it. The dragon girl said to Bodhisattva Wisdom Accumulated and to the venerable one, Shariputra, "I presented the precious jewel and the World-Honored One accepted it—was that not quickly done?"

They replied, "Very quickly!"

The girl said, "Employ your supernatural powers and watch me attain Buddhahood. It will be even quicker than that!"

At that time the members of the assembly all saw the dragon girl in the space of an instant change into a man and carry out all the practices of a bodhisattva, immediately proceeding to the Spotless World of the south, taking a seat on a jeweled lotus, and attaining impartial and correct enlightenment. With the thirty-two features and the eighty characteristics, he expounded the wonderful Law for all living beings everywhere in the ten directions.

At that time in the saha world the bodhisattvas, voice-hearers, gods, dragons and others of the eight kinds of guardians, human and non-human beings all from a distance saw the dragon girl become a Buddha and preach the Law to all the human and heavenly beings in the assembly at that time. Their hearts were filled with great joy and all from a distance paid reverent obeisance. Immeasurable living beings, hearing the Law, understood it and were able to reach the level of no regression. Immeasurable living beings received prophecies that they would gain the way. The Spotless World quaked and trembled in six different ways. Three thousand living beings of the saha world remained on the level of no regression. Three thousand living beings conceived a desire for bodhi and received prophecies of enlightenment. Bodhisattva Wisdom Accumulated, Shariputra and all the other members of the assembly silently believed and accepted these things.

13

ENCOURAGING
DEVOTION

At that time the bodhisattva and mahasattva Medicine King, along with the bodhisattva and mahasattva Great Joy of Preaching and twenty thousand bodhisattva followers who were accompanying them, all in the presence of the Buddha took this vow, saying: "We beg the World-Honored One to have no further worry. After the Buddha has entered extinction we will honor, embrace, read, recite and preach this sutra. Living beings in the evil age to come will have fewer and fewer good roots. Many will be overbearingly arrogant and greedy for offerings and other forms of gain, increasing the roots that are not good and moving farther away than ever from emancipation. But although it will be difficult to teach and convert them, we will summon up the power of great patience and will read and recite this sutra, embrace, preach and copy it, offering it many kinds of alms and never begrudging our bodies or lives."

At that time in the assembly there were five hundred arhats who received a prophecy of enlightenment. They said to the Buddha, "World-Honored One, we too will make a vow. In lands other than this one we will broadly preach this sutra."

Also there were eight thousand persons, some still learning, others with nothing more to learn, who received a prophecy of enlightenment. They rose from their seats, pressed their palms together and, turning toward the Buddha, made this vow: "World-Honored One, we too in other lands will broadly preach this sutra. Why? Because in this saha world the people are given to corruption and evil, beset by overbearing arrogance, shallow in blessings, irascible, muddled, fawning and devious, and their hearts are not sincere."

At that time the Buddha's maternal aunt, the nun Mahaprajapati, and the six thousand nuns who accompanied her, some still learning, others with nothing more to learn, rose from their seats, pressed their palms together with a single mind and gazed up at the face of the Honored One, their eyes never leaving him for an instant.

At that time the World-Honored One said to Gautami,[1] "Why do you look at the Thus Come One in that perplexed manner? In your heart are you perhaps worrying that I have failed to mention your name among those who have received a prophecy of the attainment of anuttara-samyak-sambodhi? But Gautami, I earlier made a general statement saying that all the voice-hearers had received such a prophecy. Now if you would like to know the prophecy for you, I will say that in ages to come, amid the Law of sixty-eight thousands of millions of Buddhas, you will be a great teacher of the Law, and the six thousand nuns, some still learning, some already sufficiently learned, will accompany you as teachers of the Law. In this manner you will bit by bit fulfill the way of the bodhisattva until you are able to become a Buddha with the name Gladly Seen by All Living Beings Thus Come One, worthy of offerings, of right and universal knowledge, perfect clarity and conduct, well gone, understanding the world, unexcelled worthy, trainer of people, teacher of heavenly and human

1. Gautami is another name for the nun Mahaprajapati.

beings, Buddha, World-Honored One. Gautami, this Gladly Seen by All Living Beings Buddha will confer a prophecy upon the six thousand bodhisattvas, to be passed from one to another, that they will attain anuttara-samyak-sambodhi."

At that time the mother of Rahula, the nun Yashodhara, thought to herself, The World-Honored One in his bestowal of prophecies has failed to mention my name alone!

The Buddha said to Yashodhara, "In future ages, amid the Law of hundreds, thousands, ten thousands, millions of Buddhas, you will practice the deeds of a bodhisattva, will be a great teacher of the Law, and will gradually fulfill the Buddha way. Then in a good land you will become a Buddha named Endowed with a Thousand Ten Thousand Glowing Marks Thus Come One, worthy of offerings, of right and universal knowledge, perfect clarity and conduct, well gone, understanding the world, unexcelled worthy, trainer of people, teacher of heavenly and human beings, Buddha, World-Honored One. The life span of this Buddha will be immeasurable asamkhya kalpas."

At that time the nun Mahaprajapati, the nun Yashodhara, and their followers were all filled with great joy, having gained what they had never had before. Immediately in the presence of the Buddha they spoke in verse form, saying:

> World-Honored One, leader and teacher,
> you bring tranquility to heavenly and human beings.
> We have heard these prophecies
> and our minds are peaceful and satisfied.

The nuns, having recited these verses, said to the Buddha, "World-Honored One, we too will be able to go to lands in other regions and broadly propagate this sutra."

At that time the World-Honored One looked at the eight hundred thousand million nayutas of bodhisattvas and mahasattvas. These bodhisattvas had all reached the level of avivartika, turned the unregressing wheel of the Law, and had gained dharanis. They rose from their seats, advanced before the Buddha and, pressing their palms together with a single mind, thought to themselves, If the World-Honored One should order us to embrace and preach this sutra, we would do as the

Buddha instructed and broadly propagate this Law. And then they
thought to themselves, But the Buddha now is silent and gives us no
such order. What shall we do?

At that time the bodhisattvas, respectfully complying with the
Buddha's will and at the same time wishing to fulfill their own original
vows, proceeded in the presence of the Buddha to roar the lion's roar
and to make a vow, saying: "World-Honored One, after the Thus
Come One has entered extinction we will travel here and there, back
and forth through the worlds in the ten directions so as to enable
living beings to copy this sutra, to receive, embrace, read and recite it,
understand and preach its principles, practice it in accordance with the
Law, and properly keep it in their thoughts. All this will be done
through the Buddha's power and authority. We beg that the World-
Honored One, though in another region, will look on from afar and
guard and protect us."

At that time the bodhisattvas joined their voices together and spoke
in verse form, saying:

> We beg you not to worry.
> After the Buddha has passed into extinction,
> in an age of fear and evil
> we will preach far and wide.
> There will be many ignorant people
> who will curse and speak ill of us
> and will attack us with swords and staves,
> but we will endure all these things.
> In that evil age there will be monks
> with perverse wisdom and hearts that are fawning and crooked
> who will suppose they have attained what they have
>   not attained,
> being proud and boastful in heart.
> Or there will be forest-dwelling monks
> wearing clothing of patched rags and living in retirement,
> who will claim they are practicing the true way,
> despising and looking down on all humankind.
> Greedy for profit and support,
> they will preach the Law to white-robed laymen

and will be respected and revered by the world
as though they were arhats who possess the six
   transcendental powers.
These men with evil in their hearts,
constantly thinking of worldly affairs,
will borrow the name of forest-dwelling monks
and take delight in proclaiming our faults,
saying things like this:
"These monks are greedy
for profit and support
and therefore they preach non-Buddhist doctrines
and fabricate their own scriptures
to delude the people of the world.
Because they hope to gain fame and renown thereby
they make distinctions when preaching this sutra."
Because in the midst of the great assembly
they constantly try to defame us,
they will address the rulers, high ministers,
Brahmans and householders,
as well as the other monks,
slandering and speaking evil of us,
saying, "These are men of perverted views
who preach non-Buddhist doctrines!"
But because we revere the Buddha
we will bear all these evils.
Though they treat us with contempt, saying,
"You are all no doubt Buddhas!"
all such words of arrogance and contempt
we will endure and accept.
In a muddied kalpa, in an evil age
there will be many things to fear.
Evil demons will take possession of others
and through them curse, revile and heap shame on us.
But we, reverently trusting in the Buddha,
will put on the armor of perseverance.
In order to preach this sutra
we will bear these difficult things.
We care nothing for our bodies or lives

but are anxious only for the unsurpassed way.
In ages to come we will protect and uphold
what the Buddha has entrusted to us.
This the World-Honored One must know.
The evil monks of that muddied age,
failing to understand the Buddha's expedient means,
how he preaches the Law in accordance with what
   is appropriate,
will confront us with foul language and angry frowns;
again and again we will be banished
to a place far removed from towers and temples.
All these various evils,
because we keep in mind the Buddha's orders,
we will endure.
If in the settlements and towns
there are those who seek the Law,
we will go to wherever they are
and preach the Law entrusted to us by the Buddha.
We will be envoys of the World-Honored One,
facing the assembly without fear.
We will preach the Law with skill,
for we desire the Buddha to rest in tranquility.
In the presence of the World-Honored One
and of the Buddhas who have gathered from the ten directions
we proclaim this vow.
The Buddha must know what is in our hearts.

14

PEACEFUL PRACTICES

At that time Manjushri, Dharma prince, bodhisattva and mahasattva, said to the Buddha: "World-Honored One, these bodhisattvas
undertake something that is very difficult. Because they revere and
obey the Buddha, they have taken a great vow that in the evil age
hereafter they will guard, uphold, read, recite and preach this Lotus
Sutra. World-Honored One, in the evil age hereafter, how should
these bodhisattvas and mahasattvas go about preaching this sutra?"

The Buddha said to Manjushri: "If these bodhisattvas and mahasattvas in the evil age hereafter wish to preach this sutra, they should
abide by four rules. First, they should abide by the practices and
associations proper for bodhisattvas so that they can expound this

sutra for the sake of living beings. Manjushri, what do I mean by the practices of a bodhisattva or mahasattva? If a bodhisattva or mahasattva takes his stand on perseverance, is gentle and compliant, never violent, and never alarmed in mind; and if with regard to phenomena he takes no action but observes the true entity of phenomena without acting or making any distinction, then this I call the practices of a bodhisattva or mahasattva.

"As for the associations proper for them, bodhisattvas or mahasattvas should not associate closely with rulers, princes, high ministers or heads of offices. They should not associate closely with non-Buddhists, Brahmans or Jains, or with those who compose works of secular literature or books extolling the heretics, nor should they be closely associated with Lokayatas or Anti-Lokayatas.[1] They should not be closely associated with hazardous amusements, boxing or wrestling, or with actors or others engaged in various kinds of illusionary entertainments, or with chandalas, persons engaged in raising pigs, sheep, chickens or dogs, or those who engage in hunting or fishing or other evil activities. If such persons at times come to one, then one may preach the Law for them, but one should expect nothing from it. Again one should not associate with monks, nuns, laymen or laywomen who seek to become voice-hearers, nor should one question or visit them. One should not stay with them in the same room, or in the place where one exercises, or in the lecture hall. One should not join them in their activities. If at times they come to one, one may preach the Law in accordance with what is appropriate, but should expect nothing from it.

"Manjushri, the bodhisattva or mahasattva should not, when preaching the Law to women, do so in a manner that could arouse thoughts of desire in them, nor should he delight in seeing them. If he enters the house of another person, he should not engage in talk with the young girls, unmarried women or widows. Nor should he go near the five types of unmanly men or have any close dealings with them.[2] He should not enter another person's house alone. If for some reason it is imperative to enter alone, he should concentrate his whole mind on thoughts of the Buddha. If he should preach the Law for a

---

1. The Lokáyatas expounded a materialist doctrine in the time of Shakyamuni. The anti-Lokáyatas attempted to refute them.
2. Men who are impotent or suffer from other types of sexual disabilities

woman, he should not bare his teeth in laughter or let his chest become exposed. He should not have any intimate dealings with her even for the sake of the Law, much less for any other purpose.

"He should not delight in nurturing underage disciples, shramaneras or children, and should not delight in sharing the same teacher with them. He should constantly take pleasure in sitting in meditation, being in quiet surroundings and learning to still his mind. Manjushri, these are what I call the things he should first of all associate himself with.

"Next, the bodhisattva or mahasattva should view all phenomena as empty, that being their true entity. They do not turn upside down, do not move, do not regress, do not revolve. They are like empty space, without innate nature, beyond the reach of all words. They are not born, do not emerge, do not arise. They are without name, without form, without true being. They are without volume, without limits, without hindrance, without barriers. It is only through causes and conditions that they exist, and come to be turned upside down, to be born. Therefore I say that one should constantly delight in viewing the form of phenomena as this. This is what I call the second thing that the bodhisattva or mahasattva should associate himself with."

At that time the World-Honored One, wishing to state his meaning once more, spoke in verse form, saying:

> If there are bodhisattvas
> who in the evil age hereafter
> wish with fearless hearts
> to preach this sutra,
> these are the places they should enter
> and the persons they should closely associate with.
> At all times shun rulers
> and the princes of kingdoms,
> high ministers, heads of offices,
> those engaged in hazardous amusements
> as well as chandalas,
> non-Buddhists and Brahmans.
> One should not associate with
> persons of overbearing arrogance
> or those who stubbornly adhere to the Lesser Vehicle

and are learned in its three storehouses.
Monks who violate the precepts,
arhats who are so in name only,
nuns who are fond
of jesting and laughter,
or women lay believers
who are profoundly attached to the five desires
or who seek immediate entry into extinction—
all these one should not associate with.
If there are persons
who come with good hearts
to the place of the bodhisattva
in order to hear the Buddha way,
then the bodhisattva
with a fearless heart
but without harboring expectations
should preach the Law for them.
But widows and unmarried women
and the different kinds of unmanly men—
all these he should not associate with
or treat with intimacy.
Also he must not associate with
slaughterers or flesh-carvers,
those who hunt animals or catch fish,
or kill or do harm for profit.
Those who peddle meat for a living
or display women and sell their favors—
all persons such as this
one should never associate with.
Those engaged in hazardous sports, wrestling,
or other kinds of amusements,
women of lascivious nature—
never associate with any of these.
Never go alone into an enclosed place
to preach the Law to a woman.
When you preach the Law,
let there be no jesting or laughter.
When you enter a village to beg for food,

take another monk with you;
if there is no other monk around,
with a single mind concentrate on the Buddha.
These are what I call
proper practices and associations.
By being careful about these two,
one can preach in a peaceful manner.
One should not speak in terms of
superior, medial, or inferior doctrines,
of doctrines of the conditioned or the unconditioned,
of the real or the not real.
Again one should not make distinctions
by saying, "This is a man," "This is a woman."
Do not try to apprehend phenomena,
to understand or to see them.
These are what I call
the practices of the bodhisattva.
All phenomena
are empty, without being,
without any constant abiding,
without arising or extinction.
This I call the position
the wise person associates himself with.
From upside-downness come distinctions,
that phenomena exist, do not exist,
are real, are not real,
are born, are not born.
Place yourself in quiet surroundings,
learn to still your mind,
remain tranquil, unmoving,
like Mount Sumeru.
Look upon all phenomena
as having no existence,
like empty space,
as without firmness or hardness,
not born, not emerging,
not moving, not regressing,
constantly abiding in a single form—

this I call the place to draw near to.
If after I have entered extinction
there are monks
who take up these practices
and these associations,
then when they preach this sutra
they will be free of quailing and timidity.
If a bodhisattva will at times
enter a quiet room
and with the correct mental attitude
will view phenomena according to the doctrine,
and then, rising from his meditation,
will for the sake of the ruler,
the princes, ministers and people,
the Brahmans and others,
unfold, propagate, expound
and preach this sutra,
then his mind will be tranquil,
free of quailing and timidity.
Manjushri,
these I call the first set of rules
for the bodhisattva to abide by
to enable him in later ages
to preach the Lotus Sutra.

"Furthermore, Manjushri, after the Thus Come One has passed into extinction, in the Latter Day of the Law, if one wishes to preach this sutra, he should abide by these peaceful practices. When he opens his mouth to expound or when he reads the sutra, he should not delight in speaking of the faults of other people or scriptures. He should not display contempt for other teachers of the Law or speak of other people's tastes or shortcomings. With regard to the voice-hearers he should not refer to them by name and describe their faults, or name them and praise their good points. Also he should not allow his mind to become filled with resentment or hatred. Because he is good at cultivating this kind of peaceful mind, his listeners will not oppose his ideas. If he is asked difficult questions, he should not reply in terms of the Law of the Lesser Vehicle. He should explain things solely in terms of the Great Vehicle so that people will be able to acquire wisdom embracing all species.''

At that time the World-Honored One, wishing to state his meaning once more, spoke in verse form, saying:

> The bodhisattva should at all times delight
> in preaching the Law in a tranquil manner.
> On pure clean ground
> he should spread his sitting mat,
> anoint his body with oil,
> wash away dust and impurities,
> put on a new clean robe
> and make himself both inwardly and outwardly pure.
> Seating himself comfortably in the Dharma seat,
> he should preach the Law in accordance with questions.
> If there are monks
> or nuns,
> men lay believers,
> women lay believers,
> rulers and princes,
> officials, gentlemen and common people,
> with a mild expression he should preach for them
> the subtle and wonderful doctrines.
> If there are difficult questions
> he should answer them in accordance with the doctrines,
> employing causes and conditions, similes and parables
> to expound and make distinctions,
> and through these expedient means
> cause all listeners to aspire to enlightenment,
> to increase their benefits little by little
> and enter the Buddha way.
> He should put aside all idea of laziness,
> all thought of negligence or ease,
> remove himself from cares and worries
> and with a compassionate mind preach the Law.
> Day and night constantly he should expound
> the teachings of the unsurpassed way,
> employing causes and conditions,

immeasurable similes and parables
to instruct living beings
and cause them all to be joyful.
Clothing and bedding,
food, drink, medicine—
with regard to such things
he should have no expectations
but with a single mind concentrate
upon the reasons for preaching the Law,
desiring to complete the Buddha way
and to cause those in the assembly to do likewise.
That will bring great gain to them,
an offering of peace.
After I have passed into extinction
if there are monks
who are able to expound
this Lotus Sutra of the Wonderful Law,
their minds will be free of jealousy and anger,
of all worry and hindrance.
No one will trouble them,
curse or revile them.
They will know no fear,
no attacks by sword or staff,
nor will they ever be banished,
because they abide in patience.
Wise persons will be good
at cultivating their minds like this
and be able to abide in peace
as I have described above.
The blessings of such persons
are beyond calculation, simile or parable;
thousands, ten thousands, millions of kalpas
would not suffice to describe them.

"Also, Manjushri, if a bodhisattva or mahasattva in the latter age hereafter, when the Law is about to perish, should accept and embrace, read and recite this sutra, he must not harbor a mind marked by jealousy, fawning or deceit. And he must not be contemptuous of or revile those who study the Buddha way or seek out their shortcomings.

"If there are monks, nuns, laymen, or laywomen who seek to become voice-hearers, seek to become pratyekabuddhas, or seek the bodhisattva way, one must not trouble them by causing them to have doubts or regrets, by saying to them, 'You are far removed from the way and in the end will never be able to attain wisdom embracing all species. Why? Because you are self-indulgent and willful people who are negligent of the way!'

"Also one should never engage in frivolous debate over the various doctrines or dispute or wrangle over them. With regard to all living beings one should think of them with great compassion. With regard to the Thus Come Ones, think of them as kindly fathers; with regard to the bodhisattvas, think of them as great teachers. Toward the great bodhisattvas of the ten directions at all times maintain a serious mind, paying them due reverence and obeisance. To all living beings preach the Law in an equitable manner. Because a person is heedful of the Law, that does not mean one should vary the amount of preaching. Even to those who show a profound love for the Law one should not on that account preach at greater length.

"Manjushri, if among these bodhisattvas and mahasattvas there are those who in the latter age hereafter, when the Law is about to perish, succeed in carrying out this third set of peaceful practices, then when they preach this Law they will be free of anxiety and confusion, and will find good fellow students to read and recite this sutra with. They will attract a large assembly of persons who come to listen and assent. After they have listened, they will embrace; after they have embraced, they will recite; after they have recited, they will preach; and after they have preached, they will copy, or will cause others to copy, and will present offerings to the sutra rolls, treating them with reverence, respect and praise."

At that time the World-Honored One, wishing to state his meaning once more, spoke in verse form, saying:

> If you wish to preach this sutra,
> you must set aside jealousy, hatred, arrogance,
> a mind that is fawning, deceitful, false,
> and constantly practice honest and upright conduct.

Do not look with contempt on others
or hold frivolous debates on the doctrine.
Do not cause others to have doubts or regrets
by saying, "You will never become a Buddha!"
When a son of the Buddha preaches the Law
he is at all times gentle and full of forbearance,
having pity and compassion on all,
never giving way to a negligent or slothful mind.
The great bodhisattvas of the ten directions
out of pity for the multitude carry out the way.
One should strive to respect and revere them,
saying, "These are my great teachers!"
Regarding the Buddhas, the World-Honored Ones,
learn to think of them as unsurpassed fathers.
Wipe out the mind of pride and arrogance
and preach the Law without hindrance.
Such is the third set of rules;
wise persons should guard and obey them.
If with a single mind they observe these peaceful practices,
they will be respected by immeasurable multitudes.

"Manjushri, if among these bodhisattvas and mahasattvas there are those who in the age hereafter, when the Law is about to perish, accept and embrace the Lotus Sutra, toward believers who are still in the household or those who have left the household they should cultivate a mind of great compassion, and toward those who are not bodhisattvas they should also cultivate a mind of great compassion, and should think to themselves: These persons have made a great error. Though the Thus Come One as an expedient means preaches the Law in accordance with what is appropriate, they do not listen, do not know, do not realize, do not inquire, do not believe, do not understand. But although these persons do not inquire about, do not believe and do not understand this sutra, when I have attained anuttara-samyak-sam-bodhi, wherever I may happen to be, I will employ my transcendental powers and the power of wisdom to draw them to me and cause them to abide in this Law.

"Manjushri, after the Thus Come One has entered extinction, if among these bodhisattvas and mahasattvas there are those who succeed in carrying out this fourth set of rules, then when they preach the Law they will commit no error. Monks, nuns, laymen, laywomen, rulers, princes, great ministers, common people, Brahmans and householders will constantly offer them alms and will revere, respect and praise them. The heavenly beings in the sky, in order to listen to the Law, will constantly follow and attend them. If they are in a settlement or town or in a quiet and deserted place or a forest and people come and want to ask them difficult questions, the heavenly beings day and night will for the sake of the Law constantly guard and protect them and will cause all the listeners to rejoice. Why? Because this sutra is protected by the supernatural powers of all the Buddhas of the past, future, and present.

"Manjushri, as for this Lotus Sutra, throughout immeasurable numbers of lands one cannot even hear its name, much less be able to see it, accept and embrace, read and recite it. Manjushri, suppose, for example, that there is a powerful wheel-turning sage king who wants to use his might to subdue other countries, but the petty rulers will not heed his commands. At that time the wheel-turning king calls up his various troops and sets out to attack. If the king sees any of his fighting forces who have won distinction in battle, he is greatly delighted and immediately rewards the persons in accordance with their merits, handing out fields, houses, settlements and towns, or robes and personal adornments, or perhaps giving out various precious objects such as gold, silver, lapis lazuli, seashell, agate, coral or amber, or elephants, horses, carriages, men and women servants, and people. Only the bright jewel that is in his topknot he does not give away. Why? Because this one jewel exists only on the top of the king's head, and if he were to give it away, his followers would be certain to express great consternation and alarm.

"Manjushri, the Thus Come One is like this. He uses the power of meditation and wisdom to win Dharma lands and become king of the threefold world. But the devil kings are unwilling to obey and submit. The worthy and sage military leaders of the Thus Come One engage them in battle, and when any of the Buddha's soldiers achieve distinction, the Buddha is delighted in heart and in the midst of the four kinds of believers he preaches various sutras, causing their hearts to be joyful. He presents them with meditations, emancipations, roots and powers that are free of outflows, and other treasures of the Law. He also presents them with the city of nirvana, telling them that they have attained extinction, guiding their minds and causing them all to rejoice. But he does not preach the Lotus Sutra to them.

"Manjushri, when the wheel-turning king sees someone among his soldiers who has gained truly great distinction, he is so delighted in heart that he takes that unbelievably fine jewel that has been in his topknot for so long and has never been recklessly given away, and now gives it to the man. And the Thus Come One does the same. In the threefold world he acts as the great Dharma King. He uses the Law to teach and convert all living beings, and watches his worthy and sage armies as they battle with the devils of the five components, the devils of earthly desires, and the death devil. And when they have won great distinction and merit, wiping out the three poisons, emerging from the threefold world, and destroying the nets of the devils, at that time the Thus Come One is filled with great joy. This Lotus Sutra is capable of causing living beings to attain comprehensive wisdom. It will face much hostility in the world and be difficult to believe. It has not been preached before, but now I preach it.

"Manjushri, this Lotus Sutra is foremost among all that is preached by the Thus Come Ones. Among all that is preached it is the most profound. And it is given at the very last, the way that powerful ruler did when he took the bright jewel he had guarded for so long and finally gave it away.

"Manjushri, this Lotus Sutra is the secret storehouse of the Buddhas, the Thus Come Ones. Among the sutras, it holds the highest place. Through the long night I have guarded and protected it and have never recklessly propagated it. But today for the first time I expound it for your sake."

At that time the World-Honored One, wishing to state his meaning once more, spoke in verse form, saying:

> Constantly practice perseverance,
> have pity on all beings,
> and do your best to expound and preach
> the sutra praised by the Buddha.
> In the latter age hereafter

those who embrace this sutra should,
with regard to persons in the household, persons who have
    left it,
or persons who are not bodhisattvas,
cultivate pity and compassion,
saying, "If they do not listen to
and do not believe this sutra
they will be committing a great error.
If I gain the Buddha way
I will employ expedient means
and preach this Law for them,
causing them to abide in it."
Suppose there is a powerful
wheel-turning king.
His soldiers have won merit in battle
and he rewards them with various articles,
elephants, horses, carriages,
adornments for their person,
fields and houses,
settlements and towns,
or gives them clothing,
various kinds of precious objects,
men and women servants, wealth and goods,
delightedly bestowing all these.
But if there is someone brave and stalwart
who can carry out difficult deeds,
the king will remove the bright jewel from his topknot
and present it to the man.
The Thus Come One is like this.
He acts as king of the doctrines,
possessing the great power of perseverance
and the precious storehouse of wisdom,
and with his great pity and compassion
he converts the age in accordance with the Law.
He sees all persons
as they undergo suffering and anxiety,
seeking to gain emancipation,
battling with the devils,

and for the sake of these living beings
he preaches various doctrines,
employing great expedient means
and preaching these sutras.
And when he knows that living beings
have gained power through them,
then at the very last for their sake
he preaches this Lotus Sutra,
like the king who unbinds his topknot
and gives away his bright jewel.
This sutra is to be honored
as highest among all sutras.
Constantly I guard and protect it,
and do not recklessly reveal it.
But now the time is right
for me to preach it to you.
After I have entered extinction
if someone seeks the Buddha way
and hopes to be able in tranquility
to expound this sutra,
then he should associate himself closely
with the four rules described.
Anyone who reads this sutra
will at all times be free of worry and anxiety;
likewise he will be without illness or pain,
his expression fresh and bright.
He will not be born in poverty or want,
in humble or ugly circumstances.
Living beings will delight to see him
and look up to him as a worthy or a sage.
The young sons of heavenly beings
will wait on him and serve him.
Swords and staves will not touch him
and poison will have no power to harm him.
If people speak ill and revile him,
their mouths will be closed and stopped up.
He will stroll about without fear
like the lion king.

The brilliance of his wisdom
will be like the shining of the sun;
even in his dreams
he will see only wonderful things.
He will see the Thus Come Ones
seated in their lion seats
surrounded by multitudes of monks
and preaching the Law.
And he will see dragons, spirits,
asuras and others,
numerous as Ganges sands,
reverently pressing their palms together.
He will see himself there
and will preach the Law for them.
Again he will see Buddhas,
their bodies marked by a golden hue,
emitting immeasurable rays
that light up all things,
employing brahma sounds
to expound the doctrines.
For the four kinds of believers
the Buddha will preach the unsurpassed Law,
and he will see himself among them
pressing his palms together and praising the Buddha.
He will hear the Law and delight
and will offer alms.
He will obtain dharanis
and proof of the wisdom without regression.
And when the Buddha knows that his mind
has entered deep into the Buddha way,
then he will give him a prophecy
that he will attain the highest, the correct enlightenment.
"You, good man,
in an age to come
will attain immeasurable wisdom,
the great way of the Buddha.
Your land will be adorned and pure,
incomparably broad and great,

with the four kinds of believers
who press their palms together and listen to the Law."
Again he will see himself
in the midst of mountains and forests
practicing the good Law,
understanding the true entity of all phenomena,
deeply entering meditation
and seeing the Buddhas of the ten directions.
Of Buddhas, their bodies a golden hue,
adorned with the marks of a hundred kinds of good fortune,
of listening to the Law and preaching it to people—
such will be the good dreams he constantly dreams.
Again he will dream he is king of a country
but casts aside palaces and attendants
and the superb and wonderful objects of the five desires,
repairs to the place of practice
and under the bodhi tree
seats himself in a lion seat,
seeking the way, and after seven days
gains the wisdom of the Buddhas.
Having succeeded in the unsurpassed way,
he rises and turns the wheel of the Law,
preaching the Law for the four kinds of believers,
for thousands, ten thousands, millions of kalpas
preaching the wonderful Law free of outflows,
saving immeasurable living beings.
And afterward he will enter nirvana
like smoke coming to an end when a lamp goes out.
If in that evil age hereafter
someone preaches this foremost Law,
that person will gain great benefits,
blessings such as have been described above.

15

EMERGING FROM
THE EARTH

At that time the bodhisattvas and mahasattvas who had gathered from the lands of the other directions, greater in number than the sands of eight Ganges, stood up in the midst of the great assembly, pressed their palms together, bowed in obeisance and said to the Buddha: "World-Honored One, if you will permit us in the age after the Buddha has entered extinction to diligently and earnestly protect, read, recite, copy and offer alms to this sutra in the saha world, we will preach it widely throughout this land!"

At that time the Buddha said to the bodhisattvas and mahasattvas: "Leave off, good men! There is no need for you to protect this sutra. Why? Because in this saha world of mine there are bodhisattvas and mahasattvas who are as numerous as the sands of sixty thousand Ganges, and each of these bodhisattvas has a retinue equal to the sands of sixty thousand Ganges. After I have entered extinction these persons will be able to protect, read, recite and widely preach this sutra."

When the Buddha spoke these words, the earth of the thousand-millionfold countries of the saha world all trembled and split open, and out of it emerged at the same instant immeasurable thousands, ten thousands, millions of bodhisattvas and mahasattvas. The bodies of these bodhisattvas were all golden in hue, with the thirty-two features and an immeasurable brightness. Previously they had all been dwelling in the world of empty space underneath the saha world. But when these bodhisattvas heard the voice of Shakyamuni Buddha speaking, they came up from below.

Each one of these bodhisattvas was the leader of his own great assembly, and each brought with him a retinue equal in number to the sands of sixty thousand Ganges. To say nothing of those who brought retinues equal to the sands of fifty thousand, forty thousand, thirty thousand, twenty thousand, or ten thousand Ganges. Or a retinue equal to as little as the sands of one Ganges, half a Ganges, one fourth of a Ganges, or as little as one part in a thousand, ten thousand, a million nayutas of Ganges. Or those whose retinue was only one thousand ten thousand million nayutas. Or only a million ten thousand. Or only a thousand ten thousand, a hundred ten thousand, or just ten thousand. Or only one thousand, one hundred, or ten. Or who brought with them only five, four, three, two or one disciple. Or those who came alone, preferring to carry out solitary practices. Such were they, then, immeasurable, boundless, beyond anything that can be known through calculation, simile or parable.

After these bodhisattvas had emerged from the earth, they each one proceeded to the wonderful tower of seven treasures suspended in the sky where Many Treasures Thus Come One and Shakyamuni Buddha were. On reaching it, they turned to the two World-Honored Ones, bowed their heads and made obeisance at their feet. They also all performed obeisance to the Buddhas seated on lion seats underneath the jeweled trees. Then they circled around to the right three times, pressed their palms together in a gesture of respect, utilizing the bodhisattvas' various methods of praising to deliver praises, and then took up a position to one side, gazing up in joy at the two World-

Honored Ones. While these bodhisattvas and mahasattvas who had emerged from the earth were employing the bodhisattvas' various methods of praising to praise the Buddhas, an interval of fifty small kalpas passed by.

At that time Shakyamuni Buddha sat silent, and the four kinds of believers likewise all remained silent for fifty small kalpas, but because of the supernatural powers of the Buddha, it was made to seem to the members of the great assembly like only half a day.

At that time the four kinds of believers, also because of the supernatural powers of the Buddha, saw these bodhisattvas filling the sky over immeasurable hundreds, thousands, ten thousands, and millions of lands. Among these bodhisattvas were four leaders. The first was called Superior Practices, the second was called Boundless Practices, the third was called Pure Practices, and the fourth was called Firmly Established Practices. These four bodhisattvas were the foremost leaders and guiding teachers among all the group. In the presence of the great assembly, each one of these pressed his palms together, gazed at Shakyamuni Buddha, and inquired: "World-Honored One, are your illnesses few, are your worries few, are your practices proceeding comfortably? Do those whom you propose to save readily receive instruction? Does the effort not cause the World-Honored One to become weary and spent?"

At that time the four great bodhisattvas spoke in verse form, saying:

> Is the World-Honored One comfortable,
> with few illnesses, few worries?
> In teaching and converting living beings,
> can you do so without fatigue and weariness?
> And do living beings
> receive instruction readily or not?
> Does it not cause the World-Honored One
> to become weary and spent?

At that time in the midst of the great assembly of bodhisattvas the World-Honored One spoke these words: "Just so, just so, good men! The Thus Come One is well and happy, with few ills and few worries.

The living beings are readily converted and saved and I am not weary or spent. Why? Because for age after age in the past the living beings have constantly received my instruction. And also they have offered alms and paid reverence to the Buddhas of the past and have planted various good roots. So when these living beings see me for the first time and listen to my preaching, they all immediately believe and accept it, entering into the wisdom of the Thus Come One, with the exception of those who earlier practiced and studied the Lesser Vehicle. And now I will make it possible for these persons to listen to this sutra and enter the wisdom of the Buddha."

At that time the [four] great bodhisattvas spoke in verse form, saying:

> Excellent, excellent,
> great hero, World-Honored One!
> The living beings
> are readily converted and saved.
> They know how to inquire about
> the most profound wisdom of the Buddha,
> and having heard, they believe and understand it.
> We are accordingly overjoyed.

At that time the World-Honored One praised the great bodhisattvas who led the group, saying: "Excellent, excellent, good men! You know how to rejoice in your hearts for the Thus Come One."

At that time the bodhisattva Maitreya and the multitude of bodhisattvas equal in number to the sands of eight thousand Ganges all thought to themselves: Never in the past have we seen or heard of such a great multitude of bodhisattvas and mahasattvas as these who have emerged from the earth and now stand before the World-Honored One pressing their palms together, offering alms, and inquiring about the Thus Come One!

At that time the bodhisattva and mahasattva Maitreya, knowing the thought that was in the minds of the bodhisattvas as numerous as the sands of eight thousand Ganges, and wishing also to resolve his own doubts, pressed his palms together, turned to the Buddha and made this inquiry in verse form:

Immeasurable thousands, ten thousands, millions,
a great host of bodhisattvas
such as was never seen in the past—
I beg the most honored of two-legged beings to explain
where they have come from,
what causes and conditions bring them together!
Huge in body, with great transcendental powers,
unfathomable in wisdom,
firm in their intent and thought,
with the power of great perseverance,
the kind living beings delight to see—
where have they come from?
Each one of these bodhisattvas
brings with him a retinue
immeasurable in number
like the sands of the Ganges.
Some of these great bodhisattvas
bring numbers equal to sixty thousand Ganges sands.
And this great multitude
with a single mind seek the Buddha way.
These great teachers
equal in number to sixty thousand Ganges sands
together come to offer alms to the Buddha
and to guard and uphold this sutra.
More numerous are those with followers
like the sands of fifty thousand Ganges,
those with followers like the sands of forty thousand,
   thirty thousand,
twenty thousand, ten thousand,
one thousand, one hundred,
or the sands of a single Ganges,
half a Ganges, one third, one fourth,
or only one part in a million ten thousand;
those with one thousand, ten thousand nayutas,
ten thousand, a million disciples,
or half a million—
they are more numerous still.
Those with a million or ten thousand followers,

a thousand or a hundred,
fifty or ten,
three, two, or one,
or those who come alone without followers,
delighting in solitude,
all coming to where the Buddha is—
they are even more numerous than those described above.
If one should try to use an abacus
to calculate the number of this great multitude,
though he spent as many kalpas as Ganges sands
he could never know the full sum.
This host of bodhisattvas
with their great dignity, virtue and diligence—
who preached the Law for them,
who taught and converted them and brought them to this?
Under whom did they first set their minds on enlightenment,
what Buddha's Law do they praise and proclaim?
What sutra do they embrace and carry out,
what Buddha way do they practice?
These bodhisattvas
possess transcendental powers and the power of great wisdom.
The earth in four directions trembles and splits
and they all emerge from out of it.
World-Honored One, from times past
I have seen nothing like this!
I beg you to tell me where they come from,
the name of the land.
I have constantly journeyed from land to land
but never have I seen such a thing!
In this whole multitude
there is not one person that I know.
Suddenly they have come up from the earth—
I beg you to explain the cause.
The members of this great assembly now,
the immeasurable hundreds, thousands, millions
of bodhisattvas,
all want to know these things.
Regarding the causes that govern the beginning and end

of this multitude of bodhisattvas,
possessor of immeasurable virtue, World-Honored One,
we beg you to dispel the doubts of the assembly!

At that time the Buddhas who were emanations of Shakyamuni
Buddha and had arrived from immeasurable thousands, ten thousands,
millions of lands in other directions, were seated cross-legged on lion
seats under the jeweled trees in the eight directions. The attendants of
these Buddhas all saw the great multitude of bodhisattvas who had
emerged from the earth in the four directions of the thousand-millionfold world and were suspended in the air, and each one said to his
respective Buddha: "World-Honored One, this great multitude of
immeasurable, boundless asamkhyas of bodhisattvas—where did they
come from?"

At that time each of the Buddhas spoke to his attendants, saying:
"Good men, wait a moment. There is a bodhisattva and mahasattva
named Maitreya who has received a prophecy from Shakyamuni Buddha that he will be the next hereafter to become a Buddha. He has
already inquired about this matter and the Buddha is now about to
answer him. You should take this opportunity to listen to what he
says."

At that time Shakyamuni Buddha said to the bodhisattva Maitreya:
"Excellent, excellent, Ajita, that you should question the Buddha
about this great affair. All of you with a single mind should don the
armor of diligence and determine to be firm in intent. The Thus Come
One wishes now to summon forth and declare the wisdom of the
Buddhas, the freely exercised transcendental power of the Buddhas,
the power of the Buddhas that has the lion's ferocity, the fierce and
greatly forceful power of the Buddhas."

At that time the World-Honored One, wishing to state his meaning
once more, spoke in verse form, saying:

> Be diligent and of a single mind,
> for I wish to explain this affair.
> Have no doubts or regrets—
> the Buddha wisdom is hard to fathom.
> Now you must put forth the power of faith,
> abiding in patience and goodness.

A Law which in the past was never heard
you will now all be able to hear.
Now I will bring you ease and consolation—
do not harbor doubts or fears.
The Buddha has nothing but truthful words,
his wisdom cannot be measured.
This foremost Law that he has gained
is very profound, incapable of analysis.
He will now expound it—
you must listen with a single mind.

At that time the World-Honored One, having spoken these verses, said to the bodhisattva Maitreya: "With regard to this great multitude I now say this to you. Ajita, these bodhisattvas and mahasattvas who in immeasurable and countless asamkhyas have emerged from the earth and whom you have never seen before in the past—when I had attained anuttara-samyak-sambodhi in this saha world, I converted and guided these bodhisattvas, trained their minds and caused them to develop a longing for the way. These bodhisattvas have all been dwelling in the world of empty space underneath the saha world. They read, recite, understand the various scriptures, ponder them, make distinctions and keep them correctly in mind.

"Ajita, these good men take no delight in being in the assembly and indulging in much talk. Their delight is constantly to be in a quiet place, exerting themselves diligently and never resting. Nor do they linger among human or heavenly beings, but constantly delight in profound wisdom, being free from all hindrances. And they constantly delight in the Law of the Buddhas, diligently and with a single mind pursuing unsurpassed wisdom."

At that time the World-Honored One, wishing to state his meaning once more, spoke in verse form, saying:

Ajita, you should understand this.
These great bodhisattvas
for countless kalpas
have practiced the Buddha wisdom.
All have been converted by me;
I caused them to set their minds on the great way.

These are my sons,
they dwell in this world,
constantly carrying out dhuta practices,
preferring a quiet place,
rejecting the fret and confusion of the great assembly,
taking no delight in much talk.
In this manner these sons
study and practice my way and Law.
And in order that day and night with constant diligence
they may seek the Buddha way,
in this saha world
they dwell in the empty space in its lower part.
Firm in the power of will and concentration,
with constant diligence seeking wisdom,
they expound various wonderful doctrines
and their minds are without fear.
When I was in the city of Gaya,
seated beneath the bodhi tree,
I attained the highest, the correct enlightenment
and turned the wheel of the unsurpassed Law.
Thereafter I taught and converted them,
caused them for the first time to set their minds on the way.
Now all of them dwell in the stage of no regression,
and all in time will be able to become Buddhas.
What I speak now are true words—
with a single mind you must believe them!
Ever since the long distant past
I have been teaching and converting this multitude.

At that time the bodhisattva and mahasattva Maitreya, as well as the countless other bodhisattvas, found doubts and perplexities rising in their minds. They were puzzled at this thing that had never happened before and thought to themselves: How could the World-Honored One in such a short space of time have taught and converted an immeasurable, boundless asamkhya number of great bodhisattvas of this sort and enabled them to dwell in anuttara-samyak-sambodhi?

Thereupon Maitreya said to the Buddha: "World-Honored One, when the Thus Come One was crown prince, you left the palace of the

Shakyas and sat in the place of practice not far from the city of Gaya, and there attained anuttara-samyak-sambodhi. Barely forty years or more have passed since then. World-Honored One, how in that short time could you have accomplished so much work as a Buddha? Was it through the authoritative powers of the Buddha, or through the blessings of the Buddha, that you were able to teach and convert such an immeasurable number of great bodhisattvas and enable them to achieve anuttara-samyak-sambodhi? World-Honored One, a multitude of great bodhisattvas such as this—a person might spend a thousand, ten thousand, a million kalpas counting them and never be able to reach the end or discover the limit! Since the far distant past, in the dwelling place of immeasurable, boundless numbers of Buddhas, they must have planted good roots, carried out the bodhisattva way, and engaged constantly in brahma practices. World-Honored One, it is hard for the world to believe such a thing!

"Suppose, for example, that a young man of twenty-five, with ruddy complexion and hair still black, should point to someone who was a hundred years old and say, 'This is my son!' or that the hundred year old man should point to the youth and say, 'This is my father who sired and raised me!' This would be hard to believe, and so too is what the Buddha says.

"It has in fact not been long since you attained the way. But this great multitude of bodhisattvas have already for immeasurable thousands, ten thousands, millions of kalpas applied themselves diligently and earnestly for the sake of the Buddha way. They have learned to enter into, emerge from and dwell in immeasurable hundreds, thousands, ten thousands, millions of samadhis, have acquired great transcendental powers, have over a long period carried out brahma practices, and have been able step by step to practice various good doctrines, becoming skilled in questions and answers, a treasure among persons, something seldom known in all the worlds. And today, World-Honored One, you tell us that, in the time since you attained the Buddha way, you have caused these persons for the first time to aspire to enlightenment, have taught, converted and led them, and directed them toward anuttara-samyak-sambodhi!

"World-Honored One, it is not long since you attained Buddhahood, and yet you have been able to carry out this great meritorious undertaking! We ourselves have faith in the Buddha, believing that he preaches in accordance with what is appropriate, that the words spoken by the Buddha are never false, and that the Buddha's knowledge is in all cases penetrating and comprehensive. Nevertheless, in the period after the Buddha has entered extinction, if bodhisattvas who have just begun to aspire to enlightenment should hear these words, they will perhaps not believe or accept them but will be led to commit the crime of rejecting the Law. Therefore, World-Honored One, we beg you to explain so we may put aside our doubts, and so that, in future ages when good men hear of this matter, they will not entertain doubts!"

At that time the bodhisattva Maitreya, wishing to state his meaning once more, spoke in verse form, saying:

> In the past the Buddha departed from the Shakya clan,
> left his household, and near Gaya
> sat under the bodhi tree.
> Little time has passed since then,
> yet these sons of the Buddha
> are immeasurable in number!
> Already for a long time they have practiced the Buddha way,
> dwelling in transcendental powers and the power of wisdom,
> skillfully learning the bodhisattva way,
> unsoiled by worldly things
> like the lotus flower in the water.
> Emerging from the earth,
> all display a reverent and respectful mind,
> standing in the presence of the World-Honored One.
> This is difficult to fathom—
> how can one believe it?
> The Buddha attained the way very recently,
> yet those he has helped to gain success are so many!
> We beg you to dispel the doubts of the assembly,
> to make distinctions and explain the truth of the matter.
> It is as though a young man
> just turned twenty-five
> were to point to a hundred year old man
> with gray hair and wrinkled face
> and say, 'I sired him!'
> and the old man were to say, 'This is my father!'

The father youthful, the son old—
no one in the world could believe this!
World-Honored One, your case is similar.
Only very recently you attained the way.
These bodhisattvas
are firm in will, in no way timid or immature.
For immeasurable kalpas
they have been practicing the bodhisattva way.
They are clever at difficult questions and answers,
their minds know no fear.
They have firmly cultivated a persevering mind,
upright in dignity and virtue.
They are praised by the Buddhas of the ten directions
as able and adept at preaching distinctions.
They have no wish to remain among the crowd
but constantly favor a state of meditation,
and in order to seek the Buddha way
they have been dwelling in the space under the earth.
This we have heard from the Buddha
and have no doubts in the matter.
But for the sake of future ages we beg the Buddha
to explain and bring about understanding.
If with regard to this sutra
one should harbor doubt and fail to believe,
he will fall at once into the evil paths.
So we beg you now to explain.
These immeasurable bodhisattvas—
how in such a short time
did you teach them, cause them to have aspiring minds,
and to dwell in the stage of no regression?

16

THE LIFE SPAN OF THE
THUS COME ONE

At that time the Buddha spoke to the bodhisattvas and all the great assembly: "Good men, you must believe and understand the truthful words of the Thus Come One." And again he said to the great assembly: "You must believe and understand the truthful words of the Thus Come One." And once more he said to the great assembly: "You must believe and understand the truthful words of the Thus Come One."

At that time the bodhisattvas and the great assembly, with Maitreya as their leader, pressed their palms together and addressed the Buddha, saying: "World-Honored One, we beg you to explain. We will believe and accept the Buddha's words." They spoke in this manner three times, and then said once more: "We beg you to explain it. We will believe and accept the Buddha's words."

At that time the World-Honored One, seeing that the bodhisattvas repeated their request three times and more, spoke to them, saying: "You must listen carefully and hear of the Thus Come One's secret and his transcendental powers. In all the worlds the heavenly and human beings and asuras all believe that the present Shakyamuni Buddha, after leaving the palace of the Shakyas, seated himself in the place of practice not far from the city of Gaya and there attained anuttara-samyak-sambodhi. But good men, it has been immeasurable, boundless hundreds, thousands, ten thousands, millions of nayutas of kalpas since I in fact attained Buddhahood.

"Suppose a person were to take five hundred, a thousand, ten thousand, a million nayuta asamkhya thousand-millionfold worlds and grind them to dust. Then, moving eastward, each time he passes five hundred, a thousand, ten thousand, a million nayuta asamkhya worlds he drops a particle of dust. He continues eastward in this way until he has finished dropping all the particles. Good men, what is your opinion? Can the total number of all these worlds be imagined or calculated?"

The bodhisattva Maitreya and the others said to the Buddha: "World-Honored One, these worlds are immeasurable, boundless—one cannot calculate their number, nor does the mind have the power to encompass them. Even all the voice-hearers and pratyekabuddhas with their wisdom free of outflows could not imagine or understand how many there are. Although we abide in the stage of avivartika, we cannot comprehend such a matter. World-Honored One, these worlds are immeasurable and boundless."

At that time the Buddha said to the multitude of great bodhisattvas: "Good men, now I will state this to you clearly. Suppose all these worlds, whether they received a particle of dust or not, are once more reduced to dust. Let one particle represent one kalpa. The time that has passed since I attained Buddhahood surpasses this by a hundred, a thousand, ten thousand, a million nayuta asamkhya kalpas.

"Ever since then I have been constantly in this saha world, preaching the Law, teaching and converting. And elsewhere I have led and benefited living beings in hundreds, thousands, ten thousands, millions of nayutas and asamkhyas of lands.

"Good men, during that time I have spoken about the Buddha Burning Torch and others, and described how they entered nirvana. All this I employed as an expedient means to make distinctions.

"Good men, if there are living beings who come to me, I employ my Buddha eye to observe their faith and to see if their other faculties are keen or dull, and then depending upon how receptive they are to salvation, I appear in different places and preach to them under different names, and describe the length of time during which my teachings will be effective. Sometimes when I make my appearance I say that I am about to enter nirvana, and also employ different expedient means to preach the subtle and wonderful Law, thus causing living beings to awaken joyful minds.

"Good men, the Thus Come One observes how among living beings there are those who delight in a little Law, meager in virtue and heavy with defilement. For such persons I describe how in my youth I left my household and attained anuttara-samyak-sambodhi. But in truth the time since I attained Buddhahood is extremely long, as I have told you. It is simply that I use this expedient means to teach and convert living beings and cause them to enter the Buddha way. That is why I speak in this manner.

"Good men, the scriptures expounded by the Thus Come One are all for the purpose of saving and emancipating living beings. Sometimes I speak of myself, sometimes of others; sometimes I present myself, sometimes others; sometimes I show my own actions, sometimes those of others. All that I preach is true and not false.

"Why do I do this? The Thus Come One perceives the true aspect of the threefold world exactly as it is. There is no ebb or flow of birth and death, and there is no existing in this world and later entering extinction. It is neither substantial nor empty, neither consistent nor diverse. Nor is it what those who dwell in the threefold world perceive it to be. All such things the Thus Come One sees clearly and without error.

"Because living beings have different natures, different desires, different actions, and different ways of thinking and making distinctions, and because I want to enable them to put down good roots, I employ a variety of causes and conditions, similes, parables, and phrases and preach different doctrines. This, the Buddha's work, I have never for a moment neglected.

"Thus, since I attained Buddhahood, an extremely long period of time has passed. My life span is an immeasurable number of asamkhya kalpas, and during that time I have constantly abided here without ever entering extinction. Good men, originally I practiced the bodhisattva way, and the life span that I acquired then has yet to come to an end but will last twice the number of years that have already passed. Now, however, although in fact I do not actually enter extinction, I announce that I am going to adopt the course of extinction. This is an expedient means which the Thus Come One uses to teach and convert living beings.

"Why do I do this? Because if the Buddha remains in the world for a long time, those persons with shallow virtue will fail to plant good roots but, living in poverty and lowliness, will become attached to the five desires and be caught in the net of deluded thoughts and imaginings. If they see that the Thus Come One is constantly in the world and never enters extinction, they will grow arrogant and selfish, or become discouraged and neglectful. They will fail to realize how difficult it is to encounter the Buddha and will not approach him with a respectful and reverent mind.

"Therefore as an expedient means the Thus Come One says: 'Monks, you should know that it is a rare thing to live at a time when one of the Buddhas appears in the world.' Why does he do this? Because persons of shallow virtue may pass immeasurable hundreds, thousands, ten thousands, millions of kalpas with some of them chancing to see a Buddha and others never seeing one at all. For this reason I say to them: 'Monks, the Thus Come One is hard to get to see.' When living beings hear these words, they are certain to realize how difficult it is to encounter the Buddha. In their minds they will harbor a longing and will thirst to gaze upon the Buddha, and then they will work to plant good roots. Therefore the Thus Come One, though in truth he does not enter extinction, speaks of passing into extinction.

"Good men, the Buddhas and Thus Come Ones all preach a Law such as this. They act in order to save living beings, so what they do is true and not false.

"Suppose, for example, that there is a skilled physician who is wise and understanding and knows how to compound medicines to effectively cure all kinds of diseases. He has many sons, perhaps ten, twenty, or even a hundred. He goes off to some other land far away to see about a certain affair. After he has gone, the children drink some kind of poison that makes them distraught with pain and they fall writhing to the ground.

"At that time the father returns to his home and finds that his children have drunk poison. Some are completely out of their minds, while others are not. Seeing their father from far off, all are overjoyed and kneel down and entreat him, saying: 'How fine that you have returned safely. We were stupid and by mistake drank some poison. We beg you to cure us and let us live out our lives!'

"The father, seeing his children suffering like this, follows various prescriptions. Gathering fine medicinal herbs that meet all the requirements of color, fragrance and flavor, he grinds, sifts and mixes them together. Giving a dose of these to his children, he tells them: 'This is a highly effective medicine, meeting all the requirements of color, fragrance and flavor. Take it and you will quickly be relieved of your sufferings and will be free of all illness.'

"Those children who have not lost their senses can see that this is good medicine, outstanding in both color and fragrance, so they take it immediately and are completely cured of their sickness. Those who are out of their minds are equally delighted to see their father return and beg him to cure their sickness, but when they are given the medicine, they refuse to take it. Why? Because the poison has penetrated deeply and their minds no longer function as before. So although the medicine is of excellent color and fragrance, they do not perceive it as good.

"The father thinks to himself: My poor children! Because of the poison in them, their minds are completely befuddled. Although they are happy to see me and ask me to cure them, they refuse to take this excellent medicine. I must now resort to some expedient means to induce them to take the medicine. So he says to them: 'You should know that I am now old and worn out, and the time of my death has come. I will leave this good medicine here. You should take it and not worry that it will not cure you.' Having given these instructions, he then goes off to another land, where he sends a messenger home to announce, 'Your father is dead.'

"At that time the children, hearing that their father has deserted them and died, are filled with great grief and consternation and think to themselves: If our father were alive he would have pity on us and see that we are protected. But now he has abandoned us and died in some other country far away. We are shelterless orphans with no one to rely on!

"Constantly harboring such feelings of grief, they at last come to their senses and realize that the medicine is in fact excellent in color and fragrance and flavor, and so they take it and are healed of all the effects of the poison. The father, hearing that his children are all cured, immediately returns home and appears to them all once more.

"Good men, what is your opinion? Can anyone say that this skilled physician is guilty of lying?"

"No, World-Honored One."

The Buddha said: "It is the same with me. It has been immeasurable, boundless hundreds, thousands, ten thousands, millions of na-yuta and asamkhya kalpas since I attained Buddhahood. But for the sake of living beings I employ the power of expedient means and say that I am about to pass into extinction. In view of the circumstances, however, no one can say that I have been guilty of lies or falsehoods."

At that time the World-Honored One, wishing to state his meaning once more, spoke in verse form, saying:

> Since I attained Buddhahood
> the number of kalpas that have passed
> is an immeasurable hundreds, thousands, ten thousands,
> millions, trillions, asamkhyas.
> Constantly I have preached the Law, teaching, converting
> countless millions of living beings,
> causing them to enter the Buddha way,
> all this for immeasurable kalpas.
> In order to save living beings,
> as an expedient means I appear to enter nirvana
> but in truth I do not pass into extinction.
> I am always here, preaching the Law.
> I am always here,
> but through my transcendental powers
> I make it so that living beings in their befuddlement
> do not see me even when close by.
> When the multitude see that I have passed into extinction,
> far and wide they offer alms to my relics.

All harbor thoughts of yearning
and in their minds thirst to gaze at me.
When living beings have become truly faithful,
honest and upright, gentle in intent,
single-mindedly desiring to see the Buddha,
not hesitating even if it costs them their lives,
then I and the assembly of monks
appear together on Holy Eagle Peak.
At that time I tell the living beings
that I am always here, never entering extinction,
but that because of the power of an expedient means
at times I appear to be extinct, at other times not,
and that if there are living beings in other lands
who are reverent and sincere in their wish to believe,
then among them too
I will preach the unsurpassed Law.
But you have not heard of this,
so you suppose that I enter extinction.
When I look at living beings
I see them drowned in a sea of suffering;
therefore I do not show myself,
causing them to thirst for me.
Then when their minds are filled with yearning,
at last I appear and preach the Law for them.
Such are my transcendental powers.
For asamkhya kalpas
constantly I have dwelled on Holy Eagle Peak
and in various other places.
When living beings witness the end of a kalpa
and all is consumed in a great fire,
this, my land, remains safe and tranquil,
constantly filled with heavenly and human beings.
The halls and pavilions in its gardens and groves
are adorned with various kinds of gems.
Jeweled trees abound in flowers and fruit
where living beings enjoy themselves at ease.
The gods strike heavenly drums,
constantly making many kinds of music.

Mandarava blossoms rain down,
scattering over the Buddha and the great assembly.
My pure land is not destroyed,
yet the multitude see it as consumed in fire,
with anxiety, fear and other sufferings
filling it everywhere.
These living beings with their various offenses,
through causes arising from their evil actions,
spend asamkhya kalpas
without hearing the name of the Three Treasures.
But those who practice meritorious ways,
who are gentle, peaceful, honest and upright,
all of them will see me
here in person, preaching the Law.
At times for this multitude
I describe the Buddha's life span as immeasurable,
and to those who see the Buddha only after a long time
I explain how difficult it is to meet the Buddha.
Such is the power of my wisdom
that its sagacious beams shine without measure.
This life span of countless kalpas
I gained as the result of lengthy practice.
You who are possessed of wisdom,
entertain no doubts on this point!
Cast them off, end them forever,
for the Buddha's words are true, not false.
He is like a skilled physician
who uses an expedient means to cure his deranged sons.
Though in fact alive, he gives out word he is dead,
yet no one can say he speaks falsely.
I am the father of this world,
saving those who suffer and are afflicted.
Because of the befuddlement of ordinary people,
though I live, I give out word I have entered extinction.
For if they see me constantly,
arrogance and selfishness arise in their minds.
Abandoning restraint, they give themselves up to the
   five desires

and fall into the evil paths of existence.
Always I am aware of which living beings
practice the way, and which do not,
and in response to their needs for salvation
I preach various doctrines for them.
At all times I think to myself:
How can I cause living beings
to gain entry into the unsurpassed way
and quickly acquire the body of a Buddha?

17
DISTINCTIONS
IN BENEFITS

At that time, when the great assembly heard the Buddha describe how his life span lasted such a very long number of kalpas, immeasurable, boundless asamkhyas of living beings gained a great many rich benefits.

At that time the World-Honored One said to the bodhisattva and mahasattva Maitreya: "Ajita, when I described how the life span of the Thus Come One lasts for such an exceedingly long time, living beings numerous as the sands of six hundred and eighty ten thousands, millions, nayutas of Ganges attained the truth of birthlessness. And bodhisattvas and mahasattvas a thousand times more in number gained the dharani teaching that allows them to retain all that they

hear. And bodhisattvas and mahasattvas numerous as the dust particles of an entire world gained the eloquence that allows them to speak
pleasingly and without hindrance. And bodhisattvas and mahasattvas
numerous as the dust particles of an entire world gained dharanis that
allow them to retain hundreds, thousands, ten thousands, millions,
immeasurable repetitions of the teachings. And bodhisattvas and mahasattvas numerous as the dust particles of a thousand-millionfold
world were able to turn the unregressing wheel of the Law. And
bodhisattvas and mahasattvas numerous as the dust particles of two
thousand middle sized lands were able to turn the pure wheel of the
Law. And bodhisattvas and mahasattvas numerous as the dust particles
of a thousand small lands gained assurance that they would attain
anuttara-samyak-sambodhi after eight rebirths. And bodhisattvas and
mahasattvas numerous as the dust particles of four four-continent
worlds gained assurance that they would attain anuttara-samyak-sambodhi after four rebirths. And bodhisattvas and mahasattvas numerous
as the dust particles of three four-continent worlds gained assurance
that they would attain anuttara-samyak-sambodhi after three rebirths.
And bodhisattvas and mahasattvas numerous as the dust particles of
two four-continent worlds gained assurance that they would attain
anuttara-samyak-sambodhi after two rebirths. And bodhisattvas and
mahasattvas numerous as the dust particles of one four-continent
world gained assurance that they would attain anuttara-samyak-sambodhi after one rebirth. And living beings numerous as the dust
particles of eight worlds were all moved to set their minds upon
anuttara-samyak-sambodhi.

When the Buddha announced that these bodhisattvas and mahasattvas had gained the great benefits of the Law, from the midst of the air
mandarava flowers and great mandarava flowers rained down, scattering over the immeasurable hundreds, thousands, ten thousands, millions of Buddhas who were seated on lion seats under jeweled trees,
and also scattering over Shakyamuni Buddha, and over Many Treasures Thus Come One who long ago entered extinction, both of whom
were seated on lion seats in the tower of seven treasures. They also
scattered over all the great bodhisattvas and the four kinds of believers. In addition, finely powdered sandalwood and aloes rained down,
and in the midst of the air heavenly drums sounded of their own
accord, wonderful notes deep and far-reaching. And a thousand vari-

eties of heavenly robes rained down, draped with various necklaces, pearl necklaces, mani jewel necklaces, necklaces of wish-granting jewels, spreading everywhere in nine directions. In jewel-encrusted censers priceless incenses burned, their fragrance of its own accord permeating everywhere as an offering to the great assembly. Above each one of the Buddhas there appeared bodhisattvas holding banners and canopies, in rows reaching up to the Brahma heaven. These bodhisattvas employed their wonderful voices in singing immeasurable hymns of praise to the Buddhas.

At that time the bodhisattva Maitreya rose from his seat, bared his right shoulder and, pressing his palms together and facing the Buddha, spoke in verse form, saying:

> The Buddha preaches a rarely encountered Law,
> one never heard from times past.
> The World-Honored One possesses great powers
> and his life span cannot be measured.
> The countless sons of the Buddha,
> hearing the World-Honored One make distinctions
> and describe the benefits of the Law they will gain,
> find their whole bodies filled with joy.
> Some abide in the stage of no regression,
> some have acquired dharanis,
> some can speak pleasingly and without hindrance
> or retain ten thousand, a million repetitions of the teachings.
> Some bodhisattvas numerous as the dust particles
> of a thousand major worlds
> are all able to turn
> the unregressing wheel of the Law.
> Some bodhisattvas numerous as the dust particles
> of a thousand intermediate worlds
> are all able to turn
> the pure wheel of the Law.
> And some bodhisattvas numerous as the dust particles
> of a thousand minor worlds
> are assured that after eight more rebirths
> they will be able to complete the Buddha way.
> Some bodhisattvas numerous as the dust particles

of four, three, two times
the four continents
after a corresponding number of rebirths will become Buddhas;
some bodhisattvas numerous as the dust particles
of one set of the four continents
after one more rebirth
will attain comprehensive wisdom.
Thus when living beings
hear of the great length of the Buddha's life,
they gain pure fruits and rewards
that are immeasurable and free of outflows.
Again living beings numerous as the dust particles
of eight worlds,
hearing the Buddha describe his life span,
all set their minds on the unsurpassed way.
The World-Honored One preaches a Law
that is immeasurable and cannot be fathomed,
and those who benefit from it are many,
as boundless as the open air.
Heavenly mandarava flowers
and great mandarava flowers rain down;
Shakras and Brahmas like Ganges sands
arrive from countless Buddha lands.
Sandalwood and aloes
in a jumble of fine powder rain down;
like birds flying down from the sky
they scatter as an offering over the Buddhas.
In the midst of the air heavenly drums
of their own accord emit wonderful sounds;
heavenly robes by the thousand, ten thousand, million
come whirling and fluttering down;
wonderful jewel-encrusted censers
burn priceless incense
which of its own accord permeates everywhere,
an offering to all the World-Honored Ones.
The multitude of great bodhisattvas
hold banners and canopies adorned with the seven treasures,
ten thousand, a million in kind, lofty, wonderful,

in rows reaching up to the Brahma heaven.
Before each one of the Buddhas
hang jeweled streamers and superlative banners,
while in thousands, ten thousands of verses
the praises of the Thus Come Ones are sung.
All these many things
have never been known in the past.
Hearing that the Buddha's life is immeasurable,
all beings are filled with joy.
The Buddha's name is heard in ten directions,
widely benefiting living beings,
and all are endowed with good roots
to help them set their minds on the unsurpassed way.

At that time the Buddha said to the bodhisattva and mahasattva Maitreya: "Ajita, if there are living beings who, on hearing that the life span of the Buddha is of such long duration, are able to believe and understand it even for a moment, the benefits they gain thereby will be without limit or measure. Suppose there are good men or good women who, for the sake of anuttara-samyak-sambodhi, over a period of eight hundred thousand million nayutas of kalpas practice the five paramitas—the paramitas of dana (almsgiving), shila (keeping of the precepts), kshanti (forbearance), virya (assiduousness) and dhyana (meditation), the paramita of prajna being omitted—the benefits they obtain will not measure up to even a hundredth part, a thousandth part, a hundred, thousand, ten thousand, millionth part of the benefits mentioned previously. Indeed, it is beyond the power of calculation, simile or parable to convey the comparison. For good men who have gained such benefits as those [mentioned previously] to fall back without reaching the goal of anuttara-samyak-sambodhi is utterly unimaginable."

At that time the World-Honored One, wishing to state his meaning once more, spoke in verse form, saying:

> If someone seeking the Buddha wisdom
> for a period of eight hundred thousand million
> nayutas of kalpas
> should practice the five paramitas,

during all those kalpas
distributing alms to the Buddhas
and to the pratyekabuddhas and disciples
and the multitude of bodhisattvas,
rare delicacies of food and drink,
fine garments and articles of bedding,
or building religious retreats of sandalwood
adorned with gardens and groves;
if he should distribute alms
of many varieties, all refined and wonderful,
and do this for the entire number of kalpas
to express his devotion to the Buddha way;
and if moreover he should keep the precepts,
in purity and without omission or outflow,
seeking the unsurpassed way,
praised by the Buddhas;
and if he should practice forbearance,
remaining in a posture of submission and gentleness,
even when various evils are visited on him,
not allowing his mind to be roused or swayed;
when others, convinced they have gained the Law,
harbor thoughts of overbearing arrogance
and he is treated with contempt and vexed by them,
if he can still endure it with patience;
and if he is diligent and assiduous,
ever firm in intent and thought,
for immeasurable millions of kalpas
single-minded, never lax or neglectful,
for countless kalpas
dwelling in a deserted and quiet place;
and if he practices sitting and walking exercises,
banishing drowsiness, constantly regulating his mind,
and as a result of such actions
is able to produce states of meditation,
for eighty million ten thousand kalpas
remaining calm, his mind never deranged;
and if he holds to the blessing of this single-mindedness

and with it seeks the unsurpassed way,
saying, "I will gain comprehensive wisdom
and exhaust all the states of meditation!"
If this person for a hundred, a thousand,
ten thousand, a million kalpas
should carry out these meritorious practices
as I have described above,
still those good men and women
who hear me describe my life span
and believe it for even a moment
win blessings that surpass those of such a person.
If a person is completely free
of all doubt and regret,
if in the depths of his mind he believes for one instant,
his blessings will be such as this.
These bodhisattvas
who have practiced the way for immeasurable kalpas
when they hear me describe my life span
are able to believe and accept what I say.
These persons will
gratefully accept this sutra, saying,
"Our wish is that in future ages
we may use our long lives to save living beings.
Just as today the World-Honored One,
king of the Shakyas,
roars like a lion in the place of practice,
preaching the Law without fear,
so may we too in ages to come,
honored and revered by all,
when we sit in the place of practice
describe our life span in the same manner."
If there are those profound in mind,
pure, honest and upright,
who, hearing much, can retain it all,
who follow principle in understanding the Buddha's words,
then persons such as this
will have no doubts [about my life span].

"Furthermore, Ajita, if there is someone who, hearing of the long duration of the Buddha's life span, can understand the import of such words, the benefits that such a person acquires will be without limit or measure, able to awaken in him the unsurpassed wisdom of the Thus Come One. How much more so, then, if far and wide a person listens to this sutra or causes others to listen to it, embraces it himself or causes others to embrace it, copies it himself or causes others to copy it, or presents flowers, incense, necklaces, streamers, banners, silken canopies, fragrant oil or lamps of butter oil as offerings to the sutra rolls. The benefits of such a person will be immeasurable, boundless, able to inspire in him the wisdom that embraces all species.

"Ajita, if good men and good women, hearing me describe the great length of my life span, in the depths of their mind believe and understand, then they will see the Buddha constantly abiding on Mount Gridhrakuta, with the great bodhisattvas and multitude of voice-hearers surrounding him, preaching the Law. They will also see this saha world, its ground of lapis lazuli level and well ordered, the Jambunada gold bordering its eight highways, the rows of jeweled trees, the terraces, towers and observatories all made of jewels, and all the multitude of bodhisattvas who live in their midst. If there are those who are able to see such things, you should know that it is a mark of their deep faith and understanding.

"Again, if after the Thus Come One has entered extinction there are those who hear this sutra and do not slander or speak ill of it but feel joy in their hearts, you should know that this is a sign that they have already shown deep faith and understanding. How much more in the case of persons who read, recite and embrace this sutra! Such persons are in effect receiving the Thus Come One on the crown of their heads.

"Ajita, these good men and good women need not for my sake erect towers and temples or build monks quarters or make the four kinds of offerings to the community of monks. Why? Because these good men and good women, in receiving, embracing, reading and reciting this sutra, have already erected towers, constructed monks quarters, and given alms to the community of monks. It should be considered that they have erected towers adorned with the seven treasures for the relics of the Buddha, broad at the base and tapering at the top, reaching to the Brahma heaven, hung with banners, canopies, and a multitude of jeweled bells, with flowers, incense, necklaces, powdered incense, paste incense, incense for burning, many kinds of drums, musical instruments, pipes, harps, and various types of dances and diversions, and with wonderful voices that sing and intone hymns of praise. It is as though they have already offered alms for immeasurable thousands, ten thousands, millions of kalpas.

"Ajita, if after I have entered extinction there are those who hear this sutra and can accept and uphold it, copy it themselves or cause others to copy it, then it may be considered that they have already erected monks quarters, or used red sandalwood to construct thirty-two halls, as tall as eight tala trees, lofty, spacious and beautifully adorned to accommodate hundreds and thousands of monks. Gardens, groves, pools, lakes, exercise grounds, caves for meditation, clothing, food, drink, beds, matting, medicines, and all kinds of utensils for comfort fill them, and these monks quarters and halls number in the hundreds, thousands, ten thousands, millions, and indeed are immeasurable in number. All these are presented before me as alms for me and the community of monks.

"So I say, if after the Thus Come One enters extinction there are those who accept, uphold, read and recite this sutra or preach it to others, who copy it themselves or cause others to copy it, or who offer alms to the sutra rolls, then they need not erect towers or temples or build monks quarters or offer alms to the community of monks. And how much more is this true of those who are able to embrace this sutra and at the same time dispense alms, keep the precepts, practice forbearance, and display diligence, single-mindedness and wisdom! Their virtue will be uppermost, immeasurable and boundless, as the open sky, east, west, north and south, in the four intermediate directions and up and down, is immeasurable and boundless. The blessings of such persons will be as immeasurable and boundless as this, and such persons will quickly attain the wisdom that embraces all species.

"If a person reads, recites, accepts and upholds this sutra or preaches it to others; if he copies it himself or causes others to copy it; and if he can erect towers, build monks quarters, offer alms and praise to the community of voice-hearers; if he can employ hundreds, thousands, ten thousands, millions of modes of praise to praise the merits of the bodhisattvas; and if for the sake of others he employs various causes and conditions and accords with principle in explaining and preaching this Lotus Sutra; and if he can observe the precepts with purity, keep company with those who are gentle and peaceful, be forbearing and without anger, firm in intent and thought, constantly prizing the practice of sitting in meditation, attaining various states of profound meditation, diligent and courageous, mastering all the good doctrines, keen in faculties and wisdom, good at answering difficult questions— Ajita, if after I have entered extinction there are good men and good women who accept, uphold, read and recite this sutra and have good merits such as these, you should know that they have already proceeded to the place of practice and are drawing near to anuttara-samyak-sambodhi as they sit beneath the tree of the way. Ajita, wherever these good men and good women sit or stand or circle about in exercise, there one should erect a tower, and all heavenly and human beings should offer alms to it as they would to the tower of the Buddha."

At that time the World-Honored One, wishing to state his meaning once more, spoke in verse form, saying:

If after I have entered extinction
a person can honor and uphold this sutra,
his blessings will be immeasurable,
as I have described above.
It is as though he had supplied
all manner of alms,
erecting a tower for the Buddha's relics
adorned with the seven treasures
and with a central pole very tall and wide
that tapers gradually as it reaches the Brahma heaven.
Jeweled bells by the thousand, ten thousand, million,
move in the wind, emitting a wonderful sound.
And for immeasurable kalpas
he offers alms to this tower,
flowers, incense, various kinds of necklaces,
heavenly robes and assorted musical instruments,
and burns fragrant oil and lamps of butter oil
that constantly light up the area around.
In the evil age of the Latter Day of the Law
if there is someone who can uphold this sutra,

it will be as though he supplied all the alms
described above.
If someone can uphold this sutra,
it will be as though in the presence of the Buddha
he should use ox-head sandalwood
to build monks quarters as an offering,
or thirty-two halls
as high as eight tala trees,
or supply all kinds
of superior foods and wonderful clothes and bedding,
residences for assemblies of hundreds, thousands,
gardens, groves, pools and lakes,
exercise grounds and caves for meditation,
all with various kinds of fine adornments.
If someone with a believing and understanding mind
accepts, upholds, reads, recites and copies this sutra
or causes others to copy it
or offers alms to the sutra rolls,
scattering flowers, incense and powdered incense
or constantly burning fragrant oil
extracted from sumana, champaka
or atimuktaka flowers,
if he offers alms such as these
he will gain immeasurable merits,
boundless as the open air,
and his blessings will also be like this.
How much more so if one upholds this sutra
and at the same time dispenses alms, keeps the precepts,
is forbearing, delights in meditation,
and never gives way to anger or evil speaking.
If one displays reverence toward memorial towers,
humbles himself before monks,
gives a wide berth to an arrogant mind,
constantly ponders upon wisdom
and is never angry when asked difficult questions
but responds compliantly with an explanation—
if one can carry out such practices,
his merits will be beyond measure.

If you see a teacher of the Law
who has cultivated virtues such as these,
you should scatter heavenly flowers over him,
clothe his body in heavenly robes,
bow your head before his feet in salutation,
and in your mind imagine you see the Buddha.
You should also think to yourself:
Before long he will proceed to the place of practice
and attain a state of no outflows and no action,
bringing wide benefit to heavenly and human beings!
In the place where such a person resides,
where he walks, sits or lies down,
or recites even one verse of scripture,
there you should erect a tower
adorned in a fitting and wonderful manner
and offer alms of various kinds to it.
When a son of the Buddha dwells in such places
the Buddha will accept and utilize them,
and constantly in their midst
will walk, sit or lie down.

18

THE BENEFITS OF RESPONDING WITH JOY

At that time the bodhisattva and mahasattva Maitreya said to the Buddha: "World-Honored One, if there are good men or good women who, hearing this Lotus Sutra, respond with joy, what amount of blessings do they acquire?"

Then he spoke in verse, saying:

> After the World-Honored One has passed into extinction,
> if those who hear this sutra
> are able to respond with joy,
> what amount of blessings will they acquire?

At that time the Buddha said to the bodhisattva and mahasattva Maitreya: "Ajita, after the Thus Come One has entered extinction, suppose there are monks, nuns, laymen, laywomen, or other persons of wisdom, whether old or young, who, hearing this sutra, respond with joy and, leaving the Dharma assembly, go to some other place, perhaps a monks quarters, a spot that is deserted and quiet, a city, a community, a settlement or a village, and there in accordance with what they have heard they put forth effort in preaching and expounding for the sake of their parents and relatives, their good friends and acquaintances. These persons, after hearing, respond with joy and they too set about spreading the teachings. One person, having heard, responds with joy and spreads the teachings, and the teachings in this way continue to be handed along from one to another until they reach a fiftieth person.

"Ajita, the benefits received by this fiftieth good man or good woman who responds with joy I will now describe to you—you must listen carefully. Imagine all the beings in the six paths of existence of four hundred ten thousand million asamkhya worlds, all the four kinds of living beings, those born from the egg, those born from the womb, those born from dampness, and those born by transformation, those with form, those without form, those with thought, those without thought, those who are not with thought, those who are not without thought, those without legs, those with two legs, four legs, or many legs. And imagine that, among all this vast number of living beings, a person should come who is seeking blessings and, responding to their various desires, dispenses objects of amusement and playthings to all these living beings. Each one of these living beings is given gold, silver, lapis lazuli, seashell, agate, coral, amber, and other wonderful and precious gems, as well as elephants, horses, carriages, and palaces and towers made of the seven treasures, enough to fill a whole Jambudvipa. This great dispenser of charity, having handed out gifts in this manner for a full eighty years, then thinks to himself: I have already doled out objects of amusement and playthings to these living beings, responding to their various desires. But these living beings are now all old and decrepit, their years over eighty, their hair white, their faces wrinkled, and before long they will die. Now I should employ the Law of the Buddha to instruct and guide them.

"Immediately he gathers all the living beings together and propagates the Law among them, teaching, benefiting and delighting them. In one moment all are able to attain the way of the srota-apanna, the way of the sakridagamin, the way of the anagamin, and the way of the arhat, to exhaust all outflows and enter deeply into meditation. All attain freedom and become endowed with the eight emancipations. Now what is your opinion? Are the benefits gained by this great dispenser of charity many or not?"

Maitreya said to the Buddha: "World-Honored One, this man's benefits are very many indeed, immeasurable and boundless. Even if this dispenser of charity had merely given all those playthings to living beings, his benefits would still be immeasurable. And how much more so when he has enabled them to attain the fruits of arhatship!"

The Buddha said to Maitreya: "I will now state the matter clearly for you. This man gave all these objects of amusement to the living beings in the six paths of existence of four hundred ten thousand million asamkhya worlds and also made it possible for them to attain the fruits of arhatship. But the benefits that he gains do not match the benefits of the fiftieth person who hears just one verse of the Lotus Sutra and responds with joy. They are not equal to one hundredth, one thousandth, one part in a hundred, thousand, ten thousand, a million. Indeed it is beyond the power of calculation, simile or parable to express the comparison.

"Ajita, the benefits gained by even the fiftieth person who hears the Lotus Sutra as it is handed along to him and responds with joy are immeasurable, boundless asamkhyas in number. How much greater then are those of the very first person in the assembly who, on hearing the sutra, responds with joy! His blessings are greater by an immeasurable, boundless asamkhya number, and are in fact incomparable.

"Moreover, Ajita, suppose a person for the sake of this sutra visits a monks quarters and, sitting or standing, even for a moment listens to it and accepts it. As a result of the benefits so obtained, when he is reborn in his next existence he will enjoy the finest, most superior and wonderful elephants, horses and carriages, and palanquins decked with rare treasures, and will mount up to the heavenly palaces. Or suppose there is a person who is sitting in the place where the Law is expounded, and when another person appears, the first person urges him to sit down and listen, or offers to share his seat and so persuades him to sit down. The benefits gained by this person will be such that when he is reborn he will be in a place where the lord Shakra is seated, where the heavenly king Brahma is seated, or where a wheel-turning sage king is seated.

"Ajita, suppose there is a person who speaks to another person, saying, 'There is a sutra called the Lotus. Let us go together and listen to it.' And suppose, having been urged, the other person goes and even for an instant listens to the sutra. The benefits of the first person will be such that when he is reborn he will be born in the same place as dharani bodhisattvas. He will have keen faculties and wisdom. For a hundred, a thousand, ten thousand ages he will never be struck dumb. His mouth will not emit a foul odor. His tongue will never be afflicted, nor will his mouth be afflicted. His teeth will not be stained or black, nor will they be yellow or widely spaced, nor will they be missing or fall out or be at an angle or crooked. His lips will not droop down or curl back or be rough or chapped or afflicted with sores or misshapen or twisted or too thick or too big or black or discolored or unsightly in any way. His nose will not be too broad or flat or crooked or too highly arched. His face will not be swarthy, nor will it be long and narrow, or sunken and distorted. He will not have a single unsightly feature. His lips, tongue and teeth will all be handsomely proportioned. His nose will be long and high, his face round and full, his eyebrows long and set high, his forehead broad, smooth, and well shaped, and he will be endowed with all the features proper to a human being. In each existence he is born into, he will see the Buddha, hear his Law, and have faith in his teachings.

"Ajita, just observe! The benefits gained merely by encouraging one person to go and listen to the Law are such as this! How much more, then, if one single-mindedly hears, preaches, reads, and recites the sutra and before the great assembly makes distinctions for the sake of people and practices it as the sutra instructs!"

At that time the World-Honored One, wishing to state his meaning once more, spoke in verse form, saying:

> If someone in the Dharma assembly
> is able to hear this sutra,
> even just one verse,
> and responding with joy, preaches it to others,
> and in this way the teachings are handed along

till they reach the fiftieth person,
the blessings gained by this last person
are such as I will now define.
Suppose there is a great dispenser of charity
who bestows goods on immeasurable multitudes,
doing this for a full eighty years,
responding to each person's desires.
Seeing the signs of decrepitude and old age,
the white hair and wrinkled face,
the missing teeth, the withered form,
he thinks, "Their death is not far off;
I must now teach them
so they can gain the fruits of the way!"
Immediately for their sake he employs an expedient means,
preaching the true Law of nirvana:
"Nothing in this world is lasting or firm
but all are like bubbles, foam, heat shimmer.
Therefore all of you must quickly
learn to hate it and be gone!"
When the people hear this Law,
all are able to become arhats
endowed with the six transcendental powers,
the three understandings and eight emancipations.
But the fiftieth person
who hears one verse [of the Lotus Sutra] and responds with joy
gains blessings that are far greater,
beyond description by simile or parable.
And if one who has had the teachings passed along to him
receives blessings that are immeasurable,
how much more so one who in the Dharma assembly
first hears the sutra and responds with joy.
Suppose someone encourages another person,
urging him to go and listen to the Lotus,
saying, "This sutra is profound and wonderful,
hard to encounter in a thousand, ten thousand kalpas!"
And suppose, as urged, the person goes to listen,
even though he listens for just a moment.
The blessings that the first person gets in reward

I will now describe in detail:
Age after age, no afflictions of the mouth,
no teeth missing, yellow or blackened,
lips that are not thick, curled or defective,
no hateful features,
a tongue not dry, black or too short;
nose high, long and straight,
forehead broad, smooth and well shaped,
face and eyes all properly aligned and impressive,
the kind people delight to look at,
breath free of foul odor,
a fragrance of utpala flowers
constantly emitted by the mouth.
Suppose one goes to the monks quarters
expressly to listen to the Lotus Sutra
and listens with joy for just a moment—
I will now describe his blessings.
In existences to come among heavenly and human beings
he will acquire wonderful elephants, horses, carriages,
palanquins adorned with rare jewels,
and will mount to the palaces of heaven.
If in the place where the Law is expounded
one encourages someone to sit and hear the sutra,
the blessings he acquires will enable him
to gain the seat of Shakra, Brahma and the wheel-turner.
How much more so if one listens single-mindedly,
explains and expounds the meaning,
and practices the sutra as the sutra instructs—
that person's blessings know no bounds!

19

BENEFITS OF THE TEACHER OF THE LAW

At that time the Buddha said to the bodhisattva and mahasattva Constant Exertion: "If good men or good women accept and uphold this Lotus Sutra, if they read it, recite it, explain and preach it, or transcribe it, such persons will obtain eight hundred eye benefits, twelve hundred ear benefits, eight hundred nose benefits, twelve hundred tongue benefits, eight hundred body benefits, and twelve hundred mind benefits. With these benefits they will be able to adorn their six sense organs, making all of them pure.

"These good men and good women, with the pure physical eyes they received from their parents at birth, will view all that exists in the inner and outer parts of the thousand-millionfold world, its mountains, forests, rivers and seas, down as far as the Avichi hell and up to the Summit of Being. And in the midst they will see all the living beings, and will also see and understand all the causes and conditions created by their deeds and the births that await them as a result and recompense for those deeds."

At that time the World-Honored One, wishing to state his meaning once more, spoke in verse form, saying:

> If in the midst of the great assembly
> someone with a fearless mind
> preaches this Lotus Sutra,
> listen to the benefits he will receive!
> Such a person gains eight hundred
> benefits of superior eyes.
> As a result of these adornments
> his eyes become extremely pure.
> With the eyes received at birth from his parents
> he will view all the three thousand worlds,
> their inner and outer parts, their Mount Meru,
> their Sumeru, the Iron Encircling Mountains
> and all the other mountains and forests,
> the waters of their great seas, rivers and streams,
> down as far as the Avichi hell,
> up to the Summit of Being heaven.
> And he will see all the living beings
> in their midst.
> Though he has not yet gained heavenly eyes,
> the power of his physical eyes will be such as this.

"Moreover, Constant Exertion, if good men or good women accept and uphold this sutra, if they read it, recite it, explain and preach it, or transcribe it, they will gain twelve hundred ear benefits with which to purify their ears so they can hear all the different varieties of words and sounds in the thousand-millionfold world, down as far as the Avichi hell, up to the Summit of Being, and in its inner and outer parts. Elephant sounds, horse sounds, ox sounds, carriage sounds, weeping sounds, lamenting sounds, conch sounds, drum sounds, bell sounds, chime sounds, sounds of laughter, sounds of speaking, men's voices, women's voices, boys' voices, girls' voices, the voice of the Law, the voice that is not the Law, bitter voices, merry voices, voices of common mortals, voices of sages, happy voices, unhappy voices, voices of heavenly beings, dragon voices, yaksha voices, gandharva voices, asura voices, garuda voices, kimnara voices, mahoraga voices, the sound of fire, the sound of water, the sound of wind, voices of hell dwellers, voices of beasts, voices of hungry spirits, monks' voices, nuns' voices, voices of voice-hearers, voices of pratyekabuddhas, voices of bodhisattvas and voices of Buddhas. In a word, although the person has not yet gained heavenly ears, with the pure and ordinary ears that he received at birth from his parents he will be able to hear and understand all the voices that exist in the inner and outer parts of the thousand-millionfold world. And though in this manner he can distinguish all the various different kinds of sounds and voices, this will not impair his hearing faculty."

At that time the World-Honored One, wishing to state his meaning once more, spoke in verse form, saying:

> With the ears received at birth from one's parents,
> pure and without stain or defilement,
> with these ordinary ears one can hear
> the sounds of the three thousand worlds,
> elephant, horse, carriage, ox sounds,
> bell, chime, conch, drum sounds,
> lute and harp sounds,
> pipe and flute sounds;
> the sound of pure and beautiful singing
> one can hear without becoming attached to it.
> The countless varieties of human voices—
> one can hear and understand all these.
> Again one can hear the voices of heavenly beings,
> subtle and wonderful song sounds,
> and one can hear men and women's voices,
> the voices of young boys and young girls.
> In the midst of hills, rivers and steep valleys
> the voice of the kalavinka,
> the jivakajivaka and other birds—
> all these sounds he will hear.

From the tormented multitudes of hell
the sounds of various kinds of suffering and distress,
sounds of hungry spirits driven by famine and thirst
as they search for food and drink,
of the asuras
who live on the shores of the great sea
when they talk among themselves
or emit loud cries—
he who preaches the Law
can dwell safely among all these,
hearing these many voices from afar
without ever impairing his faculties of hearing.
In the worlds of the ten directions
when beasts and birds call to one another
this person who preaches the Law
hears them all from where he is.
In the Brahma heaven and above,
the Light Sound heaven, the All Pure heaven,
and up to the Summit of Being heaven,
the sounds of the voices talking there—
the teacher of the Law, dwelling here,
can hear them all.
All the multitude of monks
and all the nuns,
whether they are reading or reciting the scriptures
or preaching them for the sake of others—
the teacher of the Law dwelling here
can hear them all.
And when there are bodhisattvas
who read and recite the sutra teachings
or preach them for the sake of others
or select passages and explain their meaning,
the sounds of their voices—
he can hear them all.
When the Buddhas, great sages and venerable ones,
teach and convert living beings,
in the midst of the great assembly
expounding and preaching the subtle and wonderful Law,

one who upholds the Lotus Sutra
can hear them all.
All the sounds in the inner and outer parts
of the thousand-millionfold world,
down to the Avichi hell,
up to the Summit of Being heaven—
he can hear all these sounds
and never impair his faculties of hearing.
Because the faculties of his ears are so keen
he can distinguish and understand all these sounds.
One who upholds the Lotus Sutra,
though he has not yet gained heavenly ears,
can do this simply through the ears he was born with—
such are the benefits he gains.

"Moreover, Constant Exertion, if good men or good women accept and uphold this sutra, if they read it, recite it, explain and preach it, or transcribe it, they will succeed in gaining eight hundred nose benefits with which to purify their faculty of smell so that they can detect all different varieties of fragrances from top to bottom and in the inner and outer parts of the thousand-millionfold world, the fragrance of sumana flowers, jatika flowers, mallika flowers, champaka flowers, patala flowers, red lotus flowers, blue lotus flowers, white lotus flowers, the fragrance of flowering trees, fruit trees, sandalwood, aloes, tamalapatra and tagara, as well as incense blended from a thousand, ten thousand ingredients, powdered incense, pellet incense or paste incense. One who upholds this sutra, while dwelling here, will be able to distinguish all these.

"Moreover he will be able to distinguish and identify the odors of living beings, of elephants, horses, oxen, sheep and so forth, the odor of a man, a woman, a boy child, a girl child, and the odors of plants, trees, thickets and forests. Whether they are near or far off, he will be able to detect all these odors and distinguish one from the other without error.

"One who upholds this sutra, though he dwells right here, will also be able to detect the odors of the various heavens in the sky above. The scent of parijataka and kovidara trees, of mandarava flowers, great mandarava flowers, manjushaka flowers, great manjushaka flowers, sandalwood, aloes, various kinds of powdered incense, and incense made of an assortment of flowers—of heavenly scents such as these, and the scents from which they are derived or blended, there are none that he cannot detect and identify.

"He will also be able to detect the scent of the bodies of heavenly beings. The scent when Shakra Devanam Indra is in his superb palace amusing himself and satisfying the five desires, or the scent when he is in the Hall of the Wonderful Law preaching the Law for the heavenly beings of Trayastrimsha, or the scent when he is wandering at leisure in his gardens, as well as the scent of the bodies of the other male and female heavenly beings—all these he will be able to detect from afar.

"He will thus be able to extend his awareness up to the Brahma heaven and even higher to the Summit of Being heaven, detecting the scent of all the bodies of the heavenly beings, and he will also detect the incense burned by the heavenly beings. Moreover the scent of voice-hearers, of pratyekabuddhas, of bodhisattvas and of the bodies of the Buddhas—all these he will detect from afar and will know where these beings are. And although he can detect all these scents, his faculty of smell will not be impaired or disordered. If he should wish to distinguish one scent from another and describe it for someone else, he will be able to recall it without error."

At that time the World-Honored One, wishing to state his meaning once more, spoke in verse form, saying:

> The purity of such a person's nose will be such
> that throughout this world
> he will be able to detect and identify
> all manner of odors, fragrant or foul,
> sumana and jatika flowers,
> tamalapatra and sandalwood,
> the scent of aloes and cassia,
> the scent of various flowers and fruits.
> And he will know the scent of living beings,
> the scent of men and women.
> Though this preacher of the Law dwells far off,
> he will detect these scents and know where the persons are.
> Wheel-turning kings of great authority,

lesser wheel-turners and their sons,
their ministers and palace attendants—
he will detect their scent and know where they are.
Precious treasures adorning the body,
treasure storehouses in the earth,
jeweled ladies of wheel-turning kings—
he will detect their scent and know where they are.
Ornaments that adorn the bodies of persons,
clothing and necklaces,
all kinds of paste incense—
by detecting these he will know who the wearers are.
When heavenly beings walk or sit,
amuse themselves or carry out magical transformations,
the upholder of the Lotus
by detecting their scent can know all this.
Blossoms and fruits of various trees,
and the aroma of butter oil—
the upholder of the sutra, dwelling here,
knows where all these are.
Deep in the mountains, in steep places
where blossoms of the sandalwood tree unfold,
living beings are in their midst—
by detecting the scent he can know all this.
Living beings in the Iron Encircling Mountains,
in the great seas or in the ground—
the upholder of the sutra detects their scent
and knows where all of them are.
When male and female asuras
and their retinues of followers
fight with one another or amuse themselves,
he detects the scent and knows all this.
On the broad plains, in narrow places,
lions, elephants, tigers, wolves,
buffaloes and water buffaloes—
by detecting their scent he knows where they are.
When a woman is pregnant
and no one can determine if the child is male or female,
if it will lack normal faculties or be inhuman,

by detecting the scent he can know all this.
And through this power to detect scents
he knows when a woman has first become pregnant,
if the pregnancy will be successful or not,
if she will be delivered safely of a healthy child.
Through his power to detect scents
he knows the thoughts of men and women,
if their minds are stained by desire, stupidity or anger,
and he knows if they are practicing good.
Hoards of goods that are stored in the earth,
gold, silver and precious treasures,
things heaped in bronze vessels—
by detecting the scent he can tell where they all are.
Various kinds of necklaces
whose value cannot be appraised—
by the scent he knows if they are precious or worthless,
where they came from and where they are now.
Flowers in the heavens above,
mandaravas, manjushakas,
parijataka trees—
detecting their scent, he knows all these.
The palaces in the heavens above
in their separate grades of upper, intermediate, and lower,
adorned with numerous jeweled flowers—
detecting their scent, he knows them all.
The heavenly gardens and groves, the superb mansions,
the observatories, the Hall of the Wonderful Law,
and those taking pleasure in their midst—
detecting their scent, he knows them all.
When heavenly beings listen to the Law
or indulge the five desires,
coming and going, walking, sitting, lying down—
detecting their scent, he knows them all.
The robes worn by heavenly women
when, adorned with lovely flowers and perfumes,
they whirl and circle in enjoyment—
detecting their scent, he knows them all.
Thus extending his awareness

upward to the Brahma heaven,
by detecting their scent, he knows all those
who enter meditation or emerge from meditation.
In the Light Sound and All Pure heavens
and up to the Summit of Being,
those born for the first time, those who have departed—
detecting their scent, he knows them all.
The multitude of monks
diligent at all times with regard to the Law,
whether sitting or walking around
or reading or reciting the sutra teachings,
sometimes under the forest trees
concentrating their energies, sitting in meditation—
the upholder of the sutra detects their scent
and knows where all of them are.
Bodhisattvas firm and unbending in will,
sitting in meditation or reading the sutras
or preaching the Law for others—
by detecting their scent he knows them all.
The World-Honored Ones, present in all quarters,
revered and respected by all,
pitying the multitude, preaching the Law—
by detecting their scent he knows them all.
Living beings who in the Buddha's presence
hear the sutra and all rejoice,
who practice as the Law prescribes—
by detecting their scent he knows them all.
Though he has not yet acquired the nose possessed
by a bodhisattva of the Law of no outflows,
the upholder of the sutra before then
will acquire a nose with the marks described here.

"Moreover, Constant Exertion, if good men or good women accept and uphold this sutra, if they read it, recite it, explain and preach it, or transcribe it, they will gain twelve hundred tongue benefits. Whether something is good tasting or vile, whether it is flavorful or not, and even things that are bitter or astringent, when encountered by the faculties of this person's tongue will all be changed into superb flavors as fine as the sweet dew of heaven, and there will be none that are not pleasing.

"If with these faculties of the tongue he undertakes to expound and preach in the midst of the great assembly, he will produce a deep and wonderful voice capable of penetrating the mind and causing all who hear it to rejoice and delight. When the men and women of heaven, Shakra, Brahma and the other heavenly beings, hear the sound of this deep and wonderful voice expounding and preaching, advancing the argument point by point, they will all gather to listen. Dragons and dragon daughters, yakshas and yaksha daughters, gandharvas and gandharva daughters, asuras and asura daughters, garudas and garuda daughters, kimnaras and kimnara daughters, mahoragas and mahoraga daughters will all gather close around its possessor in order to listen to the Law, and will revere him and offer alms. Monks, nuns, laymen, laywomen, monarchs, princes, ministers and their retinues, petty wheel-turning kings and great wheel-turning kings with their seven treasures and thousand sons and inner and outer retinues will ascend their palaces and all come to listen to the Law.

"Because this bodhisattva is so skilled at preaching the Law, the Brahmans, householders and people throughout the country will for the remainder of their lives follow and wait on him and offer him alms. Voice-hearers, pratyekabuddhas, bodhisattvas and Buddhas will constantly delight to see him. Wherever this person is, the Buddhas will all face in that direction when they preach the Law, and he will be able to accept and uphold all the doctrines of the Buddha. And in addition he will be able to emit the deep and wonderful sound of the Law."

At that time the World-Honored One, wishing to state his meaning once more, spoke in verse form, saying:

> The faculties of this person's tongue will be so pure
> that he will never experience any bad tastes,
> but all that he eats
> will become like sweet dew.
> With his deep, pure and wonderful voice
> he will preach the Law in the great assembly,
> employing causes, conditions and similes
> to lead and guide the minds of living beings.

All who hear him will rejoice
and offer him their finest alms.
Heavenly beings, dragons, yakshas,
as well as asuras and others
will all approach him with reverent minds
and together come to hear the Law.
If this preacher of the Law
wishes to use his wonderful voice
to fill the three thousand worlds
he can do so at will.
Wheel-turning kings great and small
and their thousand sons and retinues
will press their palms together with reverent minds
and constantly come to hear and accept the Law.
Heavenly beings, dragons, yakshas,
rakshasas and pishachas
likewise with rejoicing minds
will constantly delight in coming to bring alms.
The heavenly king Brahma, the devil king,
the deities Freedom and Great Freedom,
all the multitude of heavenly beings
will constantly come to where he is.
The Buddhas and their disciples,
hearing the sound of him preaching the Law,
will keep him constantly in their thoughts and guard him
and at times show themselves for his sake.

"Moreover, Constant Exertion, if good men or good women accept
and uphold this sutra, if they read it, recite it, explain and preach it,
or transcribe it, they will gain eight hundred body benefits. They will
acquire pure bodies, like pure lapis lazuli, such as living beings delight
to see. Because of the purity of their bodies, when the living beings of
the thousand-millionfold world are born or die, when they are born in
upper or lower regions, in fair or ugly circumstances, in good places
or bad, they will all be reflected [in these bodies]. The mountain kings
of the Iron Encircling Mountains, the Great Iron Encircling Mountains, Mount Meru and Mahameru, as well as the living beings in
their midst, will all be reflected therein. Down to the Avichi hell,

upward to the Summit of Being, all the regions and their living beings will all be reflected therein. Voice-hearers, pratyekabuddhas, bodhisattvas, Buddhas preaching the Law—the forms and shapes of all these will be reflected in their bodies."

At that time the World-Honored One, wishing to state his meaning once more, spoke in verse form, saying:

> If one upholds the Lotus Sutra
> his body will be very pure,
> like pure lapis lazuli—
> living beings will all delight to see it.
> And it will be like a pure bright mirror
> in which forms and shapes are all reflected.
> The bodhisattva in his pure body
> will see all that is in the world;
> he alone will see brightly
> what is not visible to others.
> Within the three thousand worlds,
> all the mass of burgeoning creatures,
> heavenly and human beings, asuras,
> hell dwellers, spirits, beasts—
> their forms and shapes in this way
> will all be reflected in his body.
> The palaces of the various heavens
> upward to the Summit of Being,
> the Iron Encircling Mountains,
> the mountains Meru and Mahameru,
> the great seas and other waters—
> all will be reflected in his body.
> The Buddhas and voice-hearers,
> Buddha sons and bodhisattvas,
> whether alone or in the assembly
> preaching the Law—all will be reflected.
> Though this person has not yet acquired
> the wonderful body of Dharma nature, free of outflows,
> because of the purity of his ordinary body
> all things will be reflected in it.

"Moreover, Constant Exertion, if good men or good women accept and uphold this sutra after the Thus Come One has entered extinction, if they read it, recite it, explain and preach it, or transcribe it, they will acquire twelve hundred mind benefits. Because of the purity of their mental faculties, when they hear no more than one verse or one phrase [of the sutra], they will master immeasurable and boundless numbers of principles. And once having understood these principles, they will be able to expound and preach on a single phrase or a single verse for a month, for four months, or for a whole year, and the doctrines that they preach during that time will conform to the gist of the principles and will never be contrary to true reality.

"If they should expound some text of the secular world or speak on matters of government or those relating to wealth and livelihood, they will in all cases conform to the correct Law. With regard to the living beings in the six realms of existence of the thousand-millionfold world, they will understand how the minds of those living beings work, how they move, what idle theories they entertain.

"Thus although they have not yet acquired the wisdom of no outflows, the purity of their minds will be such that the thoughts of these persons, their calculations and surmises and the words they speak, will in all cases represent the Law of the Buddha, never departing from the truth, and will also conform with what was preached in the sutras of former Buddhas."

At that time the World-Honored One, wishing to state his meaning once more, spoke in verse form, saying:

> The minds of these persons will be pure,
> bright, keen, without stain or defilement.
> And with these wonderful mental faculties
> they will understand the superior, intermediate, and
>   inferior Law.
> Hearing no more than one verse,
> they will master immeasurable principles
> and be able to preach them step by step in accordance with
>   the Law
> for a month, four months, or a year.
> All the living beings

in the inner and outer parts of this world,
heavenly beings, dragons, humans,
yakshas, spirits,
those in the six realms of existence
and all the various thoughts they have—
upholders of the Lotus Sutra as their reward
will know all these in an instant!
The countless Buddhas of the ten directions,
adorned with the marks of a hundred blessings,
for the sake of living beings preach the Law,
and such persons, hearing it, will be able to accept and
    uphold it.
They will ponder immeasurable principles,
preach the Law in an immeasurable number of ways,
yet from start to finish never forget or make a mistake,
because they are upholders of the Lotus Sutra.
They will understand the characteristics of all phenomena,
accord with principles, recognizing their proper order,
be masters of names and words,
and expound and preach things just as they understand them.
What these persons preach
is in all cases the Law of former Buddhas,
and because they expound this Law
they have no fear before the assembly.
Such is the purity of the mental faculties
of these upholders of the Lotus Sutra.
Though they have not yet attained freedom from outflows,
before that they will manifest the marks described here.
While these persons uphold this sutra
they will dwell safely on rare ground,
by all living beings
delighted in, loved and respected,
able to employ a thousand, ten thousand varieties
of apt and skillful words
to make distinctions, expound and preach—
because they uphold the Lotus Sutra.

20

THE BODHISATTVA
NEVER DISPARAGING

At that time the Buddha said to the bodhisattva and mahasattva Gainer of Great Authority: "You should understand this. When monks, nuns, laymen or laywomen uphold the Lotus Sutra, if anyone should speak ill of them, curse or slander them, he will suffer severe recompense for his crime, as I have explained earlier. And I have also explained earlier the benefits gained by those who uphold the sutra, namely, purification of their eyes, ears, nose, tongue, body, and mind.

"Gainer of Great Authority, long ago, an immeasurable, boundless, inconceivable number of asamkhya kalpas in the past, there was a Buddha named Awesome Sound King Thus Come One, worthy of offerings, of right and universal knowledge, perfect clarity and conduct, well gone, understanding the world, unexcelled worthy, trainer of people, teacher of heavenly and human beings, Buddha, World-Honored One. His kalpa was called Exempt from Decay and his land was called Great Achievement.

"This Buddha Awesome Sound King during the age when he lived preached the Law for heavenly and human beings and asuras. For those who were seeking to become voice-hearers he responded by preaching the Law of the four noble truths so that they could transcend birth, old age, sickness and death and eventually attain nirvana. For those seeking to become pratyekabuddhas he responded by preaching the Law of the twelve-linked chain of causation. For the bodhisattvas, as a means to lead them to anuttara-samyak-sambodhi, he responded by preaching the Law of the six paramitas so that they could eventually gain the Buddha wisdom.

"Gainer of Great Authority, this Buddha Awesome Sound King had a life span of kalpas equal to four hundred thousand million nayutas of Ganges sands. His Correct Law endured in the world for as many kalpas as there are dust particles in one Jambudvipa. His Counterfeit Law endured in the world for as many kalpas as there are dust particles in the four continents. After this Buddha had finished bringing great benefit to living beings, he passed into extinction.

"After his Correct Law and Counterfeit Law had come to an end, another Buddha appeared in the same land. He too was named Awesome Sound King Thus Come One, worthy of offerings, of right and universal knowledge, perfect clarity and conduct, well gone, understanding the world, unexcelled worthy, trainer of people, teacher of heavenly and human beings, Buddha, World-Honored One. This process continued until twenty thousand million Buddhas had appeared one after the other, all bearing the same name.

"After the original Awesome Sound King Thus Come One had passed into extinction, and after his Correct Law had also passed away, in the period of his Counterfeit Law, monks of overbearing arrogance exercised great authority and power. At this time there was a bodhisattva monk named Never Disparaging. Now, Gainer of Great Authority, for what reason was he named Never Disparaging? This monk, whatever persons he happened to meet, whether monks, nuns, laymen or laywomen, would bow in obeisance to all of them and speak words of praise, saying, 'I have profound reverence for you, I would never dare treat you with disparagement or arrogance. Why? Because you are all practicing the bodhisattva way and are certain to attain Buddhahood.'

"This monk did not devote his time to reading or reciting the scriptures, but simply went about bowing to people. And if he happened to see any of the four kinds of believers far off in the distance, he would purposely go to where they were, bow to them and speak words of praise, saying, 'I would never dare disparage you, because you are all certain to attain Buddhahood!'

"Among the four kinds of believers there were those who gave way to anger, their minds lacking in purity, and they spoke ill of him and cursed him, saying, 'This ignorant monk—where does he come from, presuming to declare that he does not disparage us and bestowing on us a prediction that we will attain Buddhahood? We have no use for such vain and irresponsible predictions!'

"Many years passed in this way, during which this monk was constantly subjected to curses and abuse. He did not give way to anger, however, but each time spoke the same words, 'You are certain to attain Buddhahood.' When he spoke in this manner, some among the group would take sticks of wood or tiles and stones and beat and pelt him. But even as he ran away and took up his stance at a distance, he continued to call out in a loud voice, 'I would never dare disparage you, for you are all certain to attain Buddhahood!' And because he always spoke these words, the overbearingly arrogant monks, nuns, laymen and laywomen gave him the name Never Disparaging.

"When this monk was on the point of death, he heard up in the sky fully twenty thousand, ten thousand, a million verses of the Lotus Sutra that had previously been preached by the Buddha Awesome Sound King, and he was able to accept and uphold them all. Immediately he gained the kind of purity of vision and purity of the faculties of the ear, nose, tongue, body and mind that have been described above. Having gained this purity of the six faculties, his life span was increased by two hundred ten thousand million nayutas of years, and he went about widely preaching the Lotus Sutra for people.

"At that time, when the four kinds of believers who were overbearingly arrogant, the monks, nuns, laymen and laywomen who had looked with contempt on this monk and given him the name Never Disparaging—when they saw that he had gained great transcendental powers, the power to preach pleasingly and eloquently, the power of great goodness and tranquility, and when they heard his preaching, they all took faith in him and willingly became his followers.

"This bodhisattva converted a multitude of a thousand, ten thousand, a million, causing them to abide in the state of anuttara-samyak-sambodhi. After his life came to an end, he was able to encounter two thousand million Buddhas, all bearing the name Sun Moon Bright, and in the midst of their Law he preached this Lotus Sutra. Through the causes and conditions created thereby, he was also able to encounter two thousand million Buddhas, all with the identical name Cloud Freedom Lamp King. In the midst of the Law of these Buddhas, he accepted, upheld, read, recited and preached this sutra for the four kinds of believers. For that reason he was able to gain purification of his ordinary eyes, and the faculties of his ears, nose, tongue, body and mind were likewise purified. Among the four kinds of believers he preached the Law with no fear in his mind.

"Gainer of Great Authority, this bodhisattva and mahasattva Never Disparaging in this manner offered alms to a vast number of Buddhas, treating them with reverence and honor and praising them. Having planted these good roots, he was later able to encounter a thousand, ten thousand, a million Buddhas, and in the midst of the Law of these Buddhas, he preached this sutra, gaining benefits that allowed him to attain Buddhahood.

"Gainer of Great Authority, what do you think? The bodhisattva Never Disparaging who lived at that time—could he be unknown to you? In fact he was none other than I myself! If in my previous existences I had not accepted, upheld, read and recited this sutra and preached it for others, I would never have been able to attain anuttara-samyak-sambodhi this quickly. Because in the presence of those earlier Buddhas I accepted, upheld, read and recited this sutra and preached it for others, I was able quickly to attain anuttara-samyak-sambodhi.

"Gainer of Great Authority, at that time the four kinds of believers, the monks, nuns, laymen and laywomen, because anger arose in their minds and they treated me with disparagement and contempt, were for two hundred million kalpas never able to encounter a Buddha, to hear the Law, or to see the community of monks. For a thousand kalpas they underwent great suffering in the Avichi hell. After they had finished paying for their offenses, they once more encountered the bodhisattva Never Disparaging, who instructed them in anuttara-samyak-sambodhi.

"Gainer of Great Authority, what do you think? The four kinds of believers who at that time constantly disparaged this bodhisattva—could they be unknown to you? They are in this assembly now, Bhadrapala and his group, five hundred bodhisattvas; Lion Moon and her group, five hundred nuns; and Thinking of Buddha and his group, five hundred laymen, all having reached the state where they will never regress in their search for anuttara-samyak-sambodhi!

"Gainer of Great Authority, you should understand that this Lotus Sutra richly benefits the bodhisattvas and mahasattvas, for it can cause them to attain anuttara-samyak-sambodhi. For this reason, after the Thus Come One has passed into extinction, the bodhisattvas and mahasattvas should at all times accept, uphold, read, recite, explain, preach and transcribe this sutra."

At that time the World-Honored One, wishing to state his meaning once more, spoke in verse form, saying:

> In the past there was a Buddha
> named Awesome Sound King,
> of immeasurable supernatural powers and wisdom,
> leading and guiding one and all.
> Heavenly and human beings, dragons, spirits
> joined in offering him alms.
> After this Buddha had entered extinction,
> when his Law was about to expire,
> there was a bodhisattva
> named Never Disparaging.
> The four kinds of believers at that time
> scrutinized and adhered to the Law.
> The bodhisattva Never Disparaging
> would go to where they were
> and speak to them, saying,
> "I would never disparage you,
> for you are practicing the way
> and all of you will become Buddhas!"
> When the people heard this,
> they gibed at him, cursed and reviled him,

but the bodhisattva Never Disparaging
bore all this with patience.
When his offenses had been wiped out
and his life was drawing to a close,
he was able to hear this sutra
and his six faculties were purified.
Because of his transcendental powers
his life span was extended,
and for the sake of others
he preached this sutra far and wide.
The many persons who adhered to the Law
all received teaching and conversion
from this bodhisattva,
who caused them to dwell in the Buddha way.
When Never Disparaging's life ended,
he encountered numberless Buddhas,
and because he preached this sutra
he gained immeasurable blessings.
Bit by bit he acquired benefits
and quickly completed the Buddha way.
Never Disparaging who lived at that time
was none other than myself.
And the four kinds of believers
who adhered to the Law then,
who heard Never Disparaging say,
"You will become Buddhas!"
and through the causes thus created
encountered numberless Buddhas—
they are here in this assembly,
a group of five hundred bodhisattvas,
and the four kinds of believers,
men and women of pure faith
who now in my presence
listen to the Law.
In previous existences
I encouraged these persons
to listen to and accept this sutra,
the foremost in the Law,

unfolding it, teaching people,
and causing them to dwell in nirvana.
So in age after age they accepted and upheld
scriptures of this kind.
A million million ten thousand kalpas,
an inconceivable time will pass
before at last one can hear
this Lotus Sutra.
A million million ten thousand kalpas,
an inconceivable time will pass
before the Buddhas, World-Honored Ones,
preach this sutra.
Therefore its practitioners,
after the Buddha has entered extinction,
when they hear a sutra like this
should entertain no doubts or perplexities
but should with a single mind
preach this sutra far and wide,
age after age encountering Buddhas
and quickly completing the Buddha way.

21

SUPERNATURAL POWERS
OF THE THUS COME ONE

At that time the bodhisattvas and mahasattvas who had emerged from the earth, numerous as the dust particles of a thousand worlds, all in the presence of the Buddha single-mindedly pressed their palms together, gazed up in reverence at the face of the Honored One, and said to the Buddha: "World-Honored One, after the Buddha has entered extinction, in the lands where the emanations of the World-Honored One are present, and in the place where the Buddha has passed into extinction, we will preach this sutra far and wide. Why? Because we ourselves wish to gain this great Law, true and pure, to accept, uphold, read, recite, explain, preach, transcribe and offer alms to it."

At that time the World-Honored One, in the presence of Manjushri and the other immeasurable hundreds, thousands, ten thousands, millions of bodhisattvas and mahasattvas who from of old had dwelled in the saha world, as well as the monks, nuns, laymen, laywomen, heavenly beings, dragons, yakshas, gandharvas, asuras, garudas, kimnaras, mahoragas, human and nonhuman beings—before all these he displayed his great supernatural powers. He extended his long broad tongue upward till it reached the Brahma heaven, and from all his pores he emitted immeasurable, countless beams of light that illuminated all the worlds in the ten directions.

The other Buddhas, seated on lion seats underneath the numerous jeweled trees, did likewise, extending their long broad tongues and emitting immeasurable beams of light. When Shakyamuni Buddha and the other Buddhas beneath the jeweled trees thus displayed their supernatural powers, they did so for fully a hundred thousand years. After that they drew in their tongues again, coughed in unison, and all together snapped their fingers. The sounds made by these two actions filled all the Buddha worlds in the ten directions, and the earth in all of them quaked and trembled in six different ways.

The living beings in their midst, the heavenly beings, dragons, yakshas, gandharvas, asuras, garudas, kimnaras, mahoragas, human and nonhuman beings, thanks to the Buddha's supernatural powers, all saw in this saha world the immeasurable, boundless hundreds, thousands, ten thousands, millions of Buddhas seated on lion seats under the numerous jeweled trees, and also saw Shakyamuni Buddha and Many Treasures Thus Come One seated together on a lion seat in the treasure tower. Moreover, they saw immeasurable, boundless hundreds, thousands, ten thousands, millions of bodhisattvas and mahasattvas and the four kinds of believers who reverently surrounded Shakyamuni Buddha.

When they had seen these things, they were all filled with great joy, having gained what they had never had before. At that time the heavenly beings in the midst of the sky cried out with loud voices, saying: "Beyond these immeasurable, boundless hundreds, thousands, ten thousands, millions of asamkhya worlds there is a land named saha, and in it a Buddha named Shakyamuni. Now for the sake of the bodhisattvas and mahasattvas he is preaching a sutra of the Great Vehicle called the Lotus of the Wonderful Law, a Law to instruct the bodhisattvas, one that is guarded and kept in mind by the Buddhas. You must respond with joy from the depths of your heart, and also offer obeisance and alms to Shakyamuni Buddha!"

When the various living beings heard the voices in the sky, they pressed their palms together, faced the saha world, and spoke these words: "Hail, Shakyamuni Buddha! Hail, Shakyamuni Buddha!"

Then they took different kinds of flowers, incense, necklaces, banners and canopies, as well as the ornaments, rare jewels and other wonderful articles that adorned their persons, and all together scattered them far off in the direction of the saha world. The objects thus scattered poured in from the ten directions like clouds gathering together. Then they changed into a jeweled curtain that completely covered the area where the Buddhas were. At that time the worlds in the ten directions were opened up so that there was unobstructed passage from one to the other and they were like a single Buddha land.

At that time the Buddha spoke to Superior Practices and the others in the great assembly of bodhisattvas, saying: "The supernatural powers of the Buddhas, as you have seen, are immeasurable, boundless, inconceivable. If in the process of entrusting this sutra to others I were to employ these supernatural powers for immeasurable, boundless hundreds, thousands, ten thousands, millions of asamkhya kalpas to describe the benefits of the sutra, I could never finish doing so. To put it briefly, all the doctrines possessed by the Thus Come One, all the freely exercised supernatural powers of the Thus Come One, the storehouse of all the secret essentials of the Thus Come One, all the most profound matters of the Thus Come One—all these are proclaimed, revealed, and clearly expounded in this sutra.

"For this reason, after the Thus Come One has entered extinction, you must single-mindedly accept, uphold, read, recite, explain, preach and transcribe it, and practice it as directed. In any of the various lands, wherever there are those who accept, uphold, read, recite, explain, preach, transcribe, or practice it as directed, or wherever the sutra rolls are preserved, whether in a garden, a forest, beneath a tree, in monks quarters, in the lodgings of white-robed laymen, in palaces, or in mountain valleys or the wide wilderness, in all these places one should erect towers and offer alms. Why? Because you should understand that such spots are places of religious practice. In such places have the Buddhas gained anuttara-samyak-sambodhi, in such places have the Buddhas turned the wheel of the Law, in such places have the Buddhas entered parinirvana."

At that time the World-Honored One, wishing to state his meaning once more, spoke in verse form, saying:

The Buddhas, saviors of the world,
abide in their great transcendental powers,
and in order to please living beings
they display immeasurable supernatural powers.
Their tongues reach to the Brahma heaven,
their bodies emit countless beams of light.
For the sake of those who seek the Buddha way
they manifest these things that are rarely seen.
The sound of the Buddhas coughing,
the sound of them snapping their fingers,
is heard throughout the lands in the ten directions
and the earth in all those lands moves in six ways.
Because after the Buddha has passed into extinction
there will be those who can uphold this sutra,
the Buddhas are all delighted
and manifest immeasurable supernatural powers.
Because they wish to entrust this sutra,
they praise and extol the person who accepts and upholds it,
and though they should do so for immeasurable kalpas
they could never exhaust their praises.
The benefits gained by such a person
are boundless and inexhaustible,
like the vast sky in the ten directions
that no one can set a limit to.
One who can uphold this sutra
has in effect already seen me,
and likewise has seen Many Treasures Buddha
and the Buddhas that are emanations of my body.
And he also sees me today
as I teach and convert the bodhisattvas.
One who can uphold this sutra
causes me and my emanations,

and Many Treasures Buddha who has already
   entered extinction,
all to be filled with joy.
The Buddhas who are present in the ten directions
and those of past and future ages—
he will see them too, offer alms to them
and cause them to be filled with joy.
The secret essentials of the Law
gained by the Buddhas who sat in the place of practice—
one who can uphold this sutra
will gain them too before long.
One who can uphold this sutra
will delight in endlessly expounding
the principles of the various doctrines
and their names and phrases,
like a wind in the open sky
moving everywhere without hindrance or block.
After the Thus Come One has passed into extinction,
this person will know the sutras preached by the Buddha,
their causes and conditions and their proper sequence,
and will preach them truthfully in accordance with principle.
As the light of the sun and moon
can banish all obscurity and gloom,
so this person as he passes through the world
can wipe out the darkness of living beings,
causing immeasurable numbers of bodhisattvas
in the end to dwell in the single vehicle.
Therefore a person of wisdom,
hearing how keen are the benefits to be gained,
after I have passed into extinction
should accept and uphold this sutra.
Such a person assuredly and without doubt
will attain the Buddha way.

22
ENTRUSTMENT

At that time Shakyamuni Buddha rose from his Dharma seat and, manifesting his great supernatural powers, with his right hand patted the heads of the immeasurable bodhisattvas and mahasattvas and spoke these words: "For immeasurable hundreds, thousands, ten thousands, millions of asamkhya kalpas I have practiced this hard-to-attain Law of anuttara-samyak-sambodhi. Now I entrust it to you. You must single-mindedly propagate this Law abroad, causing its benefits to spread far and wide."

Three times he patted the bodhisattvas and mahasattvas on the head and spoke these words: "For immeasurable hundreds, thousands, ten thousands, millions of asamkhya kalpas I have practiced this hard-to-attain Law of anuttara-samyak-sambodhi. Now I entrust it to you. You must accept, uphold, read, recite, and broadly propagate this Law, causing all living beings everywhere to hear and understand it. Why? Because the Thus Come One has great pity and compassion. He is in no way stingy or begrudging, nor has he any fear. He is able to bestow on living beings the wisdom of the Buddha, the wisdom of the Thus Come One, the wisdom that comes of itself. The Thus Come One is a great giver of gifts to all living beings. You for your part should respond by studying this Law of the Thus Come One. You must not be stingy or begrudging!

"In future ages if there are good men and good women who have faith in the wisdom of the Thus Come One, you should preach and expound the Lotus Sutra for them, so that others may hear and understand it. For in this way you can cause them to gain the Buddha wisdom. If there are living beings who do not believe and accept it, you should use some of the other profound doctrines of the Thus Come One to teach, benefit and bring joy to them. If you do all this, then you will have repaid the debt of gratitude that you owe to the Buddhas."

When the bodhisattvas and mahasattvas heard the Buddha speak these words, they all experienced a great joy that filled their bodies. With even greater reverence than before, they bent their bodies, bowed their heads, pressed their palms together and, facing the Buddha, raised their voices in unison, saying: "We will respectfully carry out all these things just as the World-Honored One has commanded. We beg the World-Honored One to have no concern on this account!"

The multitude of bodhisattvas and mahasattvas repeated these words three times, raising their voices in unison and saying: "We will respectfully carry out all these things just as the World-Honored One has commanded. Therefore we beg the World-Honored One to have no concern on this account!"

At that time Shakyamuni Buddha caused the Buddhas who were emanations of his body and had come from the ten directions to return each one to his original land, saying: "Each of these Buddhas may proceed at his own pleasure. The tower of Many Treasures Buddha may also return to its former position."

When he spoke these words, the immeasurable emanation Buddhas from the ten directions who were seated on lion seats under the jeweled trees, as well as Many Treasures Buddha, Superior Practices, and the others of the great multitude of boundless asamkhyas of bodhisattvas, Shariputra and the other voice-hearers and four kinds of believers, and the heavenly and human beings, asuras and others in all the worlds, hearing what the Buddha had said, were all filled with great joy.

23

FORMER AFFAIRS OF THE BODHISATTVA MEDICINE KING

At that time the bodhisattva Constellation King Flower spoke to the Buddha, saying: "World-Honored One, how does the bodhisattva Medicine King come and go in the saha world? World-Honored One, this bodhisattva Medicine King has carried out some hundreds, thousands, ten thousands, millions of nayutas of difficult practices, arduous practices. Very well, World-Honored One, could I ask you to explain a little? The heavenly beings, dragons, gods, yakshas, gandharvas, asuras, garudas, kimnaras, mahoragas, human and nonhuman beings, and the bodhisattvas who have come from other lands and the multitude of voice-hearers, will all be delighted to hear you."

At that time the Buddha addressed the bodhisattva Constellation

King Flower, saying: "Many kalpas in the past, immeasurable as Ganges sands, there was a Buddha named Sun Moon Pure Bright Virtue Thus Come One, worthy of offerings, of right and universal knowledge, perfect clarity and conduct, well gone, understanding the world, unexcelled worthy, trainer of people, teacher of heavenly and human beings, Buddha, World-Honored One. This Buddha had eighty million great bodhisattvas and mahasattvas and a multitude of great voice-hearers equal to the sands of seventy-two Ganges. This Buddha's life span was forty-two thousand kalpas, and the life span of the bodhisattvas was the same. In his land there were no women, hell dwellers, hungry spirits, beasts or asuras, and no kinds of tribulation. The ground was as level as the palm of a hand, made of lapis lazuli and adorned with jeweled trees. Jeweled curtains covered it over, banners of jeweled flowers hung down, and jeweled urns and incense burners filled the land everywhere. There were daises made of the seven treasures, with a tree by each dais, the tree situated an arrow-shot length from the dais. These jeweled trees all had bodhisattvas and voice-hearers sitting under them, and each of the jeweled daises had hundreds of millions of heavenly beings playing on heavenly instruments and singing the praises of the Buddha as an offering.

"At that time, for the sake of the bodhisattva Gladly Seen by All Living Beings and the other numerous bodhisattvas and multitude of voice-hearers, the Buddha preached the Lotus Sutra. This bodhisattva Gladly Seen by All Living Beings delighted in carrying out arduous practices. In the midst of the Law preached by the Buddha Sun Moon Pure Bright Virtue he applied himself diligently and traveled about here and there, single-mindedly seeking Buddhahood for a period of fully twelve thousand years. After that he was able to gain the samadhi in which one can manifest all physical forms. Having gained this samadhi, his heart was filled with great joy and he thought to himself: My gaining the samadhi in which I can manifest all physical forms is due entirely to the fact that I heard the Lotus Sutra. I must now make an offering to the Buddha Sun Moon Pure Bright Virtue and to the Lotus Sutra!

"Immediately he entered the samadhi and in the midst of the sky rained down mandarava flowers, great mandarava flowers, and finely ground, hard black particles of sandalwood; they filled the whole sky like clouds as they came raining down. He also rained down the incense of the sandalwood that grows by the southern seashore. Six taels of this incense is worth as much as the saha world. All these he used as an offering to the Buddha.

"When he had finished making this offering, he rose from his samadhi and thought to himself: Though I have employed my supernatural powers to make this offering to the Buddha, it is not as good as making an offering of my own body.

"Thereupon he swallowed various perfumes, sandalwood, kunduruka, turushka, prikka, aloes, and liquidambar gum, and he also drank the fragrant oil of champaka and other kinds of flowers, doing this for a period of fully twelve hundred years. Anointing his body with fragrant oil, he appeared before the Buddha Sun Moon Pure Bright Virtue, wrapped his body in heavenly jeweled robes, poured fragrant oil over his head and, calling on his transcendental powers, set fire to his body. The glow shone forth, illuminating worlds equal in number to the sands of eighty million Ganges. The Buddhas in these worlds simultaneously spoke out in praise, saying: 'Excellent, excellent, good man! This is true diligence. This is what is called a true Dharma offering to the Thus Come One. Though one may use flowers, incense, necklaces, incense for burning, powdered incense, paste incense, heavenly silken banners and canopies, along with the incense of the sandalwood that grows by the southern seashore, presenting offerings of all such things as these, he can never match this! Though one may make donations of his realm and cities, his wife and children, he is no match for this! Good man, this is called the foremost donation of all. Among all donations, this is the most highly prized, for one is offering the Dharma to the Thus Come Ones!'

"After they had spoken these words, they each one fell silent. The body of the bodhisattva burned for twelve hundred years, and when that period of time had passed, it at last burned itself out.

"After the bodhisattva Gladly Seen by All Living Beings had made this Dharma offering and his life had come to an end, he was reborn in the land of the Buddha Sun Moon Pure Bright Virtue, in the household of the king Pure Virtue. Sitting in cross-legged position, he was suddenly born by transformation, and at once for the benefit of his father he spoke in verse form, saying:

Great king, you should now understand this.
Having walked about in a certain place,
I immediately gained the samadhi
that allows me to manifest all physical forms.
I have carried out my endeavors with great diligence
and cast aside the body that I loved.

"When he had recited this verse, he said to his father: 'The Buddha Sun Moon Pure Bright Virtue is still present at this time. Previously I made an offering to this Buddha and gained a dharani that allows me to understand the words of all living beings. Moreover I have heard this Lotus Sutra with its eight hundred, thousand, ten thousand, millions of nayutas, kankaras, vivaras, akshobhyas of verses.[1] Great king, I must now once more make an offering to this Buddha.'

"Having said this, he seated himself on a dais made of the seven treasures, rose up into the air to the height of seven tala trees and, proceeding to the place where the Buddha was, bowed his head to the ground in obeisance to the Buddha's feet, put the nails of his ten fingers together and spoke this verse in praise of the Buddha:

A countenance so rare and wonderful,
its bright beams illuminating the ten directions!
At a previous time I made an offering,
and now once more I draw near.

"At that time, after the bodhisattva Gladly Seen by All Living Beings had spoken this verse, he said to the Buddha: 'World-Honored One, is the World-Honored One still present in the world?'

"At that time the Buddha Sun Moon Pure Bright Virtue said to the bodhisattva Gladly Seen by All Living Beings: 'Good man, the time has come for my nirvana. The time has come for extinction. You may provide me with a comfortable couch, for tonight will be my parinirvana.'

"He also commanded the bodhisattva Gladly Seen by All Living Beings, saying: 'Good man, I take this Law of the Buddha and entrust

1. Kankara, vivara, and akṣobhya are all extremely large numerical units.

it to you. In addition, the bodhisattvas and great disciples, along with the Law of anuttara-samyak-sambodhi, and the thousand-millionfold seven-jeweled world, with its jeweled trees and jeweled daises and heavenly beings who wait on and attend them—all these I hand over to you. I also entrust to you the relics of my body that remain after I have passed into extinction. You must distribute them abroad and arrange for offerings to them far and wide. You should erect many thousands of towers [to house them].'

"The Buddha Sun Moon Pure Bright Virtue, having given these commands to the bodhisattva Gladly Seen by All Living Beings, that night, in the last watch of the night, entered nirvana.

"At that time the bodhisattva Gladly Seen by All Living Beings, seeing the Buddha pass into extinction, was deeply grieved and distressed. Out of his great love and longing for the Buddha he at once prepared a pyre made of sandalwood from the seashore, and with this as an offering to the Buddha's body, he cremated the body. After the fire had burned out, he gathered up the relics, fashioned eighty-four thousand jeweled urns, and built eighty-four thousand towers, high as the three worlds, adorned with central poles, draped with banners and canopies and hung with a multitude of jeweled bells.

"At that time the bodhisattva Gladly Seen by All Living Beings once more thought to himself: Though I have made these offerings, my mind is not yet satisfied. I must make some further offering to the relics.

"Then he spoke to the other bodhisattvas and great disciples, and to the heavenly beings, dragons, yakshas, and all the members of the great assembly, saying, 'You must give your undivided attention. I will now make an offering to the relics of the Buddha Sun Moon Pure Bright Virtue.'

"Having spoken these words, immediately in the presence of the eighty-four thousand towers he burned his arms, which were adorned with a hundred blessings, for a period of seventy-two thousand years as his offering. This caused the numberless multitudes who were seeking to become voice-hearers, along with an immeasurable asamkhya of persons, to conceive a desire for anuttara-samyak-sambodhi, and all of them were able to dwell in the samadhi where one can manifest all physical forms.

"At that time the bodhisattvas, heavenly and human beings, asuras and others, seeing that the bodhisattva had destroyed his arms, were alarmed and saddened and they said: 'This bodhisattva Gladly Seen by All Living Beings is our teacher, instructing and converting us. Now he has burned his arms and his body is no longer whole!'

"At that time, in the midst of the great assembly, the bodhisattva Gladly Seen by All Living Beings made this vow, saying: 'I have cast away both my arms. I am certain to attain the golden body of a Buddha. If this is true and not false, then may my two arms become as they were before!'

"When he had finished pronouncing this vow, his arms reappeared of themselves as they had been before. This came about because the merits and wisdom of this bodhisattva were manifold and profound. At that time the thousand-millionfold world shook and trembled in six different ways, heaven rained down jeweled flowers, and all the heavenly and human beings gained what they had never had before."

The Buddha said to the bodhisattva Constellation King Flower: "What do you think? Is this bodhisattva Gladly Seen by All Living Beings someone unknown to you? He is in fact none other than the present bodhisattva Medicine King! He cast aside his body as an offering in this fashion immeasurable hundreds, thousands, ten thousands, millions of nayutas of times.

"Constellation King Flower, if there are those who have made up their minds and wish to gain anuttara-samyak-sambodhi, they would do well to burn a finger or one toe of their foot as an offering to the Buddha towers. It is better than offering one's realm and cities, wife and children, or the mountains, forests, rivers, and lakes in the 'lands of the thousand-millionfold world, or all their precious treasures. Even if a person were to fill the whole thousand-millionfold world with the seven treasures as an offering to the Buddha and the great bodhisattvas, pratyekabuddhas and arhats, the benefits gained by such a person cannot match those gained by accepting and upholding this Lotus Sutra, even just one four-line verse of it! The latter brings the most numerous blessings of all.

"Constellation King Flower, among all the rivers, streams, and other bodies of water, for example, the ocean is foremost. And this Lotus Sutra is likewise, being the most profound and greatest of the sutras preached by the Thus Come Ones. Again, just as among the

Dirt Mountains, Black Mountains, Small Iron Encircling Mountains, Great Iron Encircling Mountains, Ten Treasure Mountains and all the other mountains, Mount Sumeru is foremost, so this Lotus Sutra is likewise. Among all the sutras, it holds the highest place. And just as among all the stars and their like, the moon, a god's son, is foremost, so this Lotus Sutra is likewise. For among all the thousands, ten thousands, millions of types of sutra teachings, it shines the brightest. And just as the sun, a god's son, can banish all darkness, so too this sutra is capable of destroying the darkness of all that is not good.

"As among the petty kings the wheel-turning sage king is foremost, so this sutra is the most honored among all the many sutras. As the lord Shakra is king among the thirty-three heavenly beings, so this sutra likewise is king among all the sutras. And as the heavenly king, great Brahma, is the father of all living beings, so this sutra likewise is father of all sages, worthies, those still learning, those who have completed their learning, and those who set their minds on becoming bodhisattvas. And as among all ordinary mortals, the srota-apanna, sakridagamin, anagamin, arhats and pratyekabuddhas are foremost, so this sutra likewise is foremost among all the sutra teachings preached by all the Thus Come Ones, preached by all the bodhisattvas, or preached by all the voice-hearers. A person who can accept and uphold this sutra is likewise foremost among all living beings. Bodhisattvas are foremost among all voice-hearers and pratyekabuddhas, and in the same way this sutra is foremost among all the sutra teachings. As the Buddha is king of the doctrines, so likewise this sutra is king of the sutras.

"Constellation King Flower, this sutra can save all living beings. This sutra can cause all living beings to free themselves from suffering and anguish. This sutra can bring great benefits to all living beings and fulfill their desires, as a clear cool pond can satisfy all those who are thirsty. It is like a fire to one who is cold, a robe to one who is naked, like a band of merchants finding a leader, a child finding its mother, someone finding a ship in which to cross the water, a sick man finding a doctor, someone in darkness finding a lamp, the poor finding riches, the people finding a ruler, a traveling merchant finding his way to the sea. It is like a torch that banishes darkness. Such is this Lotus Sutra. It can cause living beings to cast off all distress, all sickness and pain. It can unloose all the bonds of birth and death.

"If a person is able to hear this Lotus Sutra, if he copies it himself or causes others to copy it, the benefits he gains thereby will be such that even the Buddha wisdom could never finish calculating their extent. If one copies these sutra rolls and uses flowers, incense, necklaces, incense for burning, powdered incense, paste incense, banners, canopies, robes, various kinds of lamps such as lamps of butter oil, oil lamps, lamps with various fragrant oils, lamps of champaka oil, lamps of sumana oil, lamps of patala oil, lamps of varshika oil, or lamps of navamalika oil to make offerings to them, the benefits that he acquires will likewise be immeasurable.

"Constellation King Flower, if there is a person who hears this chapter on the Former Affairs of the Bodhisattva Medicine King, he too will gain immeasurable and boundless benefits. If there is a woman who hears this chapter on the Former Affairs of the Bodhisattva Medicine King and is able to accept and uphold it, that will be her last appearance in a woman's body and she will never be born in that form again.

"If in the last five hundred year period after the Thus Come One has entered extinction there is a woman who hears this sutra and carries out its practices as the sutra directs, when her life here on earth comes to an end she will immediately go to the world of Peace and Delight where the Buddha Amitayus dwells surrounded by the assembly of great bodhisattvas and there will be born seated on a jeweled seat in the center of a lotus blossom. He[2] will no longer know the torments of greed, desire, anger, rage, stupidity or ignorance, or the torments brought about by arrogance, envy or other defilements. He will gain the bodhisattva's transcendental powers and the truth of the birthlessness of all phenomena. Having gained this truth, his faculty of sight will be clear and pure, and with this clear pure faculty of sight he will see Buddhas and Thus Come Ones equal in number to the sands of seven hundred twelve thousand million nayutas of Ganges.

"At that time Buddhas will join in praising him from afar, saying: 'Excellent, excellent, good man! In the midst of the Law of Shakyamuni Buddha you have been able to accept, uphold, read, recite and ponder this sutra and to preach it for others. The good fortune you gain thereby is immeasurable and boundless. It cannot be burned by

2. As the text makes clear later on, the woman has been reborn in male form.

fire or washed away by water. Your benefits are such that a thousand Buddhas speaking all together could never finish describing them. Now you have been able to destroy all devils and thieves, to annihilate the army of birth and death, and all others who bore you enmity or malice have likewise been wiped out.

" 'Good man, a hundred, a thousand Buddhas will employ their transcendental powers to join in guarding and protecting you. Among the heavenly and human beings of all the worlds, there will be no one like you. With the sole exception of the Thus Come One, there will be none among the voice-hearers, pratyekabuddhas or bodhisattvas whose wisdom and ability in meditation can equal yours!'

"Constellation King Flower, such will be the benefits and the power of wisdom successfully acquired by this bodhisattva.

"If there is a person who, hearing this chapter on the Former Affairs of the Bodhisattva Medicine King, is able to welcome it with joy and praise its excellence, then in this present existence this person's mouth will constantly emit the fragrance of the blue lotus flower, and the pores of his body will constantly emit the fragrance of ox-head sandalwood. His benefits will be such as have been described above.

"For this reason, Constellation King Flower, I entrust this chapter on the Former Affairs of the Bodhisattva Medicine King to you. After I have passed into extinction, in the last five hundred year period you must spread it abroad widely throughout Jambudvipa and never allow it to be cut off, nor must you allow evil devils, the devils' people, heavenly beings, dragons, yakshas or kumbhanda demons to seize the advantage!

"Constellation King Flower, you must use your transcendental powers to guard and protect this sutra. Why? Because this sutra provides good medicine for the ills of the people of Jambudvipa. If a person who has an illness is able to hear this sutra, then his illness will be wiped out and he will know neither old age or death.

"Constellation King Flower, if you see someone who accepts and upholds this sutra, you must take blue lotus blossoms, heap them with powdered incense, and scatter them over him as an offering. And when you have scattered them, you should think to yourself: Before long this person will pick grasses, spread them as a seat in the place of practice, and conquer the armies of the devil. Then he will sound the conch of the Law, beat the drum of the great Law, and free all living beings from the sea of old age, sickness, and death!

"For this reason when those who seek the Buddha way see someone who accepts and upholds this sutra, they should approach him with this kind of respect and reverence."

When [the Buddha] preached this chapter on the Former Affairs of the Bodhisattva Medicine King, eighty-four thousand bodhisattvas gained the dharani that allows them to understand the words of all living beings. Many Treasures Thus Come One in the midst of his treasure tower praised the bodhisattva Constellation King Flower, saying: "Excellent, excellent, Constellation King Flower. You succeeded in acquiring inconceivable benefits and thus were able to question Shakyamuni Buddha about this matter, profiting immeasurable numbers of living beings."

24
THE BODHISATTVA
WONDERFUL SOUND

At that time Shakyamuni Buddha emitted a beam of bright light from the knob of flesh [on top of his head], one of the features of a great man, and also emitted a beam of light from the tuft of white hair between his eyebrows, illuminating the Buddha worlds in the eastern direction equal in number to the sands of one hundred eighty thousand million nayutas of Ganges. Beyond these numerous worlds was a world called Adorned with Pure Light. In this realm there was a Buddha named Pure Flower Constellation King Wisdom Thus Come One, worthy of offerings, of right and universal knowledge, perfect clarity and conduct, well gone, understanding the world, unexcelled worthy, trainer of people, teacher of heavenly and human beings,

Buddha, World-Honored One. An immeasurably and boundlessly great multitude of bodhisattvas surrounded him and paid reverence, and for these he preached the Law. The beam of bright light from the white tuft of Shakyamuni Buddha illuminated the whole land.

At that time in the land Adorned with Pure Light there was a bodhisattva named Wonderful Sound, who long ago had planted numerous roots of virtue, offering alms to and waiting upon immeasurable hundreds, thousands, ten thousands, millions of Buddhas. He had succeeded in acquiring all kinds of profound wisdom, gaining the samadhi of the wonderful banner mark, the Dharma flower samadhi, the pure virtue samadhi, the samadhi of the constellation king's sport, the conditionless samadhi, the seal of wisdom samadhi, the samadhi that allows one to understand the words of all living beings, the samadhi that gathers together all benefits, the pure samadhi, the samadhi of the sport of transcendental powers, the wisdom torch samadhi, the adorned king samadhi, the pure light glow samadhi, the pure storehouse samadhi, the unshared samadhi, and the samadhi of the sun's revolving. He had gained all these great samadhis equal in number to the sands of a hundred, a thousand, ten thousand, a million Ganges.

When the light emitted by Shakyamuni Buddha illuminated his body, he immediately spoke to the Buddha Pure Flower Constellation King Wisdom, saying: "World-Honored One, I must journey to the saha world to do obeisance, wait on, and offer alms to Shakyamuni Buddha, and to see Bodhisattva Manjushri, prince of the Dharma, Bodhisattva Medicine King, Bodhisattva Brave Donor, Bodhisattva Constellation King Flower, Bodhisattva Superior Practices Intent, Bodhisattva Adorned King, and Bodhisattva Medicine Superior."

At that time the Buddha Pure Flower Constellation King Wisdom said to Bodhisattva Wonderful Sound: "You must not look with contempt on that land or come to think of it as mean and inferior. Good man, that saha world is uneven, high in places, low in others, and full of dirt, stones, mountains, foulness, and impurity. The Buddha is puny in stature and the numerous bodhisattvas are likewise small in form, whereas your body is forty-two thousand yojanas in height and mine is six million eight hundred thousand yojanas. Your body is foremost in shapeliness, with hundreds, thousands, ten thousands of blessings and a radiance that is particularly wonderful. Therefore when you journey there, you must not look with contempt on that land or come to think of the Buddha and bodhisattvas or the land itself as mean and inferior!"

Bodhisattva Wonderful Sound said to the Buddha: "World-Honored One, my journey now to the saha world is in all respects due to the power of the Thus Come One, a sport carried out by the Thus Come One's transcendental powers, an adornment to the Thus Come One's blessings and wisdom."

Thereupon the bodhisattva Wonderful Sound, without rising from his seat or swaying his body, entered into a samadhi, and through the power of the samadhi, in a place not far removed from the Dharma seat on Mount Gridhrakuta, created a jeweled mass of eighty-four thousand lotus blossoms. Their stems were made of Jambunada gold, their leaves were of silver, their stamens of diamond, and their calyxes of kimshuka jewels.

At that time the Dharma prince Manjushri, spying the lotus flowers, spoke to the Buddha, saying: "World-Honored One, what causes have brought about the appearance of this auspicious sign? Here are many ten thousands of lotus blossoms, their stems made of Jambunada gold, their leaves of silver, their stamens of diamond and their calyxes of kimshuka jewels!"

At that time Shakyamuni Buddha said to Manjushri: "This bodhisattva and mahasattva Wonderful Sound wishes to leave the land of the Buddha Pure Flower Constellation King Wisdom and, surrounded by eighty-four thousand bodhisattvas, to come to this saha world to offer alms, wait on, and pay obeisance to me. He also wishes to offer alms to and hear the Lotus Sutra."

Manjushri said to the Buddha: "World-Honored One, what good roots has this bodhisattva planted, what benefits has he cultivated, that he can exercise such great transcendental powers as this? What samadhi does he carry out? I beg you to explain for us the name of this samadhi, for we too would like to apply ourselves diligently to its practice. If we carry out this samadhi, then we will be able to observe the aspect and size of this bodhisattva and his bearing and conduct. We beg the World-Honored One to employ his transcendental powers to bring this bodhisattva here and enable us to see him!"

At that time Shakyamuni Buddha said to Manjushri, "Many Treasures Thus Come One, who entered extinction so long ago, will manifest his form for you."

Then the Buddha Many Treasures said to that bodhisattva [Wonderful Sound], "Come, good man. The Dharma prince Manjushri wishes to see your body."

With that, Bodhisattva Wonderful Sound vanished from his own land and, accompanied by eighty-four thousand bodhisattvas, appeared here [in the saha world]. The lands that he passed through on his way quaked and trembled in six different ways, and in all of them seven-jeweled lotus flowers rained down and the instruments of hundreds and thousands of heavenly musicians sounded of themselves without having been struck.

This bodhisattva's eyes were as big and broad as the leaves of the blue lotus, and a hundred, a thousand, ten thousand moons put together could not surpass the perfection of his face. His body was pure gold in color, adorned with immeasurable hundreds and thousands of blessings. His dignity and virtue were splendid, his light shone brilliantly, he was endowed with many special marks and as stalwart in body as Narayana.

Taking his place on a dais made of seven treasures, he had risen up into the air until he was raised above the earth the height of seven tala trees. Then with the host of bodhisattvas surrounding him and paying reverence, he had journeyed to Mount Gridhrakuta in this saha world. When he arrived there he descended from the dais of seven treasures. Bearing a necklace worth hundreds and thousands, he proceeded to the place where Shakyamuni Buddha was, bowed his head to the ground, made obeisance to the Buddha's feet, and presented the necklace, addressing the Buddha in these words: "World-Honored One, the Buddha Pure Flower Constellation King Wisdom wishes to inquire about the World-Honored One. Are your illnesses few, are your worries few? Can you come and go easily and conveniently, can you move about in comfort? Are the four elements properly harmonized in you? Can you endure the world's affairs? Are the living beings easy to rescue? Are they not excessive in their greed, anger, stupidity, jealousy, stinginess, and arrogance? Are they not lacking in filial conduct toward their parents? Are they not disrespectful toward shramanas and given to heterodox views and other evil? Do they not fail to control their five emotions? World-Honored One, are the living beings able to conquer and overcome the enmity of the devils? Has Many Treasures Thus Come One, who entered extinction so long ago, come in his tower of seven treasures to listen to the Law? The Buddha also wishes to inquire about Many Treasures Thus Come One, whether he is tranquil and at ease, with few worries, patient and long abiding. World-Honored One, I would like to see the body of the Buddha Many Treasures. I beg the World-Honored One to allow me to see him!"

At that time Shakyamuni Buddha said to Many Treasures Buddha, "This bodhisattva Wonderful Sound wishes to see you."

Then Many Treasures Buddha addressed Wonderful Sound, saying, "Excellent, excellent! You have come here in order to be able to offer alms to Shakyamuni Buddha and to listen to the Lotus Sutra and see Manjushri and the others."

At that time the bodhisattva Flower Virtue said to the Buddha, "World-Honored One, this bodhisattva Wonderful Sound—what good roots has he planted, what benefits has he cultivated, that he possesses these supernatural powers?"

The Buddha replied to Bodhisattva Flower Virtue: "In ages past there was a Buddha named Cloud Thunder Sound King, tathagata, arhat, samyak-sambuddha. His land was called Manifesting All Worlds and his kalpa was called Gladly Seen. For twelve thousand years the bodhisattva Wonderful Sound employed a hundred thousand types of musical instruments to provide an offering to the Buddha Cloud Thunder Sound King, and he also presented to him eighty-four thousand alms bowls made of the seven treasures. In recompense for these actions he has now been born in the land of the Buddha Pure Flower Constellation King Wisdom and possesses these supernatural powers.

"Flower Virtue, what is your opinion? The Bodhisattva Wonderful Sound who at that time made musical offerings to the Buddha Cloud Thunder Sound King and presented him with jeweled vessels—was he someone unknown to you? In fact he is none other than the bodhisattva and mahasattva Wonderful Sound who is here now!

"Flower Virtue, this bodhisattva Wonderful Sound has already made offerings to and waited on an immeasurable number of Buddhas. Long ago he planted the roots of virtue and encountered hundreds, thousands, ten thousands, millions of nayutas of Buddhas equal in number to the sands of the Ganges.

"Flower Virtue, you see only the body of Bodhisattva Wonderful Sound which is here. But this bodhisattva manifests himself in various different bodies and preaches this sutra for the sake of living beings in various different places. At times he appears as King Brahma, at times as the lord Shakra, at times as the heavenly being Freedom, at times as the heavenly being Great Freedom, at times as a great general of heaven, at times as the heavenly king Vaishravana, at times as a wheel-turning sage king, at times as one of the petty kings, at times as a rich man, at times as a householder, at times as a chief minister, at times as a Brahman, at times as a monk, a nun, a layman believer, or a laywoman believer, at times as the wife of a rich man or a householder, at times as the wife of a chief minister, at times as the wife of a Brahman, at times as a young boy or a young girl, at times as a heavenly being, a dragon, a yaksha, a gandharva, an asura, a garuda, a kimnara, a mahoraga, a human or a nonhuman being, and so preaches this sutra. The hell dwellers, hungry spirits, beasts, and the numerous others who are in difficult circumstances are thus all able to be saved. And for the sake of those who are in the women's quarters of the royal palace, he changes himself into a woman's form and preaches this sutra.

"Flower Virtue, this bodhisattva Wonderful Sound can save and protect the various living beings of the saha world. This bodhisattva Wonderful Sound performs various transformations, manifesting himself in different forms in this saha land and preaching this sutra for the sake of living beings, and yet his transcendental powers, his transformations, and his wisdom suffer no injury or diminution thereby. This bodhisattva employs various types of wisdom to illuminate the saha world, causing each one among all the living beings to acquire the appropriate understanding, and does the same in all the other worlds of the ten directions which are numerous as Ganges sands.

"If the form of a voice-hearer is what is needed to bring salvation, he manifests himself in the form of a voice-hearer and proceeds to preach the Law. If the form of a pratyekabuddha will bring salvation, he manifests himself in the form of a pratyekabuddha and preaches the Law. If the form of a bodhisattva will bring salvation, he manifests a bodhisattva form and preaches the Law. If the form of a Buddha will bring salvation, he immediately manifests a Buddha form and preaches the Law. Thus he manifests himself in various different forms, depending upon what is appropriate for salvation. And if it is appropriate to enter extinction in order to bring salvation, he manifests himself as entering extinction.

"Flower Virtue, the bodhisattva and mahasattva Wonderful Sound has acquired great transcendental powers and the power of wisdom that enable him to do all this!"

At that time the bodhisattva Flower Virtue said to the Buddha, "World-Honored One, this bodhisattva Wonderful Sound has planted the roots of goodness very deeply. World-Honored One, what samadhi does this bodhisattva dwell in, that he is able to carry out all these transformations and manifestations to save living beings?"

The Buddha said to Bodhisattva Flower Virtue, "Good man, this samadhi is called Manifesting All Kinds of Bodies. The bodhisattva Wonderful Sound, dwelling in this samadhi, is able in this manner to enrich and benefit immeasurable living beings."

When [the Buddha] preached this chapter on Bodhisattva Wonderful Sound, the eighty-four thousand persons who had come with Bodhisattva Wonderful Sound all acquired this samadhi enabling them to manifest all kinds of bodies, and the immeasurable bodhisattvas in this saha world also acquired this samadhi and dharani.

At that time the bodhisattva and mahasattva Wonderful Sound, having finished offering alms to Shakyamuni Buddha and to the tower of Many Treasures Buddha, returned to his original land. The lands that he passed through on his way quaked and trembled in six different ways, jeweled lotus flowers rained down, and hundreds, thousands, ten thousands, millions of different kinds of music played.

After he had arrived in his original land and was surrounded by his eighty-four thousand bodhisattvas, he proceeded to the place of the Buddha Pure Flower Constellation King Wisdom and addressed the Buddha, saying, "World-Honored One, I visited the saha world, enriched and benefited the living beings, saw Shakyamuni Buddha and the tower of Many Treasures Buddha, and offered obeisance and alms to them. I also saw Bodhisattva Manjushri, prince of the Dharma, as well as Bodhisattva Medicine King, Bodhisattva Gaining Diligent Exertion Power, Bodhisattva Brave Donor, and others. And I made it

possible for these eighty-four thousand bodhisattvas to gain the samadhi enabling them to manifest all kinds of bodies."

When [the Buddha] preached this chapter on the comings and
goings of Bodhisattva Wonderful Sound, forty-two thousand sons of
gods gained the truth of the birthlessness of all phenomena, and
Bodhisattva Flower Virtue gained the Dharma flower samadhi.

25

THE UNIVERSAL GATEWAY OF THE BODHISATTVA PERCEIVER OF THE WORLD'S SOUNDS

At that time the bodhisattva Inexhaustible Intent immediately rose from his seat, bared his right shoulder, pressed his palms together and, facing the Buddha, spoke these words: "World-Honored One, this Bodhisattva Perceiver of the World's Sounds—why is he called Perceiver of the World's Sounds?"

The Buddha said to Bodhisattva Inexhaustible Intent: "Good man, suppose there are immeasurable hundreds, thousands, ten thousands, millions of living beings who are undergoing various trials and suffering. If they hear of this bodhisattva Perceiver of the World's Sounds and single-mindedly call his name, then at once he will perceive the sound of their voices and they will all gain deliverance from their trials.

"If someone, holding fast to the name of Bodhisattva Perceiver of the World's Sounds, should enter a great fire, the fire could not burn him. This would come about because of this bodhisattva's authority and supernatural power. If one were washed away by a great flood and called upon his name, one would immediately find himself in a shallow place.

"Suppose there were a hundred, a thousand, ten thousand, a million living beings who, seeking for gold, silver, lapis lazuli, seashell, agate, coral, amber, pearls, and other treasures, set out on the great sea. And suppose a fierce wind should blow their ship off course and it drifted to the land of rakshasa demons. If among those people there is even just one who calls the name of Bodhisattva Perceiver of the World's Sounds, then all those people will be delivered from their troubles with the rakshasas. This is why he is called Perceiver of the World's Sounds.

"If a person who faces imminent threat of attack should call the name of Bodhisattva Perceiver of the World's Sounds, then the swords and staves wielded by his attackers would instantly shatter into so many pieces and he would be delivered.

"Though enough yakshas and rakshasas to fill all the thousand-millionfold world should try to come and torment a person, if they hear him calling the name of Bodhisattva Perceiver of the World's Sounds, then these evil demons will not even be able to look at him with their evil eyes, much less do him harm.

"Suppose there is a person who, whether guilty or not guilty, has had his body imprisoned in fetters and chains, cangue and lock. If he calls the name of Bodhisattva Perceiver of the World's Sounds, then all his bonds will be severed and broken and at once he will gain deliverance.

"Suppose, in a place filled with all the evil-hearted bandits of the thousand-millionfold world, there is a merchant leader who is guiding a band of merchants carrying valuable treasures over a steep and dangerous road, and that one man shouts out these words: 'Good men, do not be afraid! You must single-mindedly call on the name of Bodhisattva Perceiver of the World's Sounds. This bodhisattva can grant fearlessness to living beings. If you call his name, you will be delivered from these evil-hearted bandits!' When the band of merchants hear this, they all together raise their voices, saying, 'Hail to the Bodhisattva Perceiver of the World's Sounds!' And because they call his name, they are at once able to gain deliverance. Inexhaustible Intent, the authority and supernatural power of the bodhisattva and mahasattva Perceiver of the World's Sounds are as mighty as this!

"If there should be living beings beset by numerous lusts and cravings, let them think with constant reverence of Bodhisattva Perceiver of the World's Sounds and then they can shed their desires. If they have great wrath and ire, let them think with constant reverence of Bodhisattva Perceiver of the World's Sounds and then they can shed their ire. If they have great ignorance and stupidity, let them think with constant reverence of Bodhisattva Perceiver of the World's Sounds and they can rid themselves of stupidity.

"Inexhaustible Intent, the bodhisattva Perceiver of the World's Sounds possesses great authority and supernatural powers, as I have described, and can confer many benefits. For this reason, living beings should constantly keep the thought of him in mind.

"If a woman wishes to give birth to a male child, she should offer obeisance and alms to Bodhisattva Perceiver of the World's Sounds and then she will bear a son blessed with merit, virtue, and wisdom. And if she wishes to bear a daughter, she will bear one with all the marks of comeliness, one who in the past planted the roots of virtue and is loved and respected by many persons.

"Inexhaustible Intent, the bodhisattva Perceiver of the World's Sounds has power to do all this. If there are living beings who pay respect and obeisance to Bodhisattva Perceiver of the World's Sounds, their good fortune will not be fleeting or vain. Therefore living beings should all accept and uphold the name of Bodhisattva Perceiver of the World's Sounds.

"Inexhaustible Intent, suppose there is a person who accepts and upholds the names of as many bodhisattvas as there are sands in sixty-two million Ganges, and for as long as his present body lasts, he offers them alms in the form of food and drink, clothing, bedding and medicines. What is your opinion? Would this good man or good woman gain many benefits, or would he not?"

Inexhaustible Intent replied, "They would be very many, World-Honored One."

The Buddha said: "Suppose also that there is a person who accepts and upholds the name of Bodhisattva Perceiver of the World's Sounds and even just once offers him obeisance and alms. The good fortune gained by these two persons would be exactly equal and without difference. For a hundred, a thousand, ten thousand, a million kalpas it would never be exhausted or run out. Inexhaustible Intent, if one accepts and upholds the name of Bodhisattva Perceiver of the World's Sounds, he will gain the benefit of merit and virtue that is as immeasurable and boundless as this!"

Bodhisattva Inexhaustible Intent said to the Buddha, "World-Honored One, Bodhisattva Perceiver of the World's Sounds—how does he come and go in this saha world? How does he preach the Law for the sake of living beings? How does the power of expedient means apply in his case?"

The Buddha said to Bodhisattva Inexhaustible Intent: "Good man, if there are living beings in the land who need someone in the body of a Buddha in order to be saved, Bodhisattva Perceiver of the World's Sounds immediately manifests himself in a Buddha body and preaches the Law for them. If they need someone in a pratyekabuddha's body in order to be saved, immediately he manifests a pratyekabuddha's body and preaches the Law to them. If they need a voice-hearer to be saved, immediately he becomes a voice-hearer and preaches the Law for them. If they need King Brahma to be saved, immediately he becomes King Brahma and preaches the Law for them. If they need the lord Shakra to be saved, immediately he becomes the lord Shakra and preaches the Law for them. If they need the heavenly being Freedom to be saved, immediately he becomes the heavenly being Freedom and preaches the Law for them. If they need the heavenly being Great Freedom to be saved, immediately he becomes the heavenly being Great Freedom and preaches the Law for them. If they need a great general of heaven to be saved, immediately he becomes a great general of heaven and preaches the Law for them. If they need Vaishravana to be saved, immediately he becomes Vaishravana and preaches the Law for them. If they need a petty king to be saved, immediately he becomes a petty king and preaches the Law for them.

If they need a rich man to be saved, immediately he becomes a rich man and preaches the Law for them. If they need a householder to be saved, immediately he becomes a householder and preaches the Law for them. If they need a chief minister to be saved, immediately he becomes a chief minister and preaches the Law for them. If they need a Brahman to be saved, immediately he becomes a Brahman and preaches the Law for them. If they need a monk, a nun, a layman believer, or a laywoman believer to be saved, immediately he becomes a monk, a nun, a layman believer, or a laywoman believer and preaches the Law for them. If they need the wife of a rich man, of a house-holder, a chief minister, or a Brahman to be saved, immediately he becomes those wives and preaches the Law for them. If they need a young boy or a young girl to be saved, immediately he becomes a young boy or a young girl and preaches the Law for them. If they need a heavenly being, a dragon, a yaksha, a gandharva, an asura, a garuda, a kimnara, a mahoraga, a human or a nonhuman being to be saved, immediately he becomes all of these and preaches the Law for them. If they need a vajra-bearing god to be saved, immediately he becomes a vajra-bearing god and preaches the Law for them.

"Inexhaustible Intent, this Bodhisattva Perceiver of the World's Sounds has succeeded in acquiring benefits such as these and, taking on a variety of different forms, goes about among the lands saving living beings. For this reason you and the others should single-mindedly offer alms to Bodhisattva Perceiver of the World's Sounds. This bodhisattva and mahasattva Perceiver of the World's Sounds can bestow fearlessness on those who are in fearful, pressing or difficult circumstances. That is why in this saha world everyone calls him Bestower of Fearlessness."

Bodhisattva Inexhaustible Intent said to the Buddha, "World-Honored One, now I must offer alms to Bodhisattva Perceiver of the World's Sounds."

Then he took from his neck a necklace adorned with numerous precious gems, worth a hundred or a thousand taels of gold, and presented it to [the bodhisattva], saying, "Sir, please accept this necklace of precious gems as a gift in the Dharma."

At that time Bodhisattva Perceiver of the World's Sounds was unwilling to accept the gift.

Inexhaustible Intent spoke once more to Bodhisattva Perceiver of the World's Sounds, saying, "Sir, out of compassion for us, please accept this necklace."

Then the Buddha said to Bodhisattva Perceiver of the World's Sounds, "Out of compassion for this bodhisattva Inexhaustible Intent and for the four kinds of believers, the heavenly beings, dragons, yakshas, gandharvas, asuras, garudas, kimnaras, mahoragas, human and nonhuman beings, you should accept this necklace."

Thereupon Bodhisattva Perceiver of the World's Sounds, having compassion for the four kinds of believers and the heavenly beings, dragons, human and nonhuman beings and the others, accepted the necklace and, dividing it into two parts, presented one part to Shakyamuni Buddha and presented the other to the tower of the Buddha Many Treasures.

[The Buddha said,] "Inexhaustible Intent, these are the kinds of freely exercised supernatural powers that Bodhisattva Perceiver of the World's Sounds displays in his comings and goings in the saha world."

At that time Bodhisattva Inexhaustible Intent posed this question in verse form:

> World-Honored One replete with wonderful features,
> I now ask you once again
> for what reason that Buddha's son
> is named Perceiver of the World's Sounds?
> The Honored One endowed with wonderful features
> replied to Inexhaustible Intent in verse:
> Listen to the actions of the Perceiver of Sounds,
> how aptly he responds in various quarters.
> His vast oath is deep as the ocean;
> kalpas pass but it remains unfathomable.
> He has attended many thousands and millions of Buddhas,
> setting forth his great pure vow.
> I will describe him in outline for you—
> listen to his name, observe his body,
> bear him in mind, not passing the time vainly,
> for he can wipe out the pains of existence.
> Suppose someone should conceive a wish to harm you,
> should push you into a great pit of fire.
> Think on the power of that Perceiver of Sounds

and the pit of fire will change into a pond!
If you should be cast adrift on the vast ocean,
menaced by dragons, fish and various demons,
think on the power of that Perceiver of Sounds
and the billows and waves cannot drown you!
Suppose you are on the peak of Mount Sumeru
and someone pushes you off.
Think on the power of that Perceiver of Sounds
and you will hang in midair like the sun!
Suppose you are pursued by evil men
who wish to throw you down from a diamond mountain.
Think on the power of the Perceiver of Sounds
and they cannot harm a hair of you!
Suppose you are surrounded by evil-hearted bandits,
each brandishing a knife to wound you.
Think on the power of that Perceiver of Sounds
and at once all will be swayed by compassion!
Suppose you encounter trouble with the king's law,
face punishment, about to forfeit your life.
Think on the power of that Perceiver of Sounds
and the executioner's sword will be broken to bits!
Suppose you are imprisoned in cangue and lock,
hands and feet bound by fetters and chains.
Think on the power of that Perceiver of Sounds
and they will fall off, leaving you free!
Suppose with curses and various poisonous herbs
someone should try to injure you.
Think on the power of that Perceiver of Sounds
and the injury will rebound upon the originator.
Suppose you encounter evil rakshasas,
poison dragons and various demons.
Think on the power of that Perceiver of Sounds
and then none of them will dare to harm you.
If evil beasts should encircle you,
their sharp fangs and claws inspiring terror,
think on the power of that Perceiver of Sounds
and they will scamper away in boundless retreat.
If lizards, snakes, vipers, scorpions

threaten you with poison breath that sears like flame,
think on the power of that Perceiver of Sounds
and, hearing your voice, they will flee of themselves.
If clouds should bring thunder, and lightning strike,
if hail pelts or drenching rain comes down,
think on the power of that Perceiver of Sounds
and at that moment they will vanish away.
If living beings encounter weariness or peril,
immeasurable suffering pressing them down,
the power of the Perceiver of Sounds' wonderful wisdom
can save them from the sufferings of the world.
He is endowed with transcendental powers
and widely practices the expedient means of wisdom.
Throughout the lands in the ten directions
there is no region where he does not manifest himself.
In many different kinds of evil circumstances,
in the realms of hell, hungry spirits or beasts,
the sufferings of birth, old age, sickness and death—
all these he bit by bit wipes out.
He of the true gaze, the pure gaze,
the gaze of great and encompassing wisdom,
the gaze of pity, the gaze of compassion—
constantly we implore him, constantly look up in reverence.
His pure light, free of blemish,
is a sun of wisdom dispelling all darknesses.
He can quell the wind and fire of misfortune
and everywhere bring light to the world.
The precepts from his compassionate body shake us
    like thunder,
the wonder of his pitying mind is like a great cloud.
He sends down the sweet dew, the Dharma rain,
to quench the flames of earthly desires.
When law suits bring you before the officials,
when terrified in the midst of an army,
think on the power of that Perceiver of Sounds
and hatred in all its forms will be dispelled.
Wonderful sound, Perceiver of the World's Sounds,
Brahma's sound, the sea tide sound—

they surpass those sounds of the world;
therefore you should constantly think on them,
from thought to thought never entertaining doubt!
Perceiver of the World's Sounds, pure sage—
to those in suffering, in danger of death,
he can offer aid and support.
Endowed with all benefits,
he views living beings with compassionate eyes.
The sea of his accumulated blessings is immeasurable;
therefore you should bow your head to him!

At that time the bodhisattva Earth Holder immediately rose from his seat, advanced, and said to the Buddha, "World-Honored One, if there are living beings who hear this chapter on Bodhisattva Perceiver of the World's Sounds, on the freedom of his actions, his manifestation of a universal gateway, and his transcendental powers, it should be known that the benefits these persons gain are not few!"

When the Buddha preached this chapter on the Universal Gateway, a multitude of eighty-four thousand persons in the assembly all conceived a determination to attain the unparalleled state of anuttara-samyak-sambodhi.

26

DHARANI

At that time Bodhisattva Medicine King rose from his seat, bared his right shoulder, pressed his palms together and, facing the Buddha, spoke to him, saying, "World-Honored One, if there are good men or good women who can accept and uphold the Lotus Sutra, if they read and recite it, penetrate its meaning, or copy the sutra scrolls, how much merit will they gain?"

The Buddha said to Medicine King, "If there are good men or good women who offer alms to Buddhas equal in number to the sands of eight hundred ten thousand million nayutas of Ganges, what is your opinion? The merit they gain will surely be great, will it not?"

"Very great, World-Honored One."

The Buddha said, "If there are good men or good women who, with regard to this sutra, can accept and uphold even one four-line verse, if they read and recite it, understand the principle, and practice it as the sutra directs, the benefits will be very many."

At that time Bodhisattva Medicine King said to the Buddha, "World-Honored One, I will now give to those who preach the Law dharani spells, which will guard and protect them." Then he pronounced these spells:

anye manye mane mamane chitte charite shame shamitavi
shante mukte muktatame same avishame sama same kshaye
akshaye akshine shante shame dharani alokabhashe-
pratyavekshani nivishte abhyantaranivishte atyantaparishuddhi
ukkule mukkule arade parade shukakshi asamasame
buddhavilokite dharmaparikshite samghanirghoshani
bhayabhayashodhani mantre mantrakshayate rute
rutakaushalye akshaye akshayavanataya abalo amanyanataya

"World-Honored One, these dharanis, these supernatural spells, are pronounced by Buddhas equal in number to the sands of sixty-two million Ganges. If anyone should assault or injure these teachers of the Law, then he will have assaulted and injured these Buddhas!"

At that time Shakyamuni Buddha praised Bodhisattva Medicine King, saying, "Excellent, excellent, Medicine King! You keep these teachers of the Law in your compassionate thoughts, shield and guard them, and for that reason you pronounce these dharanis. They will bring great benefit to living beings."

At that time Bodhisattva Brave Donor said to the Buddha, "World-Honored One, I too will pronounce dharanis to shield and guard those who read, recite, accept, and uphold the Lotus Sutra. If a teacher of the Law acquires these dharanis, then although yakshas, rakshasas, putanas, krityas, kumbhandas or hungry spirits should spy out his shortcomings and try to take advantage of them, they will be unable to do so." Then in the presence of the Buddha he pronounced these spells:

jvale mahajvale ukke mukke ade adavati nritye nrityavati ittini
vittini chittini nrityani nrityavati

"World-Honored One, these dharanis, these supernatural spells, are pronounced by Buddhas equal in number to the sands of the Ganges, and all of them respond with joy. If anyone should assault or injure these teachers of the Law, then he will have assaulted and injured these Buddhas!"

At that time the heavenly king Vaishravana, protector of the world, said to the Buddha, "World-Honored One, I too think compassionately of living beings and shield and guard these teachers of the Law, and therefore I pronounce these dharanis." Then he pronounced these spells:

atte natte nunatte anado nadi kunadi

"World-Honored One, with these supernatural spells I shield and guard the teachers of the Law. And I will also shield and guard those who uphold this sutra, making certain that they suffer no decline or harm within the area of a hundred yojanas."

At that time the heavenly king Upholder of the Nation, who was in the assembly along with a host of thousands, ten thousands, millions of nayutas of gandharvas who surrounded him and paid him reverence, advanced to the place where the Buddha was, pressed his palms together and said to the Buddha, "World-Honored One, I too will employ dharanis, supernatural spells, to shield and guard those who uphold the Lotus Sutra." Then he pronounced these spells:

agane gane gauri gandhari chandali matangi janguli vrusani
agasti

"World-Honored One, these dharanis, these supernatural spells, are pronounced by forty-two million Buddhas. If anyone should assault or injure these teachers of the Law, then he will have assaulted and injured these Buddhas!"

At that time there were daughters of rakshasa demons, the first named Lamba, the second named Vilamba, the third named Crooked Teeth, the fourth named Flowery Teeth, the fifth named Black Teeth, the sixth named Much Hair, the seventh named Insatiable, the eighth named Necklace Bearer, the ninth named Kunti, and the tenth named Stealer of the Vital Spirit of All Living Beings. These ten rakshasa daughters, along with the Mother of Devil Children, her offspring, and her attendants, all proceeded to the place where the Buddha was and spoke to the Buddha in unison, saying, "World-Honored One, we too wish to shield and guard those who read, recite, accept, and uphold the Lotus Sutra and spare them from decline or harm. If anyone should spy out the shortcomings of these teachers of the Law and try to take advantage of them, we will make it impossible for him to do so." Then in the presence of the Buddha they pronounced these spells:

itime itime itime atime itime nime nime nime nime nime ruhe ruhe ruhe ruhe stahe stahe stahe stuhe stuhe

"Though they climb upon our very heads, they will never trouble the teachers of the Law! Whether it be a yaksha, or a rakshasa, or a hungry spirit, or a putana, or a kritya, or a vetada, or a skanda,[1] or an umaraka, or an apasmaraka, or a yaksha kritya, or a human kritya, or a fever, a one day, a two day, a three day, a four day, or up to a seven day or a constant fever, whether it be in man's form, in woman's form, in young boy's form, in young girl's form, though it be only in a dream, it will never trouble them!"

Then in the presence of the Buddha they spoke in verse form, saying:

If there are those who fail to heed our spells
and trouble and disrupt the preachers of the Law,
their heads will split into seven pieces
like the branches of the arjaka tree.
Their crime will be like that of one who kills father and mother,
or one who presses out oil,
or cheats others with measures and scales,
or, like Devadatta, disrupts the Order of monks.
Anyone who commits a crime against these teachers of the Law
will bring on himself guilt such as this!

After the rakshasa daughters had spoken these verses, they said to the Buddha, "World-Honored One, we will use our own bodies to

1. This reconstruction of the Sanskrit term from the Chinese transcription is tentative.

shield and guard those who accept, uphold, read, recite, and practice this sutra. We will see that they gain peace and tranquility, freeing them from decline and harm and nulling the effect of all poison herbs."

The Buddha said to the rakshasa daughters, "Excellent, excellent! If you can shield and guard those who accept and uphold the mere name of the Lotus Sutra, your merit will be immeasurable. How much more so if you shield and guard those who accept and uphold it in its entirety, who offer alms to the sutra rolls, flowers, incense, necklaces, powdered incense, paste incense, incense for burning, banners, canopies, music, who burn various kinds of lamps, lamps of butter oil, oil lamps, lamps of various fragrant oils, lamps of sumana flower oil, lamps of champaka flower oil, lamps of varshika flower oil, and lamps of utpala flower oil, and who in this manner offer hundreds and thousands of varieties of alms? Kunti, you and your attendants should shield and guard the teachers of the Law such as these!"

When [the Buddha] preached this Dharani chapter, sixty-eight thousand persons gained the truth of birthlessness.

27

FORMER AFFAIRS OF KING WONDERFUL ADORNMENT

At that time the Buddha addressed the great assembly, saying: "In an age long ago, an immeasurable, boundless, inconceivable number of asamkhya kalpas in the past, there was a Buddha named Cloud Thunder Sound Constellation King Flower Wisdom, tathagata, arhat, samyak-sambuddha. His land was named Light Bright Adornment and his kalpa was named Gladly Seen. In the midst of this Buddha's Law there was a king named Wonderful Adornment. This king's consort was named Pure Virtue, and he had two sons, one named Pure Storehouse and the other named Pure Eye. These two sons possessed great supernatural powers, merit, virtue, and wisdom, and for a long time they had been practicing the way appropriate to a bodhisattva, carrying out the dana-paramita, shila-paramita, kshanti-paramita, virya-paramita, dhyana-paramita, prajna-paramita, the paramita of expedient means, pity, compassion, joy, and indifference, as well as the thirty-seven aids to the way.[1] All of these they had thoroughly understood and mastered. In addition, they had gained the samadhis of the bodhisattva, namely, the pure samadhi; sun, star, and constellation samadhi; pure light samadhi; pure color samadhi; pure illumination samadhi; long adornment samadhi; and great dignity and virtue storehouse samadhi, and had thoroughly mastered all these samadhis.

"At that time that Buddha, wishing to attract and guide King Wonderful Adornment, and because he thought with compassion of living beings, preached the Lotus Sutra. The king's two sons, Pure Storehouse and Pure Eye, went to where their mother was, pressed their palms and the nails of their ten fingers together, and said to her, 'We beg our mother to go and visit the place where the Buddha Cloud Thunder Sound Constellation King Flower Wisdom is. We too will attend him, drawing near to the Buddha and offering alms and obeisance. Why? Because this Buddha is preaching the Lotus Sutra in the midst of all the multitude of heavenly and human beings and it is right that we should listen and accept it.'

"The mother announced to her sons, 'Your father puts his faith in non-Buddhist doctrines and is deeply attached to the Brahmanical Law. You should go to your father, tell him about this, and persuade him to go with you.'

"Pure Storehouse and Pure Eye pressed their palms and ten fingernails together and said to their mother, 'We are sons of the Dharma King, and yet we have been born into this family of heretical views!'

"The mother said to her sons, 'You are right to think with concern about your father. You should manifest some supernatural wonder for him. When he sees that, his mind will surely be cleansed and purified and he will permit us to go to where the Buddha is.'

"The two sons, being concerned about their father, leaped up into the air to the height of seven tala trees and there performed various types of supernatural wonders, walking, standing, sitting, and lying down in midair; making water come out of the upper part of their bodies; making fire come out of the lower part of their bodies; making

---

1. Thirty-seven ways of thinking and acting that lead one to enlightenment.

water come out of the lower part of their bodies; making fire come out of the upper part of their bodies; manifesting huge bodies that filled the sky and then making themselves small again; after becoming small, making themselves big again; disappearing in the midst of the sky and then suddenly appearing on the ground; sinking into the ground as though it were water; walking on the water as though it were land. They manifested these various types of supernatural wonders in order to cause the mind of their royal father to become pure and to make him believe and understand.

"At that time when the father saw his sons displaying supernatural powers of this kind, his mind was filled with great delight, as he experienced what he had never known before, and he pressed his palms together, faced his sons and said, 'Who is your teacher? Whose disciples are you?'

"The two sons replied, 'Great king, the Buddha Cloud Thunder Sound Constellation King Flower Wisdom is at present sitting in the Dharma seat under the seven-jeweled bodhi tree and, amid the multitudes of heavenly and human beings of all the world, is broadly expounding the Lotus Sutra. This is our teacher and we are his disciples.'

"The father said to his sons, 'I would like to go now and see your teacher. You can go with me.'

"With this the two sons descended from the air, proceeded to where their mother was, pressed their palms together and said to their mother, 'Our royal father has now come to believe and understand. He is fully capable of conceiving a desire for anuttara-samyak-sambodhi. We have finished doing the Buddha's work for the sake of our father. We beg that our mother will permit us to go to the place where the Buddha is, to leave the household life and to practice the way.'

"At that time the two sons, wishing to state their meaning once more, spoke in verse form, saying to their mother:

> We beg our mother to permit us
> to leave the household and become shramanas.
> The Buddhas are very hard to encounter;
> we will follow this Buddha and learn from him.
> Rare as is the udumbara flower,
> rarer is it to encounter a Buddha,

and escaping from difficulties is also difficult—
we beg you to allow us to leave the household.

"Their mother then said to them, 'I will permit you to leave the household life. Why? Because the Buddha is difficult to encounter.'

"The two sons then addressed their father and mother, saying: 'Excellent, father and mother! And we beg you in due time to go to the place where the Buddha Cloud Thunder Sound Constellation King Flower Wisdom is, attend him in person and offer alms. Why? Because encountering the Buddha is as difficult as encountering the udumbara flower. Or as difficult as it is for a one-eyed turtle to encounter a floating log with a hole in it. We have been blessed with great good fortune from past existences and so have been born in an age where we can encounter the Buddha's Law. For this reason our father and mother should permit us to leave household life. Why? Because the Buddhas are difficult to encounter, and the proper time is also hard to come upon.'

"At that time the eighty-four thousand persons in the women's quarters of King Wonderful Adornment were all capable of accepting and upholding the Lotus Sutra. Bodhisattva Pure Eye had long ago mastered the Dharma flower samadhi, and Bodhisattva Pure Storehouse had already, some hundreds, thousands, ten thousands, millions of kalpas in the past, mastered the samadhi of the escape from the evil realms of existence. This was because he wished to make it possible for all living beings to escape from the evil realms. The king's consort had gained the samadhi of the Buddhas' assembly and was capable of understanding the secret storehouse of the Buddhas. Her two sons, as already described, had employed the power of expedient means to improve and transform their father so that he could acquire a mind of faith and understanding and love and delight in the Buddha's Law.

"Thereupon King Wonderful Adornment, accompanied by his ranks of ministers and his attendants; his queen Pure Virtue and all the ladies-in-waiting and attendants of the women's quarters; and the king's two sons and their forty-two thousand attendants, all at the same time went to where the Buddha was. Arriving there, they bowed their heads to the ground in obeisance to his feet, circled around the Buddha three times, and then withdrew and stood at one side.

"At that time that Buddha preached the Law for the sake of the king, instructing him and bringing him benefit and joy. The king was exceedingly delighted.

"At that time King Wonderful Adornment and his queen removed from their necks necklaces of pearls worth hundreds and thousands and scattered them over the Buddha. In midair the necklaces changed into a jeweled dais with four pillars. On the dais was a large jeweled couch spread with hundreds, thousands, ten thousands of heavenly robes. Seated cross-legged on them was a Buddha who emitted a brilliant light.

"At that time King Wonderful Adornment thought to himself: The Buddha's body is rare indeed, extraordinary in dignity and adornment, constituting a form of utmost subtlety and wonder! Then the Buddha Cloud Thunder Sound Constellation King Flower Wisdom spoke to the four kinds of believers, saying, 'Do you see this King Wonderful Adornment who stands before me with his palms pressed together? In the midst of my Law this king will become a monk, diligently practicing the Law that aids the Buddha way. He will be able to become a Buddha. His name will be Sal Tree King, his land will be called Great Light, and his kalpa will be called Great Lofty King. This Buddha Sal Tree King will have an immeasurable multitude of bodhisattvas, as well as immeasurable voice-hearers. His land will be level and smooth. Such will be his benefits.'

"The king immediately turned over his kingdom to his younger brother and he himself, along with his queen, his two sons, and all their attendants, in the midst of the Buddha's Law renounced the household life to practice the way.

"After the king had left the household life, for the space of eighty-four thousand years he constantly applied himself with diligence, practicing the Lotus Sutra of the Wonderful Law. When this period had passed, he gained the samadhi of the adornment of all pure benefits. Rising into the air to the height of seven tala trees, he addressed the Buddha, saying: 'World-Honored One, these two sons of mine have carried out the Buddha's work, employing transcendental powers and transformations to turn my mind away from heresies, enabling me to abide safely in the Buddha's Law, and permitting me to see the World-Honored One. These two sons have been good friends to me. They wished to awaken the good roots from my past existences and to enrich and benefit me, and for that reason they were born into my household.'

"At that time the Buddha Cloud Thunder Sound Constellation King Flower Wisdom said to King Wonderful Adornment, 'Just so, just so. It is as you have said. If good men and good women have planted good roots, and as a result in existence after existence have been able to gain good friends, then these good friends can do the Buddha's work, teaching, benefiting, delighting, and enabling them to enter anuttara-samyak-sambodhi. Great king, you should understand that a good friend is the great cause and condition by which one is guided and led, and which enables one to see the Buddha and to conceive the desire for anuttara-samyak-sambodhi. Great king, do you see these two sons? These two sons have already offered alms to Buddhas equal in number to the sands of sixty-five hundred, thousand, ten thousand, million nayutas of Ganges, have drawn near to them with reverence, and in the presence of those Buddhas have accepted and upheld the Lotus Sutra, thinking with compassion of living beings who embrace heretical views and causing them to abide in correct views.'

"King Wonderful Adornment then descended from midair and said to the Buddha, 'World-Honored One, the Thus Come One is a very rare being! Because of his benefits and wisdom, the knob of flesh on the top of his head illuminates all with a bright light. His eyes are long, broad, and dark blue in color. The tuft of hair in between his eyebrows, one of his features, is white as a crystal moon. His teeth are white, even, closely spaced, and constantly have a bright gleam. His lips are red and beautiful as the bimba fruit.'

"At that time King Wonderful Adornment, having praised the Buddha's immeasurable hundreds, thousands, ten thousands, millions of benefits in this manner, in the presence of the Thus Come One single-mindedly pressed his palms together and addressed the Buddha once more, saying, 'World-Honored One, such a thing as this has never been known before! The Law of the Thus Come One is fully endowed with inconceivably subtle and wonderful benefits. Where his teachings and precepts are observed there will be tranquility and good feeling. From this day on I will no longer follow the whims of my own mind, nor will I give way to heretical views or to arrogance, anger, or other evil states of mind.'

"When he had spoken these words, he bowed to the Buddha and departed."

The Buddha said to the great assembly: "What is your opinion? Is this King Wonderful Adornment someone unknown to you? In fact he is none other than the present Bodhisattva Flower Virtue. And his queen Pure Virtue is Bodhisattva Light Shining Adornment Marks who is now in the Buddha's presence. Out of pity and compassion for King Wonderful Adornment and his attendants, he was born in their midst. The king's two sons are the present bodhisattvas Medicine King and Medicine Superior.

"These bodhisattvas Medicine King and Medicine Superior have already succeeded in acquiring great benefits such as these, and in the presence of immeasurable hundreds, thousands, ten thousands, millions of Buddhas have planted numerous roots of virtue and acquired inconceivably good benefits. If there are persons who are acquainted with the names of these two bodhisattvas, the heavenly and human beings of all the world will surely do obeisance to them."

When the Buddha preached this chapter on the Former Affairs of King Wonderful Adornment, eighty-four thousand persons removed themselves from dust and defilement and with respect to the various phenomena attained the pure Dharma eye.

28

ENCOURAGEMENTS OF THE BODHISATTVA UNIVERSAL WORTHY

At that time Bodhisattva Universal Worthy, famed for his freely exercised transcendental powers, dignity and virtue, in company with great bodhisattvas in immeasurable, boundless, indescribable numbers, arrived from the east. The lands that he passed through one and all quaked and trembled, jeweled lotus flowers rained down, and immeasurable hundreds, thousands, ten thousands, millions of different kinds of music played. In addition, numberless heavenly beings, dragons, yakshas, gandharvas, asuras, garudas, kimnaras, mahoragas, human and nonhuman beings surrounded him in a great assembly, each displaying his dignity, virtue, and transcendental powers.

When [Bodhisattva Universal Worthy] arrived in the midst of Mount

Gridhrakuta in the saha world, he bowed his head to the ground in obeisance to Shakyamuni Buddha, circled around him to the right seven times, and said to the Buddha: "World-Honored One, when I was in the land of the Buddha King Above Jeweled Dignity and Virtue, from far away I heard the Lotus Sutra being preached in this saha world. In company with this multitude of immeasurable, boundless hundreds, thousands, ten thousands, millions of bodhisattvas I have come to listen to and accept it. I beg that the World-Honored One will preach it for us. And good men and good women in the time after the Thus Come One has entered extinction—how will they be able to acquire this Lotus Sutra?"

The Buddha said to Bodhisattva Universal Worthy: "If good men and good women will fulfill four conditions in the time after the Thus Come One has entered extinction, then they will be able to acquire this Lotus Sutra. First, they must be protected and kept in mind by the Buddhas. Second, they must plant the roots of virtue. Third, they must enter the stage where they are sure of reaching enlightenment. Fourth, they must conceive a determination to save all living beings. If good men and good women fulfill these four conditions, then after the Thus Come One has entered extinction they will be certain to acquire this sutra."

At that time Bodhisattva Universal Worthy said to the Buddha: "World-Honored One, in the evil and corrupt age of the last five-hundred-year period, if there is someone who accepts and upholds this sutra, I will guard and protect him, free him from decline and harm, see that he attains peace and tranquility, and make certain that no one can spy out and take advantage of his shortcomings. No devil, devil's son, devil's daughter, devil's minion, or one possessed by the devil, no yaksha, rakshasa, kumbhanda, pishacha, kritya, putana, vetada, or other being that torments humans will be able to take advantage of him.

"Whether that person is walking or standing, if he reads and recites this sutra, then at that time I will mount my six-tusked kingly white elephant and with my multitude of great bodhisattvas will proceed to where he is. I will manifest myself, offer alms, guard and protect him, and bring comfort to his mind. I will do this because I too want to offer alms to the Lotus Sutra. If when that person is seated he ponders this sutra, at that time too I will mount my kingly white elephant and manifest myself in his presence. If that person should forget a single phrase or verse of the Lotus Sutra, I will prompt him and join him in reading and reciting so that he will gain understanding. At that time the person who accepts, upholds, reads, and recites the Lotus Sutra will be able to see my body, will be filled with great joy, and will apply himself with greater diligence than ever. Because he has seen me, he will immediately acquire samadhis and dharanis. These are called the repetition dharani, the hundred, thousand, ten thousand, million repetition dharani, and the Dharma sound expedient dharani. He will acquire dharanis such as these.

"World-Honored One, in that later time, in the evil and corrupt age of the last five-hundred-year period, if monks, nuns, laymen believers or laywomen believers who seek out, accept, uphold, read, recite, and transcribe this Lotus Sutra should wish to practice it, they should do so diligently and with a single mind for a period of twenty-one days. When the twenty-one days have been fulfilled, I will mount my six-tusked white elephant and, with immeasurable numbers of bodhisattvas surrounding me and with this body that all living beings delight to see, I will manifest myself in the presence of the person and preach the Law for him, bringing him instruction, benefit, and joy. I will also give him dharani spells. And because he has acquired these spells, no nonhuman being will be able to injure him and he cannot be confused or led astray by women. I too will personally guard him at all times. Therefore, World-Honored One, I hope you will permit me to pronounce these dharanis." Then in the presence of the Buddha he pronounced these spells:

adande dandapati dandavarte dandakushale dandasudhare
sudhare sudharapati buddhapashyane sarvadharani-avartani
sarvabhashyavartani su-avartani samghaparikshani
samghanirghatani asamge samgapagate tri-adhvasamgatulya-
arate-prapte sarvasamgasamatikrante sarvadharmasuparikshite
sarvasattvarutakaushalyanugate simhavikridite

"World-Honored One, if any bodhisattva is able to hear these dharanis, he should understand that it is due to the transcendental powers of Universal Worthy. If when the Lotus Sutra is propagated throughout Jambudvipa there are those who accept and uphold it, they should think to themselves: This is all due to the authority and supernatural power of Universal Worthy! If there are those who accept, uphold, read, and recite this sutra, memorize it correctly, understand its principles, and practice it as the sutra prescribes, these persons should know that they are carrying out the practices of Universal Worthy himself. In the presence of immeasurable, boundless numbers of Buddhas they will have planted good roots deep in the ground, and the hands of the Thus Come Ones will pat them on the head.

"If they do no more than copy the sutra, when their lives come to an end they will be reborn in the Trayastrimsha heaven. At that time eighty-four thousand heavenly women, performing all kinds of music, will come to greet them. Such persons will put on crowns made of seven treasures and amidst the ladies-in-waiting will amuse and enjoy themselves. How much more so, then, if they accept, uphold, read, and recite the sutra, memorize it correctly, understand its principles, and practice it as the sutra prescribes. If there are persons who accept, uphold, read, and recite the sutra and understand its principles, when the lives of these persons come to an end, they will be received into the hands of a thousand Buddhas, who will free them from all fear and keep them from falling into the evil paths of existence. Immediately they will proceed to the Tushita heaven, to the place of Bodhisattva Maitreya. Bodhisattva Maitreya possesses the thirty-two features and is surrounded by a multitude of great bodhisattvas. He has hundreds, thousands, ten thousands, millions of heavenly women attendants, and these persons will be reborn in their midst. Such will be the benefits and advantages they enjoy.

"Therefore persons of wisdom should single-mindedly copy the sutra themselves, or cause others to copy it, should accept, uphold, read, and recite it, memorize it correctly and practice it as the sutra prescribes. World-Honored One, I now therefore employ my transcendental powers to guard and protect this sutra. And after the Thus Come One has entered extinction, I will cause it to be widely propagated throughout Jambudvipa and will see that it never comes to an end."

At that time Shakyamuni Buddha spoke these words of praise: "Excellent, excellent, Universal Worthy! You are able to guard and assist this sutra and cause many living beings to gain peace and happiness and advantages. You have already acquired inconceivable benefits and profound great pity and compassion. Since long ages in the past you have shown a desire for anuttara-samyak-sambodhi, and have taken a vow to use your transcendental powers to guard and protect this sutra. And I will employ my transcendental powers to guard and protect those who can accept and uphold the name of Bodhisattva Universal Worthy.

"Universal Worthy, if there are those who accept, uphold, read, and recite this Lotus Sutra, memorize it correctly, practice and transcribe it, you should know that such persons have seen Shakyamuni Buddha. It is as though they heard this sutra from the Buddha's mouth. You should know that such persons have offered alms to Shakyamuni Buddha. You should know that the Buddha has praised such persons as excellent. You should know that such persons have been patted on the head by Shakyamuni Buddha. You should know that such persons have been covered in the robes of Shakyamuni Buddha.

"They will no longer be greedy for or attached to worldly pleasures, they will have no taste for the scriptures or jottings of the non-Buddhists. They will take no pleasure in associating with such people, or with those engaged in evil occupations such as butchers, raisers of pigs, sheep, chickens, or dogs, hunters, or those who offer women's charms for sale. These persons will be honest and upright in mind and intent, correct in memory, and will possess the power of merit and virtue. They will not be troubled by the three poisons, nor will they be troubled by jealousy, self-importance, ill-founded conceit, or arrogance. These persons will have few desires, will be easily satisfied, and will know how to carry out the practices of Universal Worthy.

"Universal Worthy, after the Thus Come One has entered extinction, in the last five-hundred-year period, if you see someone who accepts, upholds, reads, and recites the Lotus Sutra, you should think to yourself: Before long this person will proceed to the place of practice, conquer the devil hosts, and attain anuttara-samyak-sambodhi. He will turn the wheel of the Dharma, beat the Dharma drum, sound the Dharma conch, and rain down the Dharma rain. He is worthy to sit in the lion seat of the Dharma, amid the great assembly of heavenly and human beings.

"Universal Worthy, in later ages if there are those who accept, uphold, read, and recite this sutra, such persons will no longer be greedy for or attached to clothing, bedding, food and drink, or other necessities of daily life. Their wishes will not be in vain, and in this present existence they will gain the reward of good fortune. If there is anyone who disparages or makes light of them, saying, 'You are mere idiots! It is useless to carry out these practices—in the end they will gain you nothing!', then as punishment for his offense that person will be born eyeless in existence after existence. But if there is anyone who offers alms to them and praises them, then in this present existence he will have manifest reward for it.

"If anyone sees a person who accepts and upholds this sutra and tries to expose the faults or evils of that person, whether what he speaks is true or not, he will in his present existence be afflicted with white leprosy. If anyone disparages or laughs at that person, then in existence after existence he will have teeth that are missing or spaced far apart, ugly lips, a flat nose, hands and feet that are gnarled or deformed, and eyes that are squinty. His body will have a foul odor, with evil sores that run pus and blood, and he will suffer from water in the belly, shortness of breath, and other severe and malignant illnesses. Therefore, Universal Worthy, if you see a person who accepts and upholds this sutra, you should rise and greet him from afar, showing him the same respect you would a Buddha."

When this chapter on the Encouragements of the Bodhisattva Universal Worthy was preached, bodhisattvas immeasurable and boundless as Ganges sands acquired dharanis allowing them to memorize a hundred, a thousand, ten thousand, a million repetitions of the teachings, and bodhisattvas equal to the dust particles of the thousand-millionfold world perfected the way of Universal Worthy.

When the Buddha preached this sutra, Universal Worthy and the other bodhisattvas, Shariputra and the other voice-hearers, along with the heavenly beings, dragons, human and nonhuman beings—the entire membership of the great assembly were all filled with great joy. Accepting and upholding the words of the Buddha, they bowed in obeisance and departed.

GLOSSARY

The Glossary contains definitions of all important personal and place names appearing in the translation, as well as major Sanskrit terms and numerical categories. A few names of very minor figures and some Sanskrit names of flowers, birds, types of perfume, etc., that appear only once or twice in the text have been omitted. Sanskrit words are given with full diacritical marks when that form differs from the one in which the word appears in the translation: Skt = Sanskrit; Ch = Chinese; J = Japanese.

Ajatashatru (Ajātaśatru). A king of the state of Magadha in Shakyamuni's time. He made Magadha into the most powerful kingdom in India at that period. Later in his life he converted to Buddhism.

Ajnata Kaundinya (Ājñāta Kauṇḍinya). One of the five ascetics who heard Shakyamuni's first sermon and converted to his teachings. The eighth chapter of the Lotus Sutra predicts that he will become a Buddha named Universal Brightness.

Akanishtha (Akaniṣṭha). The highest heaven in the world of form. Beings living in this heaven possess a pure body, free from all suffering and illness.

Akshobhya (Akṣobhya). A Buddha mentioned in the seventh chapter of the Lotus Sutra. He became an important figure in esoteric Buddhism.

Amitayus (Amitāyus). A Buddha mentioned in chapters seven and twenty-three of the Lotus Sutra. Also known as Amitābha, he became the central figure in the Pure Land teachings of Chinese and Japanese Buddhism.

anagamin (anāgāmin). One of the four kinds of shravakas or voice-hearers. The anagamin is a voice-hearer who does not have to return to the world of human beings anymore.

Ananda (Ānanda). A cousin of Shakyamuni and one of his ten major disciples. He accompanied Shakyamuni for many years as his personal attendant and heard more of his teachings than any other disciple. He is accordingly known as foremost in hearing the Buddha's teachings. At the First Council held after Shakyamuni's death to put in order his teachings, Ananda is said to have recited the sutras from memory. The words "This is what I heard" that appear at the beginning of most sutras refer to this recitation.

Aniruddha (also called Anuruddha). A cousin of Shakyamuni and one of his ten major disciples, known as foremost in divine insight. The eighth chapter of the Lotus Sutra predicts that he will become a Buddha named Universal Brightness.

anuttara-samyak-sambodhi (anuttara-samyak-saṃbodhi). Supreme perfect enlightenment, the enlightenment of a Buddha.

arhat. A "worthy," one who has attained the highest stage of Hinayana enlightenment, the highest among the four kinds of shravakas or voice-hearers. Such a person has gained freedom from transmigration in the six paths of existence. The Lotus Sutra urges one to reject the goal of arhat and instead strive for the highest level of enlightenment, that of Buddhahood.

asamkhya (asaṃkhya). An ancient Indian numerical unit, indicating an un-countably large number.

Asita. The name of a seer who in a later existence became Devadatta, as related in the twelfth chapter of the Lotus Sutra.

asura. A class of contentious demons in Indian mythology who fight continually with the god Indra. In Buddhism the asuras constitute one of the eight kinds of nonhuman beings who protect Buddhism.

Avichi (Avīci). The hell of incessant suffering, the most terrible of the eight hot hells. One who commits one of the five cardinal sins or slanders the True Law is said to fall into this hell.

avivartika. Also rendered as avaivartika. Terms for the stage at which one is certain never to regress in religious practice, or for a person who has reached that stage.

Bhadrapala (Bhadrapāla). A bodhisattva who was among the assembly described in chapter one of the Lotus Sutra.

bodhi. Enlightenment or Buddhahood.

bodhi tree. The pipal tree at Buddhagayā under which Shakyamuni attained enlightenment.

bodhisattva. A being who aspires to attain Buddhahood and carries out various altruistic practices in order to achieve that goal. Compassion is the outstanding characteristic of the bodhisattva, who postpones his or her own entry into nirvana in order to assist others to gain enlightenment. The bodhisattva figure is particularly important in Mahayana Buddhism.

Brahma (Brahmā). Also called Mahābrahman. An Indian deity regarded as the personification of the fundamental universal principle. In Buddhism he was adopted as a protective deity. He lives in the first of the four meditation heavens in the world of form above Mt. Sumeru and rules the saha world.

Brahma (Brahmā) heaven. Another name for the first of the four meditation heavens in the world of form.

Brahma (Brahmā) king. A king of the Brahma heaven, a deity who has attained supremacy in a particular universe. In the Lotus Sutra a great number of Brahma kings appear.

brahma practices. Religious practices of a pure nature.

brahma sound. 1. A pure sound or pure voice. 2. The voice of a Brahma king.

Brahman. A member of the priestly class, the highest of the four classes in ancient Indian society.

Buddha. An "awakened one," one who has reached the highest level of enlightenment. In Mahayana Buddhism, the number of Buddhas is infinite, but the term often refers specifically to Shakyamuni Buddha, the Buddha of our present saha world.

chandala (caṇḍāla). An untouchable class, below the lowest of the four classes in ancient India. People in this class handled corpses, butchered animals, and carried out other tasks associated with the killing of living creatures.

Correct Law (Ch cheng-fa, J shōbō). According to Buddhist belief, after the death of a Buddha, his teachings pass through three periods or phases of development. In the first, known as the period of the Correct Law, Buddhism is a living religion and those who practice it attain enlightenment through its teachings. The period of the Correct Law following the death of Shakyamuni Buddha is usually said to be a thousand years in length, though some sources describe it as five hundred years long. *See also* Counterfeit Law *and* Latter Day of the Law.

Counterfeit Law (Ch hsiang-fa, J zōbō). Second period following the death of a Buddha. During this period, Buddhism becomes increasingly formalized, people's connection with it weakens, and progressively fewer of them are able to gain enlightenment through its teachings. Some sources describe the period of the Counterfeit Law following Shakyamuni's death as a thousand years in length, others as five hundred years.

Devadatta. A disciple of Shakyamuni and, according to some sources, Shakyamuni's cousin. He was at first diligent in religious practice but later, growing envious of Shakyamuni, worked to foment dissension within the Order and made several attempts on Shakyamuni's life. He is regarded as the epitome of evil and is said to have fallen into hell alive, but chapter twelve of the Lotus Sutra predicts that he will attain Buddhahood in a future existence.

dharani (dhāraṇī). A spell or formula said to protect the one who recites it and benefit the person by virtue of its mystic power.

dharma (Ch fa, J hō). 1. The Law or body of the Buddhist teachings; when this meaning is intended, the word has been translated as Law or written as Dharma. 2. Phenomena, things, facts, existences, as in the phrase "the true entity of all phenomena" (Ch chu-fa shih-hsiang, J shohō jissō).

Dharma King. A term for the Buddha.

Dharma prince, A term for a bodhisattva.

Dharma seal. The emblem of the Law or essence of the Buddha's teachings.

dhuta (dhūta). A discipline or ascetic practice carried out in order to purify the body and mind and free one from the desire for food, clothing and shelter.

dragon (Skt nāga, Ch lung, J ryū). One of the eight kinds of nonhuman beings who protect Buddhism and appear frequently in the Lotus Sutra. The first chapter of the Lotus Sutra lists eight dragon kings who attended the preaching of the sutra.

eighteen unshared properties. Properties possessed by a Buddha and not shared by others. They are freedom from illusions, eloquence, absence of attachments, impartiality, constant concentration of mind, knowledge of all things, untiring intention to lead people to salvation, incessant endeavor, consistency of teachings with those of other Buddhas, perfect wisdom, perfect emancipation, perfect insight, consistency of deeds with wisdom, consistency of words with wisdom, consistency of mind with wisdom, knowledge of the past, knowledge of the future, and knowledge of the present.

eight emancipations. They are emancipation from the view that the body is pure, from the view that the outside world is pure, from illusions, from the view that matter exists, from the view that consciousness has limits, from the view that a thing has its own property, from the view that thought exists or that thought does not exist, and from the view that mentality exists in any sense.

eighty characteristics. Extraordinary features which only Buddhas and bodhisattvas possess. There are various explanations of the eighty characteristics; some of the characteristics duplicate the thirty-two features.

evil paths of existence. The three lowest of the six paths or realms in which unenlightened beings transmigrate. They are hell, the realm of hungry spirits, and that of beasts. Sometimes the realm of the asuras is included to make four evil paths.

expedient means (Skt upāya, Ch fang-pien, J hōben). A device or temporary means adopted in order to relieve suffering and lead beings to enlightenment, often by offering provisional teachings as a means of guiding them to the truth. It is the title of the second chapter of the Lotus Sutra.

five ascetics. Five men whom Shakyamuni's father sent to accompany Shakyamuni when he embarked on ascetic practices. Later, when Shakyamuni forsook extreme asceticism, they thought he had abandoned the search for truth and accordingly left him. After Shakyamuni had attained enlightenment, he sought them out and preached to them at the Deer Park in Varanasi, converting them to his teachings. One of them was Ajnata Kaundinya, who is mentioned in the Lotus Sutra.

five components. Also called the five skandas. Form, perception, conception, volition, and consciousness.

five desires. The desires that arise from the contact of the five sense organs, eyes, ears, nose, tongue, and body, with their respective objects. Sometimes the five desires are defined as the desire for wealth, sex, food and drink, fame, and sleep.

five emotions. Another term for the five desires.

five impurities. Sometimes called the five defilements; they are (1) the impurity of the age, such as war or other disruptions of the social or natural environment; (2) impurity of desire, the tendency to be ruled by emotions such as greed or anger; (3) impurity of living beings, the physical and spiritual decline of human beings; (4) impurity of view, impurity deriving from mistaken views or values; and (5) impurity of life span, the distortion of life itself, which leads to a disordered and shortened life span.

five obstacles. Five limitations set forth in some Buddhist teachings which women face in their religious practice. According to this view, a woman can never become a Brahma heavenly king, can never become the lord Shakra, can never become a devil king, can never become a wheel-turning sage king, and can never become a Buddha. In chapter twelve of the Lotus Sutra, this view is refuted.

five transcendental powers. The first five of the six transcendental powers; see six transcendental powers.

four elements. The four basic elements which according to ancient Indian belief make up all things. They are earth, water, fire, and wind. In addition to these, Buddhism postulates a fifth element, emptiness or space, which serves to integrate and harmonize the four elements.

Four Heavenly Kings. Lords of the four quarters who serve Indra as his generals and protect the four continents. They are Dhrtarāṣṭra, who appears in the Lotus Sutra under the name Upholder of the Nation, guardian of the east; Virūḍhaka, guardian of the south; Virūpākṣa, who guards the west; and Vaiśravaṇa, who guards the north.

four kinds of believers. Monks, nuns, laymen, and laywomen.

four kinds of fearlessness. Four aspects of the Buddha's fearlessness in preaching. The Buddha is fearless in declaring that he is enlightened to the truth of all phenomena; fearless in proclaiming he has extinguished all desires and illusions; fearless in teaching that desires and karma can be obstacles to enlightenment; and fearless in teaching that one can overcome all sufferings by practicing Buddhism.

four kinds of offerings to the community of monks. Clothing, food and drink, bedding, and medicine.

four methods of winning people. Four methods employed by bodhisattvas to attract others to their teachings. They are to give alms and expound the Law; to speak in a kindly manner; to work to benefit others; and to share their hardships and cooperate with them.

four noble truths. A fundamental doctrine of early Buddhism, it teaches that (1) all existence is marked by suffering; (2) suffering is caused by craving; (3) by doing away with craving one can gain release from suffering; (4) there is a method for achieving this goal. The method is that known as the eightfold path, which enjoins one to cultivate right views, right thinking, right speech, right action, right way of life, right endeavor, right mindfulness, and right meditation.

four unlimited kinds of knowledge. Unlimited powers of understanding and preaching that Buddhas and bodhisattvas possess. They are complete understanding of the Law; complete mastery of the meanings deriving from the Law; complete freedom in expressing the teachings in various languages and dialects; and the ability to preach to all people at will by employing the first three powers.

gandharva. A heavenly musician, one of the eight kinds of nonhuman beings who protect Buddhism.

garuda (garuḍa). In Indian mythology, a giant bird that is said to feed on dragons. One of the eight kinds of nonhuman beings who protect Buddhism.

gatha (gāthā). In Buddhist scriptures, a verse stating a Buddhist teaching or praising a Buddha or bodhisattva. Some sutras are made up entirely of such verses, while others have extensive verse sections, often restating the meaning of a preceding prose section.

Gaya (Gayā). City in present day Bihar. In Shakyamuni's time it was a city of the state of Magadha. Some seven miles south of the city is the site where Shakyamuni sat beneath the bodhi tree and gained enlightenment, at the place called Buddhagayā. Buddhagayā is sometimes referred to in Buddhist scriptures by the name Gaya.

Gayakashyapa (Gayākāśyapa). A disciple of Shakyamuni, a younger brother of Uruvilvakashyapa and Nadikashyapa. When his two brothers converted to Shakyamuni's teachings, he also converted along with his two hundred disciples.

Great Katyayana, *see* Mahakatyayana.

Great Maudgalyayana, *see* Maudgalyayana.

Great Vehicle, *see* Mahayana.

Gridhrakuta (Gṛdhrakūṭa). Mountain northeast of the city of Rajagriha where Shakyamuni is said to have preached the Lotus Sutra and other teachings. The name is often translated in English as Vulture Peak, but because Kumārajīva in his Chinese translation of the Lotus Sutra calls it Eagle Peak, that translation has been adopted here. It is also referred to as Holy Eagle Peak.

Hinayana (Hinayāna, Ch hsiao-ch'eng, J shōjō). The term *Hinayana* or "Lesser Vehicle" is used by followers of the Mahayana teachings to designate the other major branch of Buddhism. Hinayana teaches that, since Buddhahood is almost impossible to attain, one should aim for a "lesser" goal, that of arhat. It is the form of Buddhism that prevails today in Sri Lanka, Burma, Thailand, Cambodia, and Laos, where it is known as Theravāda or the Teaching of the Elders.

Holy Eagle Peak, *see* Gridhrakuta.

Indra, *see* Shakra Devanam Indra.

Jambudvipa (Jambudvīpa). The continent lying to the south of Mt. Sumeru, the "continent of the jambu trees." It is populated by people with bad karma, and hence Buddhism spreads there in order to bring them salvation.

Jambunada (Jambūnada) gold. Gold found in the river running through the forest of jambu trees in Jambudvipa.

kalavinka (kalaviṅka). A bird with a very melodious voice found in the valleys of the Himalayas.

kalpa. An extremely long period of time.

Katyayana, *see* Mahakatyayana

Kaundinya, *see* Ajnata Kaundinya

kimnara (kiṃnara). A type of heavenly being who excels in singing and dancing, one of the eight kinds of nonhuman beings who protect Buddhism.

kritya (kṛtya). A kind of demon.

kumbhanda (kumbhāṇḍa). A kind of evil spirit.

last five-hundred-year period. The first two five-hundred-year periods after the parinirvana of Shakyamuni constitute the era of the Correct Law. The following two five-hundred-year periods constitute the period of the Counterfeit Law. The last or fifth five-hundred-year period marks the beginning of the Latter Day of the Law, when the teachings of the Buddha lose their effectiveness.

Latter Day of the Law (Ch mo-fa, J mappō). Third of the three periods which the teachings of a Buddha pass through after his death. In this third and last period, the teachings of the Buddha lose their power to lead people to enlightenment. It is said to last for ten thousand years or more.

Lesser Vehicle, see Hinayana.

level of no regression The stage one reaches in religious practice where one is certain never to regress or backslide. In Sanskrit it is known as avivartika or avaivartika.

Mahakashyapa (Mahākāśyapa). One of Shakyamuni's ten major disciples, known as foremost in ascetic practice. After Shakyamuni's death, he became head of the Order. The sixth chapter of the Lotus Sutra predicts that he will in future become a Buddha named Light Bright.

Mahakatyayana (Mahākātyāyana). One of Shakyamuni's ten major disciples, known as foremost in debate. He is also called simply Katyayana. The sixth chapter of the Lotus Sutra predicts that he will become a Buddha named Jambunada Gold Light.

Mahamaudgalyayana, see Maudgalyayana.

Mahaprajapati (Mahāprajāpatī). Also known as Gautami. Younger sister of Māyā, Shakyamuni's mother. When Māyā died shortly after Shakyamuni's birth, Mahaprajapati raised him. Later she renounced secular life and became the first nun to be admitted to the Buddhist Order. The thirteenth chapter of the Lotus Sutra predicts that she will become a Buddha named Gladly Seen by All Living Beings.

mahasattva (mahāsattva). A "great being," another term for a bodhisattva.

Mahayana (Mahāyāna, Ch ta-ch'eng, J daijō). One of the two main branches of Buddhism. It calls itself Mahayana or the "Great Vehicle" because its teachings enable all beings to attain Buddhahood. It lays particular emphasis upon the bodhisattva, who vows to attain Buddhahood for himself and to assist all others to do so. The Mahayana teachings arose around the 1st cen.

BCE and 1st cen. CE in India and spread to China, Tibet, Korea, Japan, and Vietnam.

mahoraga. A being with the head of a snake, one of the eight kinds of nonhuman beings who protect Buddhism.

Maitreya. A bodhisattva, also called Ajita, who figures in chapter seventeen of the Lotus Sutra. It is said that he will succeed Shakyamuni as the Buddha of the future and that he will appear in this world 5,670 million years after Shakyamuni's death. Meanwhile he dwells in the Tushita heaven.

mandarava (māndārava) flower. Also called mandara (māndāra) flower. A kind of fragrant red flower that blooms in heaven.

mani (maṇi) jewel. A globe-shaped gem, said to be efficacious in warding off sickness and evil and in purifying water.

manjushaka (mañjūṣaka) flower. A species of white flower that blooms in heaven.

Manjushri (Mañjuśrī). A bodhisattva who plays an important role in the Lotus Sutra and other sutras. He is symbolic of the perfection of wisdom and is revered as chief of the bodhisattvas. In Buddhist art he is usually depicted riding a lion. In the twelfth chapter of the Lotus Sutra he is shown guiding the dragon king's daughter to enlightenment.

Many Treasures (Skt Prabhūtaratna, Ch To-pao, J Tahō). A Buddha who appears, seated inside the Treasure Tower, to bear witness to the truth of Shakyamuni's teachings in the Lotus Sutra. While still a bodhisattva, he vowed that, even after he had entered nirvana, he would appear and attest to the validity of the Lotus Sutra wherever anyone might preach it.

Maudgalyayana (Maudgalyāyana). One of Shakyamuni's ten major disciples, known as foremost in occult powers. The sixth chapter of the Lotus Sutra predicts that he will become a Buddha named Tamalapatra Sandalwood Fragrance.

Medicine King (Skt Bhaiṣajyarāja, Ch Yao-wang, J Yakuō). A bodhisattva who is the subject of chapter twenty-three of the Lotus Sutra.

men of lifelong wisdom. A term of respect for monks, indicating the lasting quality of their wisdom.

Nadikashyapa (Nadīkāśyapa). A disciple of Shakyamuni and one of the Kashyapa brothers.

Narayana (Nārāyaṇa). Another name for the god Vishnu in Indian mythology. Incorporated into Buddhism as a protective deity, he is represented in Buddhist scriptures as possessing great physical strength.

nayuta. A numerical unit, defined differently in different texts but clearly indicating an extremely large number.

nirvana (nirvāṇa). The word, which means "blown out," indicates the state in which one has escaped from the cycle of birth and death. In Mahayana Buddhism, it is taken to mean awakening to the true nature of phenomena, or the perfection of Buddha wisdom. In Hinayana teaching there are two types of nirvana. First is that of the arhat who has eliminated all illusions and will no longer be reborn in the six paths, but who still possesses a body. This is called the nirvana of remainder. Second is that which the arhat achieves at death, when both body and mind are extinguished. This is called the nirvana of no remainder or complete nirvana.

outflows. That which flows out ceaselessly from the six sense organs, that is, illusions. Outflows is another term for earthly desires. Hence to be free of outflows is to be without illusions or desires.

Papiyas (Pāpīyas). Another name for the Devil or Māra, a personification of evil.

paramita, *see* six paramitas.

parinirvana (parinirvāṇa). A term similar to nirvana, it is used in reference to the apparent passing away of the physical body of a Buddha.

Perceiver of the World's Sounds (Skt Avalokiteśvara, Ch Kuan-shih-yin or Kuan-yin, J Kanzeon or Kannon). A bodhisattva, the subject of chapter twenty-five of the Lotus Sutra, who assumes thirty-three different forms and manifests himself anywhere in the world to save people from danger and suffering. The bodhisattva was originally conceived of as a male figure, but in China and Japan frequently came to be depicted in female form and worshiped as a protector of women and children.

pishacha (piśāca). A kind of devil or goblin.

place of practice. The place where one carries out religious practice and gains enlightenment, often referring specifically to the place where Shakyamuni gained enlightenment.

pratyekabuddha. A "self-enlightened" being, one who has won an understanding of the truth through his or her own efforts but makes no effort to enlighten others.

Purna (Pūrṇa). Sometimes called Purna Maitrayaniputra (Maitrāyaṇīputra). One of Shakyamuni's ten major disciples, known as foremost in preaching the Law. Chapter eight of the Lotus Sutra predicts that he will gain enlightenment as a Buddha named Law Bright.

putana (pūtana). A class of demons.

Rahula (Rāhula). The son of Shakyamuni and Yashodhara and later one of Shakyamuni's ten major disciples, known as foremost in inconspicuous practice. The ninth chapter of the Lotus Sutra predicts that he will become a Buddha named Stepping on Seven Treasure Flowers.

Rajagriha (Rājagṛha). Capital of the kingdom of Magadha in northeastern India.

rakshasa (rākṣasa). An evil or malignant demon who sometimes appears in Buddhist scriptures as a protector of Buddhism.

Saddharma-pundarika Sutra (Saddharma-puṇḍarīka Sūtra). "The Sutra of the Lotus of the Wonderful Law," the Sanskrit title of the Lotus Sutra.

Sagara (Sāgara). A dragon king whose daughter plays an important role in chapter twelve of the Lotus Sutra.

saha (saha) world. Our present world, which is full of sufferings to be endured. The Sanskrit word saha means "endurance."

sakridagamin (sakṛdāgāmin). One of the four kinds of shravakas or voice-hearers. The sakridagamin is a voice-hearer who is destined to return to the world of human beings only once more.

sal tree. The sal or śāla grows in northern India, reaching a considerable height and bearing light yellow blossoms. Shakyamuni passed away in a grove of sal trees on the outskirts of Kushinagara.

samadhi (samādhi). A state of intense concentration of the mind, which produces a sense of inner serenity.

Samgha (Saṃgha). The Buddhist Order, one of the Three Treasures, the Buddha, the Dharma, and the Samgha.

samsara (saṃsāra). The ordinary world of suffering and cyclical birth and death.

samyak-sambuddha (samyak-saṃbuddha). A being "of right and universal knowledge," one of the ten epithets for a Buddha.

seven Buddhas. Shakyamuni and the six Buddhas who are said to have preceded him. The seven are Vipaśyin, Śikhin, Viśvabhū, Krakucchanda, Kanakamuni, Kāśyapa, and Śākyamuni.

seven treasures. Seven precious substances mentioned in the Buddhist scriptures. The list varies from text to text. In the Lotus Sutra the seven are gold, silver, lapis lazuli, seashell, agate, pearl, and carnelian.

Shakra Devanam Indra (Śakra Devānām Indra). Also called simply Shakra or Indra. Originally the god of thunder in Indian mythology, he was later incorporated into Buddhism as a protective deity.

Shakyamuni (Śākyamuni). The "Sage of the Shakyas," the historical founder of Buddhism. He is also known by his family name Gautama.

Shariputra (Śāriputra). One of Shakyamuni's ten major disciples, known as foremost in wisdom. The third chapter of the Lotus Sutra predicts that he will become a Buddha named Flower Glow.

Shikhin (Śikhin). One of the great Brahma kings.

shramana (śramaṇa). In India the word originally referred to any ascetic, recluse, or religious practitioner who has renounced the world in order to seek the way. Later it came to mean chiefly one who has renounced the world to practice Buddhism.

shramanera (śrāmaṇera). A male novice in the Buddhist Order who has vowed to uphold the ten precepts.

shravaka (śrāvaka). A "voice-hearer," that is, one who listens to the teachings of Shakyamuni Buddha. The term originally applied to Shakyamuni's immediate disciples, but later came to mean all those who follow the teachings of Hinayana Buddhism. The way of the shravaka constitutes one of the three vehicles. There are four kinds of voice-hearers: the srota-apanna, sakridagamin, anagamin, and arhat.

shunyata (śūnyatā). Emptiness or Void, the underlying reality that unites all being, according to the doctrine of nondualism in Mahayana Buddhism.

six faculties. The faculties of the six sense organs, the eyes, ears, nose, tongue, body, and mind.

six paramitas (pāramitās). Six practices required of Mahayana bodhisattvas in order to attain Buddhahood. The Sanskrit word paramita means "perfection" or "having reached the other shore," that is, having crossed over from the shore of delusion to that of enlightenment. The six practices are (1) almsgiving, which includes material almsgiving, almsgiving of the Law, and almsgiving of fearlessness; (2) keeping of the precepts; (3) forbearance or bearing up patiently under opposition and hardship; (4) assiduousness or diligence in practice; (5) meditation; and (6) wisdom. The Sanskrit names for the six paramitas are dāna, śīla, kṣānti, vīrya, dhyāna, and prajña. Sometimes four more are added, (7) skill in expedient means, (8) vows, (9) power, and (10) knowledge, to make ten paramitas.

six paths. The six realms or worlds in which unenlightened beings transmigrate. Counting up from the lowest level, they are (1) hell; (2) the realm of hungry spirits; (3) beasts; (4) asuras; (5) human beings; and (6) heavenly beings.

six transcendental powers. Powers which Buddhas, bodhisattvas, and arhats are said to possess. They are the power of being anywhere at will; power of seeing anything anywhere; power of hearing any sound anywhere; power of knowing the thoughts of all other minds; power of knowing past lives; and power of eradicating illusions.

srota-apanna (srota-āpanna). One of the four kinds of shravakas or voice-hearers. The srota-apanna is a voice-hearer who has entered the way to enlightenment.

stupa (stūpa). A shrine, usually dome-shaped, built to house the relics of Shakyamuni or other holy persons. The early Mahayana movement was said to have centered around the worship of such stupas or memorial towers housing Shakyamuni's relics.

Subhuti (Subhūti). One of Shakyamuni's ten major disciples, depicted in the Wisdom sutras as foremost in the understanding of nondualism. The sixth chapter of the Lotus Sutra predicts that he will become a Buddha named Rare Form.

Sumeru. A huge mountain that stands at the center of the world. The god Shakra or Indra resides on the top, while the Four Heavenly Kings live halfway down the four sides. At its base are four continents, the most important of which is that lying to the south called Jambudvipa, where Buddhism spreads.

Summit of Being heaven. Another name for the Akanishtha heaven, the highest heaven in the world of form.

sweet dew (Skt amṛta). In ancient Indian lore, a wonderful sweet nectar that makes the drinker an immortal. In the Mahayana sutras, the teachings of the Buddha are often likened to such sweet dew.

tala (tāla) tree. The palmyra tree or fan palm.

tamalapatra (tamālapatra). The leaf of the tamala, which is a kind of sandalwood tree.

tathagata (tathāgata), *see* Thus Come One.

ten directions. Eight points of the compass, plus up and down.

ten epithets. Ten honorable titles for a Buddha; (1) Thus Come One; (2) worthy of offerings; (3) of right and universal knowledge; (4) perfect clarity and conduct; (5) well gone; (6) understanding the world; (7) unexcelled worthy; (8) trainer of people; (9) teacher of heavenly and human beings; (10) Buddha, World-Honored One.

ten powers. The powers of a Buddha, namely, the power of knowing what is true and what is not; power of knowing the karmic causality at work in the lives of all beings past, present and future; power of knowing all stages of concentration, emancipation and meditation; power of knowing the life-condition of all people; power of judging all people's understanding; power of discerning the superiority or inferiority of all people's capacity; power of knowing the effects of all people's actions; power of remembering past lifetimes; power of knowing when each person will be born and die and in what realm that person will be reborn; power of eradicating all illusions.

ten worlds. The ten paths or realms of existence in which all beings exist. In ascending order they are (1) hell; (2) realm of hungry spirits; (3) beasts; (4) asuras; (5) human beings; (6) heavenly beings or gods; (7) shravakas or voice-hearers; (8) pratyekabuddhas; (9) bodhisattvas; (10) Buddhas.

thirty-two features. Remarkable physical characteristics possessed by great beings such as Buddhas and wheel-turning kings. They are flat soles; markings of the wheel of the Law on the soles; long slender fingers; broad flat heels; webbed feet and hands; extremely flexible limbs; protuberant insteps; slender legs like those of a deer; hands that extend past the knees even when standing; concealed genitals; body height equal to armspan; body hair that turns upward; one hair growing from each pore; golden skin; light radiating from the body; thin pliant skin; well-developed muscles in hands, feet, shoulders, nape of neck; well-developed muscles below armpits; dignified torso like that of a lion; large straight body; substantial shoulders; forty teeth; even teeth; four white fangs; full cheeks like those of a lion; unexcelled sense of taste; long broad tongue; voice that can reach to the Brahma heaven; eyes the color of blue lotus blossoms; long eyelashes like those of a cow; protuberant knot of flesh like a topknot on crown of head; tuft of white hair between the eyebrows curling to the right.

thousand-millionfold world. A major world system in ancient Indian cosmology. A world consists of a Mt. Sumeru, its surrounding seas and mountains, heavenly bodies, etc., extending upward to the first meditation heaven in the world of form and downward to the circle of wind which forms the basis of a world. One thousand such worlds make up a minor world system, one thousand minor world systems constitute an intermediate world system, and one thousand intermediate world systems form a major world system. Therefore, one major world system comprises one billion worlds. There were thought to be countless major world systems in the universe.

three existences. The past, present, and future, or the entire span of time.

threefold world. The world of desire, the world of form, and the world of formlessness. The realms inhabited by unenlightened beings who transmigrate within the six paths. Beings in the world of desire are ruled by various desires. Those in the world of form have material form but no desires. Those in the world of formlessness are free from both desire and form.

three poisons. The fundamental evils inherent in life that give rise to human suffering, namely, greed, anger, and ignorance.

three storehouses. Another name for the Tripitaka, the three-part collection of the Buddhist scriptures. It is made up of the sutras, which contain the teachings of the Buddha; the vinayas, which deal with the rules of monastic discipline; and the abhidharmas, the treatises or commentaries on Buddhist doctrine.

three sufferings. Three types of suffering, namely, suffering that results from undesirable causes or conditions; suffering that results from the loss of something desirable; and suffering that results from the impermanence of phenomena.

three thousand worlds. Another name for a thousand-millionfold world.

Three Treasures. The three things that all Buddhists are enjoined to serve and revere, namely, the Buddha, the Law or Dharma, and the Samgha or Order.

three understandings. Three of the six transcendental powers: the power of seeing anything anywhere, the power of knowing past lives, and the power of eradicating illusions.

three vehicles. The path or career of the shravaka or voice-hearer; of the pratyekabuddha; and of the bodhisattva or Buddha.

Thus Come One (Skt tathāgata, Ch ju-lai, J nyorai). One of the ten epithets for a Buddha.

Trayastrimsha (Trāyastriṃśa) heaven. Heaven of the Thirty-Three Gods, second of the six heavens of the world of desire. It is located on a plateau at the top of Mt. Sumeru, where thirty-three gods, including Indra, live. Beings in this heaven have a life span of one thousand years, each day of which is equal to a hundred years in the saha world.

Tushita (Tuṣita) heaven. Heaven of Satisfaction, the fourth of the six heavens in the world of desire. It is said that bodhisattvas are reborn there just before their last rebirth in the world when they will attain Buddhahood. The future Buddha Maitreya is at present dwelling in the Tushita heaven.

twelve divisions of the sutras. Another name for the sutras or scriptures of Buddhism as a whole. The scriptures are classified into twelve categories on the basis of their style of exposition.

twelve-linked chain of causation. Also called the doctrine of dependent origination, an important part of the teaching of early Buddhism. It illustrates step by step the causal relationship between ignorance and suffering. It is described in chapter seven of the Lotus Sutra.

udumbara. A type of plant said to bloom only once in three thousand years. Used in Buddhist literature to symbolize the rarity of encountering a Buddha.

Universal Worthy (Skt Samantabhadra, Ch P'u-hsien, J Fugen). A bodhisattva who is the subject of chapter twenty-eight of the Lotus Sutra. He is symbolic of religious practice and is usually depicted riding a white elephant.

Uruvilvakashyapa (Uruvilvākāśyapa). A disciple of Shakyamuni, the eldest of the three Kashyapa brothers. When Shakyamuni came to Uruvilva village to preach, he became one of the Buddha's early converts along with his two brothers.

Vaidehi (Vaidehī). Wife of Bimbisāra, king of Magadha, and mother of Ajatashatru.

Vaishravana (Vaiśravaṇa). One of the Four Heavenly Kings, he watches over the north and listens to the Buddhist teachings, protecting the place where the Buddha expounds them.

Varanasi (Vārāṇasī). The capital of Kashi (Kāśī), one of the sixteen major states of ancient India. It corresponds to the present-day Benares. The Deer Park, where Shakyamuni preached his first sermon, was in Varanasi.

wheel-turning sage king (Skt cakravarti-rāja). An ideal ruler in Indian mythology. In Buddhism the wheel-turning kings are kings who rule by justice rather than force. They possess the thirty-two features and rule the four continents surrounding Mt. Sumeru.

wisdom embracing all species. Knowledge of the equality and differences that distinguish all things and phenomena.

Wise Kalpa. The present major kalpa in which we live. It is so called because it is said that a thousand Buddhas of great wisdom will appear in the course of it to save living beings.

World-Honored One. One of the ten epithets for a Buddha.

yaksha (yakṣa). A type of demon, one of the eight kinds of nonhuman beings who protect Buddhism.

Yashodhara (Yaśodharā). Wife of Shakyamuni and mother of Rahula. After Shakyamuni renounced secular life and gained enlightenment, he converted her to his teachings and she became a nun. The thirteenth chapter of the Lotus Sutra predicts that she will become a Buddha named Endowed with a Thousand Ten Thousand Glowing Marks.

yojana. A unit of measurement in ancient India, equal to the distance that the royal army could march in a day.

INDEX

OTHER WORKS IN
THE COLUMBIA
ASIAN STUDIES SERIES

The Manyōshū, Nippon Gakujutsu Shinkōkai edition 1965

Su Tung-p'o: Selections from a Sung Dynasty Poet, tr. Burton Watson. Also in paperback ed. 1965

Bhartrihari: Poems, tr. Barbara Stoler Miller. Also in paperback ed. 1967

Basic Writings of Mo Tzu, Hsün Tzu, and Han Fei Tzu, tr. Burton Watson. Also in separate paperback eds. 1967

The Awakening of Faith, Attributed to Aśvaghosha, tr. Yoshito S. Hakeda. Also in paperback ed. 1967

Reflections on Things at Hand: The Neo-Confucian Anthology, comp. Chu Hsi and Lü Tsu-ch'ien, tr. Wing-tsit Chan 1967

The Platform Sutra of the Sixth Patriarch, tr. Philip B. Yampolsky. Also in paperback ed. 1967

Essays in Idleness: The Tsurezuregusa of Kenkō, tr. Donald Keene. Also in paperback ed. 1967

The Pillow Book of Sei Shō, tr. Ivan Morris, 2 vols. 1967

Two Plays of Ancient India: The Little Clay Cart and the Minister's Seal, tr. J.-A.-B. van Buitenen 1968

The Complete Works of Chuang Tzu, tr. Burton Watson 1968

The Romance of the Western Chamber (Hsi Hsiang chi), tr. S.-I. Hsiung. Also in paperback ed. 1968

The Manyōshū, Nippon Gakujutsu Shinkōkai edition. Paperback ed. only. 1969

Records of the Historian: Chapters from the Shih chi of Ssu-ma Ch'ien, tr. Burton Watson. Paperback ed. only. 1969

Cold Mountain: 100 Poems by the T'ang Poet Han-shan, tr. Burton Watson. Also in paperback ed. 1970

Twenty Plays of the Nō Theatre, ed. Donald Keene. Also in paperback ed. 1970

Chūshingura: The Treasury of Loyal Retainers, tr. Donald Keene. Also in paperback ed. 1971; rev. ed. 1997

The Zen Master Hakuin: Selected Writings, tr. Philip B. Yampolsky 1971

Chinese Rhyme-Prose: Poems in the Fu Form from the Han and Six Dynasties Periods, tr. Burton Watson. Also in paperback ed. 1971

Kūkai: Major Works, tr. Yoshito S. Hakeda. Also in paperback ed. 1972

The Old Man Who Does as He Pleases: Selections from the Poetry and Prose of Lu Yu, tr. Burton Watson 1973

The Lion's Roar of Queen Śrīmālā, tr. Alex and Hideko Wayman 1974

Courtier and Commoner in Ancient China: Selections from the History of the Former Han by Pan Ku, tr. Burton Watson. Also in paperback ed. 1974

Japanese Literature in Chinese, vol. 1: *Poetry and Prose in Chinese by Japanese Writers of the Early Period*, tr. Burton Watson 1975

Japanese Literature in Chinese, vol. 2: *Poetry and Prose in Chinese by Japanese Writers of the Later Period*, tr. Burton Watson 1976

Scripture of the Lotus Blossom of the Fine Dharma, tr. Leon Hurvitz. Also in paperback ed. 1976

Love Song of the Dark Lord: Jayadeva's Gītagovinda, tr. Barbara Stoler Miller. Also in paperback ed. Cloth ed. includes critical text of the Sanskrit. 1977; rev. ed. 1997

Ryōkan: Zen Monk-Poet of Japan, tr. Burton Watson 1977

Calming the Mind and Discerning the Real: From the Lam rim chen mo of Tsoṇ-kha-pa, tr. Alex Wayman 1978

The Hermit and the Love-Thief: Sanskrit Poems of Bhartrihari and Bilhaṇa, tr. Barbara Stoler Miller 1978

The Lute: Kao Ming's P'i-p'a chi, tr. Jean Mulligan. Also in paperback ed. 1980

A Chronicle of Gods and Sovereigns: Jinnō Shōtōki of Kitabatake Chikafusa, tr. H. Paul Varley 1980

Among the Flowers: The Hua-chien chi, tr. Lois Fusek 1982

Grass Hill: Poems and Prose by the Japanese Monk Gensei, tr. Burton Watson 1983

Doctors, Diviners, and Magicians of Ancient China: Biographies of Fangshih, tr. Kenneth J. DeWoskin. Also in paperback ed. 1983

Theater of Memory: The Plays of Kālidāsa, ed. Barbara Stoler Miller. Also in paperback ed. 1984

The Columbia Book of Chinese Poetry: From Early Times to the Thirteenth Century, ed. and tr. Burton Watson. Also in paperback ed. 1984

Poems of Love and War: From the Eight Anthologies and the Ten Long Poems of Classical Tamil, tr. A.-K. Ramanujan. Also in paperback ed. 1985

The Bhagavad Gita: Krishna's Counsel in Time of War, tr. Barbara Stoler Miller 1986

The Columbia Book of Later Chinese Poetry, ed. and tr. Jonathan Chaves. Also in paperback ed. 1986

The Tso Chuan: Selections from China's Oldest Narrative History, tr. Burton Watson 1989

Waiting for the Wind: Thirty-six Poets of Japan's Late Medieval Age, tr. Steven Carter 1989

Selected Writings of Nichiren, ed. Philip B. Yampolsky 1990

Saigyō, Poems of a Mountain Home, tr. Burton Watson 1990

The Book of Lieh Tzu: A Classic of the Tao, tr. A.-C. Graham. Morningside ed. 1990

The Tale of an Anklet: An Epic of South India — The Cilappatikāram of Iḷaṅ kō Aṭikaḷ, tr. R. Parthasarathy 1993

Waiting for the Dawn: A Plan for the Prince, tr. and introduction by Wm. Theodore de Bary 1993

Yoshitsune and the Thousand Cherry Trees: A Masterpiece of the Eighteenth-Century Japanese Puppet Theater, tr., annotated, and with introduction by Stanleigh H. Jones, Jr. 1993

The Classic of Changes: A New Translation of the I Ching as Interpreted by Wang Bi, tr. Richard John Lynn 1994

Beyond Spring: Tz'u Poems of the Sung Dynasty, tr. Julie Landau 1994

The Columbia Anthology of Traditional Chinese Literature, ed. Victor H. Mair 1994

Scenes for Mandarins: The Elite Theater of the Ming, tr. Cyril Birch 1995

Letters of Nichiren, ed. Philip B. Yampolsky; tr. Burton Watson et al. 1996

Unforgotten Dreams: Poems by the Zen Monk Shōtetsu, tr. Steven D. Carter 1997

The Vimalakirti Sutra, tr. Burton Watson 1997

Japanese and Chinese Poems to Sing: The Wakan rōei shū, tr. J.-Thomas Rimer and Jonathan Chaves 1997

Breeze Through Bamboo: Kanshi of Ema Saikō, tr. Hiroaki Sato 1998

A Tower for the Summer Heat, Li Yu, tr. Patrick Hanan 1998

Traditional Japanese Theater: An Anthology of Plays, Karen Brazell 1998

The Original Analects: Sayings of Confucius and His Successors (0479 – 0249), E. Bruce Brooks and A. Taeko Brooks 1998

The Classic of the Way and Virtue: A New Translation of the Tao-te ching *of Laozi as Interpreted by Wang Bi,* tr. Richard John Lynn 1999

The Four Hundred Songs of War and Wisdom: An Anthology of Poems from Classical Tamil, The Puranāṇūru, eds. and trans. George L. Hart and Hank Heifetz 1999

Original Tao: Inward Training (Nei-yeh) *and the Foundations of Taoist Mysticism,* by Harold D. Roth 1999

Lao Tzu's Tao Te Ching: *A Translation of the Startling New Documents Found at Guodian,* Robert G. Henricks 2000

The Shorter Columbia Anthology of Traditional Chinese Literature, ed. Victor H. Mair 2000

Mistress and Maid (Jiaohongji) by Meng Chengshun, tr. Cyril Birch 2001

Chikamatsu: Five Late Plays, tr. and ed. C. Andrew Gerstle 2001

The Essential Lotus: Selections from the Lotus Sutra, tr. Burton Watson 2002

Early Modern Japanese Literature: An Anthology, 1600–1900, ed. Haruo Shirane 2002

The Sound of the Kiss, or The Story That Must Never Be Told: Pingali Suranna's Kalapurnodayamu, tr. Vecheru Narayana Rao and David Shulman 2003

The Selected Poems of Du Fu, tr. Burton Watson 2003

Far Beyond the Field: Haiku by Japanese Women, tr. Makoto Ueda 2003

Just Living: Poems and Prose by the Japanese Monk Tonna, ed. and tr. Steven D. Carter 2003

Han Feizi: Basic Writings, tr. Burton Watson 2003

Mozi: Basic Writings, tr. Burton Watson 2003

Xunzi: Basic Writings, tr. Burton Watson 2003

Zhuangzhi: Basic Writings, ed. and tr. Burton Watson 2003

MODERN ASIAN LITERATURE

Modern Japanese Drama: An Anthology, ed. and tr. Ted. Takaya. Also in paperback ed. 1979

Mask and Sword: Two Plays for the Contemporary Japanese Theater, by Yamazaki Masakazu, tr. J. Thomas Rimer 1980

Yokomitsu Riichi, Modernist, Dennis Keene 1980

Nepali Visions, Nepali Dreams: The Poetry of Laxmiprasad Devkota, tr. David Rubin 1980

Literature of the Hundred Flowers, vol. 1: *Criticism and Polemics*, ed. Hualing Nieh 1981

Literature of the Hundred Flowers, vol. 2: *Poetry and Fiction*, ed. Hualing Nieh 1981

Modern Chinese Stories and Novellas, 1919–1949, ed. Joseph S.-M. Lau, C.-T. Hsia, and Leo Ou-fan Lee. Also in paperback ed. 1984

A View by the Sea, by Yasuoka Shōtarō, tr. Kären Wigen Lewis 1984

Other Worlds: Arishima Takeo and the Bounds of Modern Japanese Fiction, by Paul Anderer 1984

Selected Poems of Sō Chōngju, tr. with introduction by David R. McCann 1989

The Sting of Life: Four Contemporary Japanese Novelists, by Van C. Gessel 1989

Stories of Osaka Life, by Oda Sakunosuke, tr. Burton Watson 1990

The Bodhisattva, or Samantabhadra, by Ishikawa Jun, tr. with introduction by William Jefferson Tyler 1990

The Travels of Lao Ts'an, by Liu T'ieh-yün, tr. Harold Shadick. Morningside ed. 1990

Three Plays by Kōbō Abe, tr. with introduction by Donald Keene 1993

The Columbia Anthology of Modern Chinese Literature, ed. Joseph S.-M. Lau and Howard Goldblatt 1995

Modern Japanese Tanka, ed. and tr. by Makoto Ueda 1996

Masaoka Shiki: Selected Poems, ed. and tr. by Burton Watson 1997

Writing Women in Modern China: An Anthology of Women's Literature from the Early Twentieth Century, ed. and tr. by Amy D. Dooling and Kristina M. Torgeson 1998

American Stories, by Nagai Kafū, tr. Mitsuko Iriye 2000

The Paper Door and Other Stories, by Shiga Naoya, tr. Lane Dunlop 2001

Grass for My Pillow, by Saiichi Maruya, tr. Dennis Keene 2002

For All My Walking: Free-Verse Haiku of Taneda Santō with excerpts from His Diary, tr. Burton Watson 2003

STUDIES IN ASIAN CULTURE

The Ōnin War: History of Its Origins and Background, with a Selective Translation of the Chronicle of Ōnin, by H. Paul Varley 1967

Chinese Government in Ming Times: Seven Studies, ed. Charles O. Hucker 1969

The Actors' Analects (Yakusha Rongo), ed. and tr. by Charles J. Dunn and Bungō Torigoe 1969

Self and Society in Ming Thought, by Wm. Theodore de Bary and the Conference on Ming Thought. Also in paperback ed. 1970

A History of Islamic Philosophy, by Majid Fakhry, 2d ed. 1983

Phantasies of a Love Thief: The Caurapañcāśikā Attributed to Bilhaṇa, by Barbara Stoler Miller 1971

Iqbal: Poet-Philosopher of Pakistan, ed. Hafeez Malik 1971

The Golden Tradition: An Anthology of Urdu Poetry, ed. and tr. Ahmed Ali. Also in paperback ed. 1973

Conquerors and Confucians: Aspects of Political Change in Late Yüan China, by John W. Dardess 1973

The Unfolding of Neo-Confucianism, by Wm. Theodore de Bary and the Conference on Seventeenth-Century Chinese Thought. Also in paperback ed. 1975

To Acquire Wisdom: The Way of Wang Yang-ming, by Julia Ching 1976

Gods, Priests, and Warriors: The Bhṛgus of the Mahābhārata, by Robert P. Goldman 1977

Mei Yao-ch'en and the Development of Early Sung Poetry, by Jonathan Chaves 1976

The Legend of Semimaru, Blind Musician of Japan, by Susan Matisoff 1977

Sir Sayyid Ahmad Khan and Muslim Modernization in India and Pakistan, by Hafeez Malik 1980

The Khilafat Movement: Religious Symbolism and Political Mobilization in India, by Gail Minault 1982

The World of K'ung Shang-jen: A Man of Letters in Early Ch'ing China, by Richard Strassberg 1983

The Lotus Boat: The Origins of Chinese Tz'u Poetry in T'ang Popular Culture, by Marsha L. Wagner 1984

Expressions of Self in Chinese Literature, ed. Robert E. Hegel and Richard C. Hessney 1985

Songs for the Bride: Women's Voices and Wedding Rites of Rural India, by W.-G. Archer; eds. Barbara Stoler Miller and Mildred Archer 1986

The Confucian Kingship in Korea: Yŏngjo and the Politics of Sagacity, by JaHyun Kim Haboush 1988

COMPANIONS TO ASIAN STUDIES

Approaches to the Oriental Classics, ed. Wm. Theodore de Bary 1959

Early Chinese Literature, by Burton Watson. Also in paperback ed. 1962

Approaches to Asian Civilizations, eds. Wm. Theodore de Bary and Ainslie T. Embree 1964

The Classic Chinese Novel: A Critical Introduction, by C.-T. Hsia. Also in paperback ed. 1968

Chinese Lyricism: Shih Poetry from the Second to the Twelfth Century, tr. Burton Watson. Also in paperback ed. 1971

A Syllabus of Indian Civilization, by Leonard A. Gordon and Barbara Stoler Miller 1971

Twentieth-Century Chinese Stories, ed. C.-T. Hsia and Joseph S.-M. Lau. Also in paperback ed. 1971

A Syllabus of Chinese Civilization, by J. Mason Gentzler, 2d ed. 1972

A Syllabus of Japanese Civilization, by H. Paul Varley, 2d ed. 1972

An Introduction to Chinese Civilization, ed. John Meskill, with the assistance of J. Mason Gentzler 1973

An Introduction to Japanese Civilization, ed. Arthur E. Tiedemann 1974

Ukifune: Love in the Tale of Genji, ed. Andrew Pekarik 1982

The Pleasures of Japanese Literature, by Donald Keene 1988

A Guide to Oriental Classics, eds. Wm. Theodore de Bary and Ainslie T. Embree; 3d edition ed. Amy Vladeck Heinrich, 2 vols. 1989

INTRODUCTION TO ASIAN CIVILIZATIONS
Wm. Theodore de Bary, General Editor

Sources of Japanese Tradition, 1958; paperback ed., 2 vols., 1964. 2d ed., vol. 1, 2001, compiled by Wm. Theodore de Bary, Donald Keene, George Tanabe, and Paul Varley

Sources of Indian Tradition, 1958; paperback ed., 2 vols., 1964. 2d ed., 2 vols., 1988

Sources of Chinese Tradition, 1960, paperback ed., 2 vols., 1964. 2d ed., vol. 1, 1999, compiled by Wm. Theodore de Bary and Irene Bloom; vol. 2, 2000, compiled by Wm. Theodore de Bary and Richard Lufrano

Sources of Korean Tradition, 1997; 2 vols., vol. 1, 1997, compiled by Peter H. Lee and Wm. Theodore de Bary; vol. 2, 2001, compiled by Yŏngho Ch'oe, Peter H. Lee, and Wm. Theodore de Bary

NEO-CONFUCIAN STUDIES

Instructions for Practical Living and Other Neo-Confucian Writings by Wang Yang-ming, tr. Wing-tsit Chan 1963

Reflections on Things at Hand: The Neo-Confucian Anthology, comp. Chu Hsi and Lü Tsu-ch'ien, tr. Wing-tsit Chan 1967

Self and Society in Ming Thought, by Wm. Theodore de Bary and the Conference on Ming Thought. Also in paperback ed. 1970

The Unfolding of Neo-Confucianism, by Wm. Theodore de Bary and the Conference on Seventeenth-Century Chinese Thought. Also in paperback ed. 1975

Principle and Practicality: Essays in Neo-Confucianism and Practical Learning, eds. Wm. Theodore de Bary and Irene Bloom. Also in paperback ed. 1979

The Syncretic Religion of Lin Chao-en, by Judith A. Berling 1980

The Renewal of Buddhism in China: Chu-hung and the Late Ming Synthesis, by Chün-fang Yü 1981

Neo-Confucian Orthodoxy and the Learning of the Mind-and-Heart, by Wm. Theodore de Bary 1981

Yüan Thought: Chinese Thought and Religion Under the Mongols, eds. Hok-lam Chan and Wm. Theodore de Bary 1982

The Liberal Tradition in China, by Wm. Theodore de Bary 1983

The Development and Decline of Chinese Cosmology, by John B. Henderson 1984

The Rise of Neo-Confucianism in Korea, by Wm. Theodore de Bary and JaHyun Kim Haboush 1985

Chiao Hung and the Restructuring of Neo-Confucianism in Late Ming, by Edward T. Ch'ien 1985

Neo-Confucian Terms Explained: Pei-hsi tzu-i, by Ch'en Ch'un, ed. and trans. Wing-tsit Chan 1986

Knowledge Painfully Acquired: K'un-chih chi, by Lo Ch'in-shun, ed. and trans. Irene Bloom 1987

To Become a Sage: The Ten Diagrams on Sage Learning, by Yi T'oegye, ed. and trans. Michael C. Kalton 1988

The Message of the Mind in Neo-Confucian Thought, by Wm. Theodore de Bary 1989

The Columbia Anthology of Modern Chinese Literature, 2d ed., ed. Joseph S. M. Lau and Howard Goldblatt